The Problem of Embodiment in Early African American Narrative

The Problem of Embodiment in Early African American Narrative

Katherine Fishburn

Contributions in Afro-American and African Studies,
Number 183

GREENWOOD PRESS
Westport, Connecticut • London

Library of Congress Cataloging-in-Publication Data

Fishburn, Katherine, 1944–
    The problem of embodiment in early African American narrative /
Katherine Fishburn.
      p.   cm. — (Contributions in Afro-American and African
studies, ISSN 0069–9624 ; no. 183)
    Includes bibliographical references (p.   ) and index.
    ISBN 0–313–30359–2 (alk. paper)
    1. American prose literature—Afro-American authors—History and
criticism. 2. American fiction—Afro-American authors—History and
criticism. 3. Afro-Americans in literature. 4. Body, Human, in
literature. 5. Slavery in literature. 6. Slaves in literature.
7. Narration (Rhetoric) I. Title. II. Series.
PS366.A35F57   1997
818′.08—dc21   96–50295

British Library Cataloguing in Publication Data is available.

Library of Congress Catalog Card Number: 96–50295
ISBN: 0–313–30359–2
ISSN: 0069–9624

First published in 1997

Greenwood Press, 88 Post Road West, Westport, CT 06881
An imprint of Greenwood Publishing Group, Inc.

Printed in the United States of America

The paper used in this book complies with the
Permanent Paper Standard issued by the National
Information Standards Organization (Z39.48–1984).

10 9 8 7 6 5 4 3 2 1

Copyright Acknowledgments

The author and publisher gratefully acknowledge permission to use the following:

Excerpts from *Frederick Douglass: Autobiographies* by Frederick Douglass. Copyright © 1994. Reprinted by permission of The Library of America.

Excerpts from *Incidents in the Life of a Slave Girl, Written by Herself* by Harriet Jacobs and edited by Jean Fagan Yellin. Copyright © 1987 by the President and Fellows of Harvard College. Reprinted by permission of Harvard University Press.

As I was writing this book, my father died.
The loving response I have seen from my mother's own community of friends
in these difficult days has reaffirmed for me the argument I make in these pages
on behalf of the potential and need for human interconnectedness that we all
bear within our body-selves.
As for my father himself, no doubt he would have been surprised to see the
direction my thinking has taken—
but his own thinking helped to make the journey possible.

Everything depends upon this alone, that the truth of Being come to language and that thinking attain to this language.

Martin Heidegger (1947)

Every experience worthy of the name thwarts an expectation.

Hans-Georg Gadamer (1989)

These new objects and problems are necessarily *invisible* in the field of the existing theory, because they are not objects of this theory, because they are *forbidden* by it—they are objects and problems necessarily without any necessary relations with the field of the visible as defined by this problematic.

Louis Althusser and Etienne Balibar (1968)

Contents

Preface: What the Body Knows

Reflection is the courage to make the truth of our own presuppositions and the realm of our own goals into the things that most deserve to be called into question.

Martin Heidegger
"The Age of the World Picture" (1938, 116)

What the surprise encounter with otherness should do is lay bare some hint of an ignorance one never knew one had.

Barbara Johnson
A World of Difference (1987, 16)

When I first envisioned this book—and applied for the two grants that would fund its composition—I planned to examine African American narrative from what has become detectable as a major trend in recent literary theory and criticism. That is to say, I planned to investigate the matter of bodies in the composition, contents, and reception of African American fiction. Recognizing that I could not treat African American fiction without reconsidering the nineteenth-century slave narratives, I knew that I would need to find some evidence in these earlier texts that would help me make my case that the problem of embodiment in African American fiction was a *formal* problem. In making my pitch for this project, I confidently asserted, therefore, that in composing the narratives that would prove them rational, the ex-slaves were faced with the dilemma of how to represent the body that had been the occasion of their enslavement and the impediment to their freedom. Contrasting my approach to other books in the field, I proposed, in part, that in these texts the issue of em-

bodiment exceeds what Myra Jehlen would call the "merely thematic" in order
to function formally as a major organizing principle of African American literature, determining what has been permitted in texts and what has been excluded.
Because black slaves were identified with and by their bodies (that is, by the
visible or legal determination of their blackness), I planned to argue that the indisputable fact of their embodiment in a culture that valued the mind at the expense of the debased body faced these early writers with two interrelated
narrative dilemmas. One was how to demonstrate their own capacity to reason
without minimizing the physical horrors of enslavement, the accounts of which
were necessary to the abolitionist cause. The other, which is the obverse of the
first, was how to demonstrate the fact that, however imbued with reason they already were, African Americans still needed a fundamental change in their material circumstances if they were ever to achieve their full human potential.

It seemed an elegant argument and, indeed, got me the funding I requested.
But the more I read and the more I thought about my thesis, the more it seemed
somewhat misdirected. I liked the idea, especially its argument about the formal
limitations on narratives that would admit the body, but it seemed to be missing
something important. Then I stumbled upon a book that would change everything for how I conceived this project—David Michael Levin's *The Body's
Recollection of Being* (1985). It was Levin who took me back to Martin Heidegger's critique of metaphysics and to the concept of the flesh found in the later
writings of the great French phenomenologist Maurice Merleau-Ponty. Reading
Levin, and rereading Heidegger and Merleau-Ponty, helped me see what my
project as I initially had envisioned it was missing. And that was the *importance*
of the body to the slaves and the ex-slaves. Schooled both formally and infor-
mally in the thinking of metaphysics, as other twentieth-century Westerners
have been (the latter more than the former in my case), I had assumed, as my
own organizing principle, that for the slaves to have been identified with and by
their bodies necessarily meant that for them the problem of embodiment was a
problem to be overcome. But somehow the narratives themselves resisted my
reading them from this Western prejudice—that is, this pre-understanding that
has come out of my own exposure to metaphysics. Far better, I discovered, was
to treat the problem of embodiment in slave narratives as the same kind of intellectual problem with which philosophers like Levin and Merleau-Ponty work,
one that attempts to elude the dualistic thinking that separates mind from body,
by valorizing mind over body. What a difference this new approach made to my
understanding of those narratives. Rather than seeing the ex-slaves' embodiment
as something to be denied, underplayed, or overcome, I began to see it as the
route to a new kind of knowing—one based in the body, or, as I prefer to call it,
one based in the body-self. The more I reread the narratives themselves, the
more I became convinced that the ex-slaves were not trying to write themselves
into Western metaphysics as equal to whites, but were instead, more radically
and daringly, rethinking metaphysics itself. After a friend pointed out William
Spanos's recent book, *Heidegger and Criticism: Retrieving the Cultural Politics
of Destruction* (1993), I became even more convinced that I was right. Putting it

in slightly different (but complementary) terms, I could now see that the slaves were offering their own form of anti-humanism—not the so-called "virulent" kind disparaged by Frederick Olafson (1995, 9), but an anti-metaphysical critique that was premised on recalling the body and honoring its recollection of Being. In sum, I began to see the slave narratives not as devaluing the body but as reminding us of its foundational necessity to the experience of human be-ing. Without bodies, the narratives remind us, we humans would have no presence in the world. Without bodies, we humans would not even *have* a world. So, as far as the slave narratives go, it is not bodies that must be overcome, but metaphysics.

This discovery put a whole new spin on my project. Rather than looking for evidence of the ex-slaves' negative experiences with their bodies, I began to look for what their embodiment taught them that was positive and even different from what the rest of us know. Then I began to ask myself how we lost this knowledge, how this unconcealment became concealed all over again—and what the consequences were to later African American narrative to have this bodily knowing of the slaves lost from sight.

This, then, is the origin of *The Problem of Embodiment in Early African American Narrative*. I hope this project will be received in the spirit it is being offered: as a respectful interrogation into the question of what the slaves knew and how this knowing has informed subsequent generations of texts. It required of me as I wrote this book, and will require of its readers, that we give up—as much as we can—the virulent hatred of the body that marks so much Western thought and religion, a hatred that itself helped make possible, if not entirely inevitable, the enslavement of Africans in the New World and the Nazi Holocaust. It is a hatred, on my view, that the slaves could not afford, however much they were encouraged to adopt it by the professional philosophy and dominant ideology of their time. For what, in the economy of the slavocracy, were the slaves free to love if not the body? How else were they free to know if not by the body? The fruits of their bodily labor might have enriched the slavocrats instead of themselves, but the fruits of their *bodily knowing*, though they indeed entered into their own form of economic exchange, could not be stolen from them. In the economy of the slave narratives, the ex-slaves could only gain by making known what their bodies knew. For the more their narratives were products of public consumption, the more understanding was increased, to the benefit of writers and readers alike. But the hatred of the body that the slave narratives attempted to counter would not be so easily vanquished as subsequent generations of African American texts make only too clear.

This virulent hatred of the body is one that we ourselves, the inheritors of the world the slaves helped make, can ill afford to cherish. It costs too much to think we can stand outside our bodies, unencumbered by the very entity that makes us human. What form will our hatred of the body take in the next generation if we find ourselves unable to overcome it in this one?

That the body knows I hope will be taken as a given. *What* the body knows is the subject of this book.

Acknowledgments

I could not have written this book without the current generation of scholars of African American literature, who not only performed their own acts of unconcealment in finding lost and out-of-print novels and slave narratives but who also documented their origins and saw to it that they were reprinted. I am particularly grateful to my friend and colleague at the University of Wisconsin-Madison, Professor Nellie Yvonne McKay, who has always welcomed me at the table. I am also grateful to my friend and colleague at the University of New Hampshire, Professor John Ernest, who has given me help and encouragement in the preparation of this manuscript and recently published a very fine book on nineteenth-century African American literature.

I could not have finished this book in the timely fashion I did without the support of Michigan State University. Thanks to my colleagues within the Department of English for a research leave during spring semester 1996, and thanks to my colleagues outside the department for an All-University Research Initiation Grant fall semester 1995. I hope they will think I spent my time well.

As always, I owe an enormous debt of gratitude to my many students for helping me work through my thought process. I especially want to recognize Kevin Asman, Wayne Smith, and Sherry Wynn, all of whom have given more than they realized. Additionally, Tonita Branan deserves recognition for the research she did; without her, this project might never have got off the ground.

It also would not have materialized without Nancy Eckelbarger and her staff, whose own work continues to help make mine possible.

I wish to acknowledge the loving support of my husband, Tom, and all the four-legged creatures who populate our household—Charlie-Boy Fishburn Lab, Chloe Gene Fishburn Beagle (the Beagle Queen), and Princess Callie Cat.

Finally, I wish to thank my mother, Ruth O. Richards, and my sister-in-law, Nancy Fink, for the friendship and conversations that help sustain me.

Introduction: Seeing Otherwise

This project pivots on a series of paradoxes—an all-too-appropriate kind of ful-crum for a study of the literature generated by the only people to have been born into slavery in a country founded on the principles of natural rights and individ-ual freedom. My basic argument is in itself paradoxical. That is to say, I plan to argue that the very bodies that were the occasion of African peoples' enslave-ment in the New World—the bodies that were shackled, tortured, and worked to exhaustion, the bodies that were the *sign* of debasement and enslavement, the bodies that were despised both by the Judeo-Christian tradition[1] and Cartesian metaphysics—these bodies carried with them a tacit, inborn knowledge of our "relatedness-to-Being," a knowledge that infused the slave narratives with a fundamental challenge to what Alison Jaggar has called the "normative dualism" of Western liberalism, which promotes the fallacious and harmful "assumption that human individuals are essentially solitary, with needs and interests that are separate from if not in opposition to those of other individuals" and at the same time "encourages liberal theorists to ignore human biology"—the facts of which, on her view, "must form the starting point" of any political philosophy.[2] It will be my further argument that the slave narrators challenge the disembod-ied rationalism of Western liberalism even as they employ its democratic ideals in order to define themselves as equal to—if not indistinguishable from—white subjects. That is to say, I will argue that the slave narratives offered one of the most effective, if heretofore overlooked, pre-Heideggerian critiques of human-ism and metaphysics[3] ever attempted in the West.

My major purpose in this book, therefore, is to theorize the founding im-pulse that lies behind the production of African American narrative literatures. In so doing, I respond to Houston Baker's work on the blues (Baker 1984) and Henry Louis Gates's work on "words, signs, and the 'racial' self" (Gates 1989)—and I do so by grounding their ideas in the material experience of black embodiment. What remains vital to but often only implicit in their work—that is, the quotidian experience of black bodies—I thematize in mine. As a comprehensive (though hardly exhaustive) study of early African American narrative, my work also functions as a supplementary text to Trudier Harris's work on ritualized violence (Harris 1984), Ann duCille's work on African American women's sexuality and the marriage plot (duCille 1993), Laura Doyle's reconfiguration of modernism through a study of women's bodies in African American and white American narratives (Doyle 1994), and Karen Sánchez-Eppler's work on the role of bodies in abolitionist and feminist literature (Sánchez-Eppler 1988, 1993). While Harris organizes her study around questions of lynching, she does not address the larger issue of black embodiment and its relationship to imaginative texts. While duCille attends to the physical appearance and experience of African Americans, she mostly confines her discussion to women. While Doyle offers a rereading of modernism through the trope of female bodies and while Sánchez-Eppler attends to physical description in nineteenth-century literature, neither author offers a comprehensive theory of the origins of African American narrative per se. In contrast, my project argues that early African American narrative itself depends upon and philosophizes about the more fundamental dependence of human be-ing on human embodiment—a dependence that, more often than not, has been denied in Western culture. This tension between needing to acknowledge the fact of human embodiment and wishing to overcome its negative consequences in a racist society is particularly obvious in the antebellum American slave narratives but can still be easily detected in their immediate literary successors, the post-Reconstruction novels of racial uplift and passing.

Underlying this tension and increasing its significance tenfold, however, is the momentous insight inhering in the slave narratives themselves that we are all related to and through *being*[4]—and that this relatedness is known in and by our bodies. It is this deeply philosophical understanding of the human condition that made the slave narratives therapeutic in their own time and can make them therapeutic in our own alienated, pain-driven time when any number of countries are split apart by seemingly endless tribal warfare and the fabric of our own society is threatened by racial and class conflict. By recalling us to our bodies, these narratives can help, in a Heideggerian sense, recollect us to *being* itself. In short, I intend to argue that the slave narrators knew their pre-conceptual relatedness to *being*-as-a-whole—knew it first and foremost in their bodies. Though much has changed in the century and a half since slavery was legally abolished in this country and much is made of the so-called global village, very little of our political philosophy has changed. As is still true of the world we Westerners inhabit today, the world the slaves inhabited socialized its members to "forget" or otherwise ignore the bodily knowledge of relatedness with which we are all born—and which, on David Michael Levin's view, the body itself never forgets.[5] It is my argument that because the slaves were to a larger extent than white Americans identified with their bodies (however debased they were), because slaves on a daily basis had to use their bodies (however unwillingly) in grueling physical labor for the enrichment of others, and because slaves retained some knowledge (however attenuated or modified) of what has been called a West African world view, they (or at any rate, many of those who survived to write their narratives) did not completely forget the bodily knowledge of our relatedness-to-*being*.[6] It was this knowledge—sometimes conscious, sometimes unconscious—that helped them resist the otherwise dehumanizing conditions of enslavement and recognize the philosophical truth expressed by Maurice Merleau-Ponty that alterity resides in, is a condition of, ontology.[7] That is to say, it permitted them to see that black slave and white master were dependent upon one another; not in the classic Hegelian sense,[8] but intertwined—part of one another, flesh of the same flesh, the very insight that the concepts of race and racism were invented to conceal.

As Barbara Jeanne Fields and others have demonstrated, the by-now thoroughly familiar and naturalized concept of "race," which we so take for granted in the late twentieth century and which is one of the controlling tropes of this study, had in its origins actually very little to do with biology and virtually everything to do with ideology, economics, psychology, and politics (on this, see also Appiah 1992).[9] In "Slavery, Race and Ideology in the United States of America," Fields enumerates the social, political, and economic changes of the seventeenth century that led to the invention of "race" in the colonies. It is with a combination of hope and horror that we follow her argument, as we are reminded that things did not have to turn out the way they did. Instead, external events converged around human needs, human weakness, and human greed to invent an ideology that allowed Euro-Americans to despise, enslave, and totalize a diverse group of peoples whose single but fateful flaw it was to have been born in Africa of darker skin than theirs.

Fields begins her argument by looking at conditions in colonial Virginia, where the major source of wealth was growing tobacco, a venture that, to be profitable, required a huge force of impressed laborers. At the beginning this force was composed of white European indentured servants, a class of people who, according to Fields, experienced every indignity and degradation *except* "perpetual enslavement" (Fields 1990, 102). But even though these immigrant servants had lost much of the dignity and freedom their ancestors had wrested from the English aristocracy, they were still relatively safe from perpetual enslavement because the colonial landowners were fearful of reigniting the centuries-long struggle between peasant and patrician. On Fields's view, such a thorough-going degradation of working-class immigrants would have been a decidedly "dangerous undertaking considering that servants were well-armed, that they outnumbered their masters, and that the Indians could easily take advantage of the inevitably resulting warfare among the enemy" (103). Because Africans had not participated in or benefited from this centuries-long struggle to secure the legal rights of poor people, they were both suitable for and susceptible to enslavement for life "in a way that English servants were not" (104). Even if the Africans had no historical legacy of contesting their rights with the European landowners and were also readily available from the slavers for importation into the colonies after 1619, slavery itself was not systematized until 1661.[10] As Fields remarks, the first African slaves "enjoyed rights that, in the nineteenth century, not even free black people could claim" (104). It was not until it became economically feasible to enslave people for life that slavery became systematized.

By the 1660s a series of events combined to make this both practical and desirable.[11] It was during this time, just as the price of tobacco declined, that fewer Europeans were immigrating to the colonies. Those who did come as indentured servants began in large numbers to survive the period of servitude and thus began also to demand the land and the freedom due them now as free white European settlers. "By the 1670s," Fields reports, "the rulers of Virginia faced a potentially serious problem: a large class of young (white) freedmen, landless, single, discontented—and well armed" (105). What better solution was there than to avoid this problem altogether by replacing European servants with African ones—a solution made even more appealing by the fact that Africans were now living long enough to more than offset the slave owners' original investment in them. Still, "race" was not yet what Fields calls "a coherent ideology" (106). Just as it had taken time to systematize slavery (from the concept of limited indenture to that of slavery for life), it took time to invent the concept of race. Reversing the common-sense view that oppression follows perceived inferiority, Fields argues that the slaves' so-called state of natural inferiority was an ideological concept that grew out of their oppression (106).[12] She then goes on to trace the invention of race in the colonies—the invention and maintenance of what she calls the ideology of race, whereby a group of people (immigrant Africans) was said to deserve and benefit from enslavement for life in a "republic founded on radical doctrines of liberty and natural rights" (114).[13] The slaves themselves, she reminds us, needed no "racial explanation" (114). It was, of course, the whites who needed a racial distinction in order to convince themselves that in enslaving other people for life they were engaged in an act that was legal, ethical, and moral. Through the invention of race, on Fields's view, they attempted to conceal from themselves what the Africans already knew: that the country was locked in a paralyzing, immoral, political paradox. It is thus a central purpose of this project to help us find a way out of this paradox by returning to what in our own combined African and Euro-American tradition is most therapeutic: the world the slave narrators knew in and transmitted through their own bodies. To do so we must consider how it is that the slaves were so well positioned to critique liberal humanism—a consideration that will constitute the rest of this introduction.

First, however, a word about my critical approach. My project is very like the slave narratives in that it too challenges liberal humanism and Western metaphysics, but it also presents a challenge to the aestheticism of New Criticism and the ahistoricism of structuralism. As such, it goes against the grain of those attempts by some critics of African American literature to aestheticize the African American narrative in order to rescue it from what they consider to be the backwaters of sociological or anthropological criticism.[14] While it can certainly be argued that treating African American narratives as "case histories" of social oppression and/or pathology has contributed little to our understanding of them as artful or fictional accounts of African American life in all its complexity and variability, I do not think the solution is to subject them to New Critical readings. Close reading, after all, is not zero-degree reading; it is the politically interested method of reading that was promulgated by politically invested middle- and upper-class, white male American and English critics who, above all else it would appear, tried to convince themselves and others of the apoliticality of their endeavors—not to mention the disembodiment of their reading selves.[15] I, personally, can think of few critical transgressions as grave as trying to lift these African American texts out of their time and place, as New Critics would have us do. It is my further argument, inspired by the texts themselves and by such philosophers as the American neo-pragmatist Richard Rorty and the French postmodernist Jean-François Lyotard, that these nineteenth-century narratives as well as their twentieth-century successors *think being*. That is to say, these narratives philosophize and, in so doing, they meditate on the fundamental question of what (a) human being is. They also offer what Lyotard (1984) reminds us the West—in its obsession with legitimation and scientific instrumentalism—more often than not disparages: that is to say, a kind of narrative knowledge. By helping us to see otherwise, these narratives dare to call into question the very ideas that make us who we are as Westerners. The slave narratives in particular call to the best in us—yet challenge some of our most cherished ideals and ideas. In so doing, they offer what we might call an anti-humanist or alternative modernism. While they cannot help but forward the liberal humanist ideals of progress and reason, they redefine what progress and reason entail—especially challenging reason's disembodiment.[16] In so doing, they necessarily return a temporal-historical dimension to these reified ideals, reminding us that even "reason" is what we say it is. These Enlightenment ideals, in other words, may indeed be revolutionary concepts but they are nothing more, or less, than the influential political-philosophical constructs that a particular group of people has agreed to value at a particular time and place. That they have furthered Enlightenment and emancipation for some goes without question; that they have denied it to others is equally certain, no matter how influential these ideas are today at the so-called "End of History."[17]

While the slave narratives also forward the notion of rights and that of the individual, they also modify these concepts, as they were understood in the nineteenth century—and as they are understood today. For the slave narratives, progress seems to involve the advancement not just of individuals but of the Race itself.[18] Progress is thus dependent upon a positive sense of community, one that is not defined in opposition to the individual; or, to put it in Rorty's terms (1989), there is a strong sense of human solidarity in the slave narratives. Where Western philosophers, including Rorty, cannot conceptualize how individual rights (the private sphere) and communal needs (the public sphere) might be successfully reconciled, the slave narrators seem to have little difficulty in imagining that what is good for the community is good for the individual because our lives always already overlap with the lives of others.[19] The narrators have more success at conceptualizing this reconciliation, on my view, because they are working in the everyday experience of the slaves' body-selves. Like Heidegger after them, the slave narrators offer a negative critique, or what William Spanos would describe as a "radical interrogation of the founding (ontotheological) discourses that have 'written' the discourse and practice of humanist/patriarchal/bourgeois/capitalist modernity" (Spanos 1993, 19). Unlike Heidegger, however, they do not limit themselves to a relatively abstract conception of history—to what we might call, pejoratively, Heidegger's ungrounded anti-humanism. Instead, the slave narratives are grounded in particularity; they gain their power from moving from quotidian details to compelling human truths.[20] Much more so than Heidegger, they also admit the body into their discourse and, on my view, utilize the body and its knowledge to forward a new kind of rationality.[21] These texts, like bodies themselves, are moreover temporal in be-ing (see Spanos 1993, 23). They are not, as I have already averred, metaphysical or verbal icons; they are not to be admired but experienced. It is thus that in my reading of these narratives there is always a full congregation of bodies present: the body of the author, the body of the text, the body of the reader, and the bodies in the text.

Let me now turn at some length to two of the major influences on this project: Michel Foucault and Martin Heidegger.[22] First, Foucault, who explains that in referring to "humanism" he means:

the totality of discourse through which Western man is told: "Even though you don't exercise power, you can still be a ruler. Better yet, the more you deny yourself the exercise of power, the more you submit to those in power, then the more this increases your sovereignty." Humanism invented a whole series of subjected sovereignties: the soul (ruling the body, but subjected to God), consciousness (sovereign in a context of judgment, but subjected to the necessities of truth), the individual (a titular control of personal rights subjected to the laws of nature and society), basic freedom (sovereign within, but accepting the demands of an outside world and "aligned with destiny"). In short, humanism is everything in Western civilization that restricts *the desire for power*: it prohibits the desire for power and excludes the possibility of power being seized. The theory of the subject (in the double sense of the word) is at the heart of humanism and this is why our culture has tenaciously rejected anything that could weaken its hold upon us. (Foucault 1971, 221–22)

Of this critique of humanism, first of all, I would ask rhetorically: How could anyone understand better than those Africans who were designated slaves for life in the United States of America the thrust of Foucault's claims that deal with the false promises of liberal humanism? It will be my argument, pursued in the pages that follow, that Foucault's sociopolitical anti-humanism and Heidegger's ontological anti-humanism—both of which, as Spanos shows us (1993), stand in supplementary relation to and need of one other[23]—were, in fact, anticipated by the anti-humanism of nineteenth-century American slave narratives. In making this claim, I am clearly breaking ranks with those who read the slave narratives as evidence of the slaves' own claim to humanistic principles. I do not, of course, mean to suggest that the slaves were anything less than human or that their project in any way undermined their desire to be seen as fully human. What I do mean to suggest is that the composition of these narratives should be seen as a thorough-going yet finally incomplete critique of liberal humanism.[24] More successful, yet still incomplete, as it needs must be, was their related critique of the metaphysical principles on which much of Western humanism founded its own arguments. I base the first part of my argument on the fact that, by legal and philosophical definition, African slaves in the eighteenth and nineteenth centuries were excluded from humanistic principles and the liberal society to which these principles gave birth. As far as the slaves were concerned, they were homeless; there was literally no place for them in Western humanism. As a result, the very lives of these slaves, who, for purposes of representation, counted only as three-fifths of a "person,"[25] thematized the dirty little secrets upon which liberal humanism built its elegant universalizing edifice. Among these are (1) the complicity of the discourse of so-called disinterested truth (whether scientific or philosophic) with the repressive, indeed colonizing, practices of Western sociopolitical power[26]; (2) the metaphysical reification of *being* as Being, which effectively masks its temporal dimension and the sociohistorical construction of human truths; (3) the denial of the human body as a source of either knowledge or understanding, which contributes to the notion of a disembodied universal subject, thus making possible what Jaggar (1983) has called the abstract individualism of liberal humanism; and yet (4) the identification of only particular human beings as subjects and, thus, in the political realm, the identification of only particular human beings as qualifying for full representation and legal rights.[27] In sum, in writing themselves as fully human beings, the slave narrators necessarily redefined what it means to be human. In so doing they not only anticipated Foucault's and Heidegger's anti-humanism, but they also, as I shall argue at length in the chapters that follow, anticipated Maurice Merleau-Ponty's concept of the flesh and his efforts to challenge the reign of Western metaphysics.[28]

For the purposes of my argument, "humanism" should be read as that body of philosophical and political discourse that has given shape to the West as we know it today. Deeply influenced by the French Enlightenment, it is largely by now (although it was not always) a secular discourse that looks to reason ("man's" reason) rather than religion to solve the world's problems and give meaning, morals, and direction to human life. It traces its complex roots variously back from the secular humanism and scientific instrumentalism of the late twentieth century to the agnostic or atheistic scientific rationalism of the nineteenth century, to the skepticism of Hume in the eighteenth centuries, to the

European Renaissance of the fifteenth and sixteenth century, until, finally, it finds itself all the way back to Rome. Heidegger argues in his "Letter on Humanism" that "[e]very humanism is either grounded in a metaphysics or is itself made to be the ground of one" (Heidegger 1947, 225). By this he means that "[i]n defining the humanity of man [in taking it for granted, that is] humanism not only does not ask about the relation of Being to the essence of man; because of its metaphysical origin *humanism even impedes the question* by neither recognizing nor understanding it" (226; emphasis added). If humanism is itself reliant on, beholden to, or even blinded by metaphysics, one must also see that in its elevation of and commitment to the notion of *individual* rights, in contrast to communal good, the philosophical discourse (or political ideology) of liberalism is also implicated in, or necessary to, our concept of Western humanism.[29] From liberalism, humanism also takes the metaphysical urge to seek eternal truths, since liberalism seeks to ground its principles of individual freedom in universals, most particularly those human rights that are said to be inherent in each person, irrespective of any external sociohistoric factors—a belief most eloquently and famously stated in the opening words of our own Declaration of Independence: "We hold these truths to be self-evident, that all men are created equal, that they are endowed by their Creator with certain unalienable Rights, that among these are Life, Liberty, and the pursuit of Happiness."[30] Thus, the discourse of liberal humanism and the social polity to which it gave birth was peopled by disembodied, universalized, and individualized subjects, valued for and noted by their rationality.[31]

With these definitions in place, let us walk our way through Foucault's postmodern critique, point by point. As we have seen, Foucault begins by unpacking the emancipatory discourse of liberal humanism, revealing the hidden—and unexpressed—discourse of repression upon which it relies.[32] For Foucault, in fact, humanism is most oppressive when it represents itself as liberating. "By humanism," he writes, therefore, "I mean the totality of discourse through which Western man is told: 'Even though you don't exercise power, you can still be a ruler. Better yet, the more you deny yourself the exercise of power, the more you submit to those in power, then the more this increases your sovereignty'" (1971, 221). In reply to Foucault's pointed critique, to which I shall return momentarily with additional glosses, I want to ask: Does his statement not describe the advice given to slaves by owners and ministers alike? To remain fully themselves, as slaves, were not the enslaved taught to obey their master—and in remaining obedient were they not said to fulfill the will of God? As Harriet Jacobs recalls, for example, this was the message of the Reverend Mr. Pike, who chose Ephesians 6:5 as his text: "Servants, be obedient to your masters according to the flesh, with fear and trembling, in singleness of your heart, as unto Christ" (Jacobs 1861, 68).[33] Henry Bibb recalls in his *Narrative* that preaching of this sort had the unexpected outcome of turning slaves away from religion because the slaveholders "preach a pro-slavery doctrine. They say, 'Servants be obedient to your masters[']—and he that knoweth his master's will and doeth it not, shall be beaten with many stripes;—means that God will send

them to hell, if they disobey their masters. This kind of preaching has driven
thousands into infidelity" (Bibb 1850, 24). Even though, as I shall argue shortly,
slaves were definitionally, philosophically, and legally denied the status of at-
omized, disembodied, rational subjects, does not their daily experience disclose
what being a (humanistic) subject really involved? In other words, does not the
experience of slaves thematize the underbelly of humanism? Does it not reveal
that subjects were subjected by the discourse of liberation? Or, to put it in
Althusserian terms, does not the experience of slaves reveal the effects of interpellation, wherein the individual is "hailed" by a combination of the openly
"Repressive State Apparatus" and the more subtle "Ideological State Apparatuses" (the ISAs) into a subject position?[34] Do not the African slaves reveal that,
to one degree or another, all Westerners are slaves to the ISAs? In other words,
does their existence not reveal a kind of interpellation continuum, wherein all
are enslaved, but some are more enslaved than others?[35]

Foucault's de[con]struction of humanism continues: "Humanism invented a
whole series of subjected sovereignties: the soul (ruling the body, but subjected
to God), consciousness (sovereign in a context of judgment, but subjected to the
necessities of truth), the individual (a titular control of personal rights subjected
to the laws of nature and society), basic freedom (sovereign within, but accepting the demands of an outside world and 'aligned with destiny')" (1971, 221).
Did not the slaves always already have a conflicted relationship to these humanist sovereignties? To some, slaves, not being fully human, had no soul, so definitionally they could not be sheltered in the so-called emancipatory embrace of
humanism. If they *were* granted a soul, and it was subjected to God, its keeping,
as we have just seen, was in the hands of their worldly masters—as were, of
course, their bodies. Similarly, was not the possible sovereignty of their judgment always already precluded by the purported "truth" of their inferiority? If
Heidegger can claim that humanism is metaphysical in not interrogating the so-
called humanity of man and questioning its relationship to *being*, surely we, too,
can claim it metaphysical in assuming *ipso facto* that certain human beings—by
virtue of their physical appearance and place of origin—did not deserve inclusion in the category "human being." Further, was not the concept of the individual perverted beyond recognition in the case of the slave, who did not even have
titular control of personal rights, such as when to sleep and eat, whom to marry,
where to live? Did not the laws of society—most proximally in the person of
their master, himself a subject par excellence—always already hold sway over
any potential titular rights of the (individual) slave? Is not calling a slave an
"individual" in this context therefore empty of meaning? Finally, was not the
basic freedom of slaves literally unthinkable? It stood to reason, after all, that if
slaves themselves were absent of a disembodied and reified reason they technically were not subjects, and thus they had no rights. With guidance and education, they might later acquire reason, or so some arguments went, but they were
not born with it—which goes to show how sociohistorically specific humanism's foundational thinking was, after all. Either everybody has reason at birth
or its so-called universality is a made truth.[36] Eager to ground their emancipa-

tory ideas in universal truths, eighteenth- and nineteenth-century political philosophers simply could not see the discursive origins of their own revolutionary
claims.

"In short," Foucault argues, "humanism is everything in Western civilization
that restricts *the desire for power*: it prohibits the desire for power and excludes
the possibility of power being seized" (1971, 221–22). If, more than anything
else, slaves desired freedom and the power to govern their own lives—as the
slave narratives themselves testify—they need must, in this desire and its exe-
cution, in one way or another overcome humanism and the universal truths it
produced and promulgated.[37] In this context, one could argue that, whereas the
slaves' bodies were regarded as chattel and thus, in legal and humanistic terms,
were not their own, their *body-selves* (their *real* selves, by which they experienced the world, irrespective of who legally owned them) nonetheless experienced another kind freedom—one that if not, strictly speaking, outside the prison
walls of metaphysics that enclose us, still gave them the capacity to take the
measure of our shared epistemological prison.[38] I want to be very careful here,
as I make this claim. I want it clearly understood that I am most assuredly not
arguing for or on behalf of any form of slavery. I do not for a minute contest
that slaves paid a terrible, historically unequaled price for the destructive hermeneutics they practiced. Instead, I am arguing that by virtue of their being
outside the formal parameters of metaphysics (and, to a degree, at least somewhat outside its language)[39] the slave narrators could see what metaphysics
hides from us—and this, I am arguing, is a gift of their body-selves to our own.
Unlike the rest of us, they were free to think differently, to see otherwise. Thus,
when Houston Baker asks his pointed and poignant question, "[w]here . . . in
Douglass's *Narrative* does a prototypical black American self reside?" (Baker
1980, 43), I would respond it resides in the flesh—in the ability of Douglass's
body-self to see otherwise. It is, in short, a kind of freedom, since, in Heideggerian terms, the essence of freedom is not just a lack of controls or an ability to
act but, more fundamentally, "engagement in the disclosure of beings as such"
(Heidegger 1961, 126).

My argument, in sum, is that the slaves were better positioned than their
owners to ask—and to answer—the fundamental questions about existence, such
as "What is *being*?" and "What is human be-ing?" or "What is a human being?"
More than anything else, having opened themselves to the disclosedness and
interrelatedness of all beings (human and otherwise), what the slaves needed
was to translate their insight into effective political action, so their body-selves
would no longer be treated as human chattel. What they produced *mirabile dictu*
was the slave narrative—a counter-hegemonic discourse that challenged the
dominant thinking of the time, not all of it but enough to make a difference. If
the slaves' nineteenth-century readers could not see that metaphysics, liberal
humanism, and their own social polity were all being challenged, they could at
least admire the process of thinking that was on display and could not but conclude that, indeed, it was a man and brother, or a woman and sister, whose
words they read. In this effort to change minds, the slave narrators were not all

that different from their contemporaries, for, as Rorty reminds us, "[w]hat was glimpsed at the end of the eighteenth century was that anything could be made to look good or bad, important or unimportant, useful or useless, by being redescribed" (Rorty 1989, 7; see also Foucault 1970). What ultimately matters on Rorty's view, a view I will adopt here for my own purposes, is whether the metaphors by which you choose to write your life become literalized in the next generation. That is, for the slave narrators the question was not the one facing Hamlet, "To be or not to be," but the one facing Nietzsche: to be described by others or to describe oneself (see Rorty 1989, 29). Always relevant to and attendant upon this question is whether or not the slaves would have the political and discursive power to change not just the words themselves, but the very meaning of the words used to describe them. That is to say, would they be, following Michel Pêcheux (1975), in a position to call themselves human and in the process redefine what the expressions "human being" and "slave" meant in society at large?[40] In the weak sense they succeeded, in that at least some whites, having heard and read the ex-slaves' narratives, acknowledged they were in the presence of other fully rational human beings, that is to say, subjects. In the strong sense they probably failed, in that their audience remained deaf and blind to the fact of our bodies' recollection of *being*. That is, the whites were willing to admit ex-slaves into the subject category but they could not see that doing so, by definition, changed the category itself because of the bodily knowledge the slaves brought with them.

Let us finish, then, with Foucault's twentieth-century critique of humanism, which I have been using to structure this discussion. "The theory of the subject (in the double sense of the word)," he concludes, "is at the heart of humanism and this is why our culture has tenaciously rejected anything that could weaken its hold upon us" (1971, 222). Yes, I would agree—but the theory of the atomistic, universal and individualized, rational subject (before which the world stands and time stops) has since its coeval conception with the birth of humanism had its grip on us compromised by its inability (that is, its unwillingness) either to represent itself as historically, culturally, and racially specific or, conversely, to permit the "other" access to this representation.[41] By not designating all human beings as subjects, the hegemonic humanistic discourse ensured the rise of a counter-discourse. Or, as David Theo Goldberg sums it up, the great irony in modernism (a term equivalent to what I am calling liberal humanism) is that while "modernity commits itself progressively to idealized principles of liberty, equality, and fraternity, as it increasingly insists upon the moral irrelevance of race, there is a multiplication of racial identities" (Goldberg 1993, 6). Because liberalism, on Goldberg's view, is "key in establishing racialized reasoning and its racist implications as central to modernity's common moral and sociopolitical sense," philosophical discourse itself has been implicated in the fostering of racism at the heart of modernity (1). It therefore falls, in part, to philosophical discourse to challenge "the culture of racisms" (2)—as I contend is already taking place in the nineteenth-century American slave narrative.

In "The Age of the World Picture," Heidegger argues similarly for the necessity of the subject-object dualism to humanism. For Heidegger, modernity it-self is characterized by the world turning into what we recognize as "picture" (Heidegger 1938, 130). Further, this is exactly "the same event with the event of man's becoming *subiectum* in the midst of that which is" (132). So it is that the more completely and effectively "the world stands at man's disposal as con-quered, and the more objectively the object appears, all the more subjectively, i.e., the more importunately, does the *subiectum* rise up"; at the same time, our understanding of the world is transformed "into a doctrine of man, into anthro-pology" (133). But where, I ask, in all of this does the slave stand? Certainly not as a humanistic subject before whom the world appears as object. The slave stands, as the world (picture) stands, as an object before the self-described zero-degree raced subject.[42] Or, to draw from another of Heidegger's essays, we might even argue that the slaves went beyond the status of object and were al-ways already part of the "standing-reserve [*Bestand*]" (Heidegger 1954a, 17). In "The Question Concerning Technology," from which I have taken this quota-tion, Heidegger characterizes the essence of technology as a form of "uncon-cealment" that is a "challenging revealing" (17, 16). In the standing-reserve "[e]verywhere everything is ordered to stand by, to be immediately at hand" to ensure that it is always available "for a further ordering" (17).[43] On my view, it was no coincidence that the anthropologies that arose to describe, classify, and explain other peoples arose with the emergence of liberal humanism; for, very simply, anthropology is humanism writ large. Neither was it a coincidence that the slaves themselves invented their own destructive hermeneutics, 100 years before Heidegger. How could the slaves possibly have seen the world the way their masters did? To continue this introductory argument, therefore, let me now cite a key passage from Heidegger's *Being and Time* (1927a):

In anticipating [zum] the indefinite certainty of death, Dasein opens itself to a constant *threat* arising out of its own 'there'. In this very threat Being-towards-the-end must maintain itself. So little can it tone this down that it must rather cultivate the indefinite-ness of the certainty. How is it existentially possible for this constant threat to be genu-inely disclosed? All understanding is accompanied by a state-of-mind. Dasein's mood brings it face to face with the thrownness of its 'that it is there'. *But the state-of-mind which can hold open the utter and constant threat to itself arising from Dasein's own-most individualized Being, is anxiety.* In this state-of-mind, Dasein finds itself *face to face* with the 'nothing' of the possible impossibility of its existence. Anxiety is anxious *about* the potentiality-for-Being of the entity so destined, and in this way it discloses the uttermost possibility (266).[44]

Earlier I suggested that African American peoples who had been designated slaves for life were in a unique position to anticipate Foucault's critique of hu-manism; to that I now wish to add the suggestion that they were in a unique position to experience the feelings of anxiety (or dread) in the face of human finitude that Heidegger describes in this passage.[45] As I shall suggest at various other points throughout this study, I mean here to suggest that the quotidian ex-

periences of African American slaves can be seen to thematize various philosophical claims that underlie and underwrite Western thought. Though I am
suggesting that Heidegger himself offers an effective ontological critique of
humanism—and a less complete critique of metaphysics—he is one of the most
influential figures of twentieth-century Western philosophy and thus is constrained to critique philosophy entirely from within the very boundaries he
would question. The slaves, however, were not constrained to the same degree.
Condemned both to perpetual bondage and to standing outside the boundaries of
professional philosophy, the ex-slave narrators were, paradoxically, free to avail
themselves of their formal exclusion from metaphysics and could thus offer a
more pointed critique of its principles. I have already acknowledged in a previous footnote that no one, not even the slaves, could escape metaphysics entirely.
But, like Merleau-Ponty in his use of the flesh (as I will suggest in the following
chapter), the slaves in their embodiment have done better than most in eluding
the terms of metaphysics. As I have stated repeatedly, their critique of metaphysics emerges from the equally inescapable fact of human embodiment, the
sine qua non of human be-ing. In this famous passage from his early major
work, *Being and Time*, Heidegger describes the dread (the *Angst* or anxiety) that
accompanies the human condition of finitude. Faced with the incomparable, in-
expressible, and unimaginable prospects of our own temporarily delayed but always impending death, we recoil in dread from the incomprehensible abyss of
nothingness. But this dread-ful recoiling from our own future non-being is what
makes authentic being possible. The dread we feel in the face of our own ex-
tinction makes possible the questions: What is being? What is the relationship
between being and *being*? As Spanos puts it in his reading of this passage: "As
irreducibly temporal 'being,' Heidegger's *Sein* implies . . . a permanent absence,
or absenting. . . . In 'always already' . . . destroying presence, it always already
disseminates being:[46] disperses and defers what in the metaphysical tradition is
taken to be eternal, identical, proper, and thus plenary—certain and graspable—
into indeterminate and ineffable (uncanny) temporal difference" (Spanos 1993,
112).

Is not this the human condition—to know that we must die and yet be incapable of imagining a time that is no time? If we are, if we exist in time (as we
do), if we have been thrown into time (as we have), there will come a time when
time is no longer there for us—and when we are no longer there for time. Anxiety is the state of mind that reveals this possibility (which is a certainty still delayed in our lifetime). Was not this same anxiety the state of mind of the African
American slaves for life?[47] Heidegger distinguishes between this profound, ungrounded anxiety and the more manageable experience of fear. Anxiety is without object; fear domesticates anxiety by offering specific objects for its
attention. I am not talking about the fears of being a slave—the fear of being
traded, the fear of being beaten, the fear of not getting sufficient food, clothing,
or rest. I am instead talking about an undifferentiated, pervasive dread, a necessary talent for coming face to face with their own mortality that haunted the
daily experience of the slaves, a state of mind that was more than fleeting or oc-

casional. It was this ability—no doubt less welcome than endured—to entertain anxiety that combined with their self-conscious, *ek-static* bodily presence to set the slaves apart and force them to see the world differently. It was this combination of unremitting dread and thematized bodily presence that made possible—if not inevitable—the ex-slaves' pre-Heideggerian critique of metaphysics and liberal humanism. It was this combination, in short, that made possible the interrogation of be-ing that we know as the slave narratives.[48]

What, then, has happened to conceal this interrogation from us? How is it that we cannot see the destructive hermeneutics that informs the slave narratives? How is it that we have lost what the body-selves of the slaves knew? How is it that we find it so very difficult to retrieve a sense of the body's recollection of *being* that lies at the heart of the slave narratives? The answers to these questions lie most generally in our Western allegiance to humanism and largely unquestioning acceptance of its underlying metaphysical principles.[49] But the answers also lie more specifically in the postbellum novels produced by other African Americans, when so many writers worked so hard to uplift the race and enter the middle class. Once it became feasible for large numbers of African Americans to imagine themselves becoming part of the respectable black middle class, I think the pervasive but often cryptic anti-humanism of the slave narratives went even further underground—especially as their destructive hermeneutics could be construed by black and white readers alike as threatening the progress of the race. What had been the slave narrators' embodied knowledge of our human connectedness thus seemed to become the postbellum novelists' disembodied ambition to enter the middle class as social, moral, and economic equals to whites. What had been before the war an unexpected advantage to the slave narrators—an inability to deny the body-self—became during the reign of terror that succeeded the war strictly a liability.

It was not so much that postbellum African American writers no longer saw the world differently but that they had to represent their difference in terms that were not so obviously bodily-based. Apparently turning away from the anti-liberal humanist, destructive hermeneutics of the slave narrators, a significant number of influential late nineteenth- and early twentieth-century African American novelists seemed, therefore, to be taking pen in hand figuratively to write themselves out of their bodies: to prove to the white world that while their souls might be housed in black bodies—the visible sign of their ancestors' enslaved status and purported lack of reason—their own probity, purity, and industriousness were ultimately more important than the color of their skin. Intent on demonstrating in their fiction their own brand of racial superiority and their race's accompanying claim to genteel respectability, these writers tried to repress the fact of their characters' racialized embodiment. But just as the suffering, hard-working, productive bodies of the ex-slaves themselves could not be completely silenced or eradicated, neither could those of their immediate descendants. It is this persistence on the part of the body-self to be remembered in narrative even when its presence was unwelcome that ultimately led to the need for formal strategies of control and containment. It thus becomes a narrative project of the postbellum sentimental novelists—ambitious to uplift the race, enter the middle class, and be accepted by the white hegemony—to write out these troublesome bodies so their presence would not become an impediment to the ongoing project of racial uplift.[50] But the body could not be denied—no bodies can forever. And in a racist society like ours, how could a racialized subject ever forget the body?

These are the very problems, of course, that plagued W. E. B. Du Bois for much of his distinguished career. In his famous 1897 address to the American Negro Academy, Du Bois accepted the nineteenth-century premise of racial differences, only to invert its conclusions by arguing (against Hegel, surely) that it was precisely *because* they were different that "the Negro people, as a race, have a contribution to make to civilization and humanity, which no other race can make" (Du Bois 1897, 825). Given this unrealized potential, it was thus incumbent upon African Americans, as the century turned, for them "to maintain their race identity until this mission of the Negro people is accomplished, and the ideal of human brotherhood has become a practical possibility" (825). Such stirring, brave words. Would that their promise had come true, whatever the premise it rested upon. But even Du Bois, as Kwame Anthony Appiah argues, was unable to ignore the growing scientific evidence of his own time that "there are no races: there is nothing in the world that can do all we ask 'race' to do for us" (Appiah 1985–86, 25).[51] Du Bois, then, was caught on the horns of a dilemma—to believe in race or not to believe in it. In "The Conservation of 'Race,'" Appiah warns us further of the dangers that lie within "categories of difference" as they have been (and are being) defined by the hegemons (Appiah 1989, 56). Having argued in the earlier essay against a genetically founded concept of race, here Appiah defends himself against Houston Baker's ill-tempered attack (in Baker 1985–86) that scholars like himself have "been co-opted by the ideology that is the instrument of our domination" (Appiah 1989, 42). Appiah rebuts Baker's argument by retorting that "it may be those who accept rather than those who reject the language of 'race' that risk co-optation by the hegemons" (Appiah 1989, 42). For Appiah, "the very category of the Negro is at root a European product: for the 'whites' invented the Negroes in order to dominate them" (Appiah 1992, 62). I will leave it to others to continue this debate.[52] What I want to extract from this particular exchange is Appiah's adaptation of an argument made by John B. Thompson in *Studies in the Theory of Ideology* (1984). Unconvinced that the canonical wars being fiercely waged within the academy have the potential to change much outside it, Appiah looks to academicians to "[disrupt the] discourse of difference" (55). He turns then to Thompson to argue that "the stability of today's capitalist society may require 'a pervasive *fragmentation* of the social order and a proliferation of divisions between its members'" (56).[53] Such fragmentation, which at one time or another we have all either witnessed or fostered (see Fields 1990),[54] has on Thompson's, Appiah's, and my view, the pernicious capacity to keep us so at odds with one another that we cannot form "a coherent alternative view which would provide a basis for political action" (Thompson 1984, 63).[55]

It is my abiding belief that the slave narratives provide us with just such an alternative view—and do so by recollecting us to *being* itself. That the voices of the slave narrators have not been heard in this way is in part a function of the reign of metaphysics itself and our Western ideology—the one the product of the other—and both of which teach us to deny what (or even that) the body knows. It is also a function of the fact that the narrators themselves had to speak (as must we all) in the language of metaphysics and operate, at least to a degree, within the normative dualism it spawned. (That the slaves were also signifying on the very language they employed, not surprisingly, has often gone unnoticed.)[56] Finally, it is a function of the fact that subsequent generations of African American writers (most particularly those postbellum novelists who followed hard on the heels of the slave narrators) set their sights on racial uplift and in so doing seem to have left the poor body behind. For where in the genteel middle-class novel do we ever find bodies? Alas, only in the fallen characters— or those about to fall—and, of course, always already in the plenitude of metaphor. It will be part of my task in this project, therefore, to flesh out the metaphors, to uncover what they seem to conceal—to argue that they are in and of themselves an unconcealment, speaking truths we have been taught not to hear. In redeeming the body in the text, of the text, and before the text, I also redeem the more transparent body of language.

More than being just a controlling theme of African American narrative, therefore, the conflicted fact of black embodiment became, immediately after Reconstruction, one of the tradition's most compelling "structuring assumptions."[57] That is to say, the problem of embodiment became a problem of form, virtually determining what could and could not appear in certain African American fiction, certainly helping to determine how it might appear there, and, furthermore, once it was there, helping to determine how a particular text would be received by its readers.[58] For the ex-slaves the problem of their embodiment led most immediately to the problem of representation: how to document the terrible abuse of their enslaved bodies without appearing to identify their "better selves" with what their liberal humanist audience would perceive as a debased physicality. But, at the same time, the problem of embodiment was the problem of enslavement. In other words, the ex-slaves had a certain cultural permission and narrative expectation that they would talk about the body. The dilemma facing them was what to do with this expectation. Some shied away from providing too much detail, either unwilling to offend their audience too much or out of a basic reluctance to share such private experiences with even a sympathetic public. For some it might have been an understandable question of shame, a conviction that talking about pain and torture was tantamount to talking about such other private matters as sexual relations. For others it might have been a misplaced sense of shame, that somehow they themselves were to blame for the suffering they had had to endure. But still others, like Mary Prince and William Grimes, wrote in detail about the physical demands placed on their working bodies. Even Harriet Wilson, a free black woman living in the North, enumerated in wracking detail all the chores her autobiographical heroine was compelled to perform and the cost to her body of performing them. Frederick Douglass clearly took pride in his body and his strength, as did Venture Smith. And, as I will argue in the pages that follow, all to one degree or another, acknowledged and drew on their bodies' *ek-static* presence in the world.

But whereas the slave narrators challenged metaphysics and interrogated liberal humanism, and did so through their body-selves, there is reason to believe, as I have already averred, that their post-Reconstruction successors back away from this project, accepting without apparent reservations the bourgeois conventions of late nineteenth-century domestic fiction and endorsing, however reluctantly or inadvertently, the era's accompanying neo-Hegelian ideology—an endorsement that, ironically enough, seems to be most evident in late nineteenth-century and early twentieth-century novels of the racial uplift school. I have already suggested why these sentimental novelists, who were struggling to enter the American mainstream as artists and citizens equal to whites, felt they could not afford an eruption of funky black bodies into their genteel bourgeois "fictions."[59] Neither did their educated, light-skinned heroes and heroines, except in their oft-expressed desire to elevate all members of the race, necessarily see much of a connection between themselves and their darker brethren.[60] Much is said of social equality among the blacks in this fiction, but very little is shown. Additionally, the authors' combined distrust of white culture and their adoption of many of its values seem to manifest themselves in the main characters' idealized "white" appearance or in their relative disembodiment, which is characteristic of virtually all bourgeois fiction of the nineteenth century. For those persons who have their material needs met—who eat well, live comfortably, and have servants to attend them—can pretend, at least in novels, to be completely unmarked by the daily needs of the body for adequate food, sleep, clothes, and shelter. Only the poor are always reminded, in their own deprivation, of their bodies' requirements. Although, as I shall argue later, the lives of field hands, sharecroppers, and other working-class blacks provide little more than a colorful backdrop to the lives of the more prosperous protagonists in most post-Reconstruction African American fiction, their continuing debasement and impoverishment represent the racial uplift that remains to be done and an indirect admonition to those who would fall from the ranks of the black middle class—since theirs is a fate that functions metonymically in these bourgeois novels as a reminder of the unwelcome, perdurable heritage of enslavement. At the very least, the poor, uneducated rural folk are portrayed as requiring the help of the middle-class mulattos to achieve their own racial advancement—this even though they are already decent, hard-working people.

The residuals of a postbellum complicity with neo-Hegelian thought seem also to be evident in early twentieth-century novels about passing—such as James Weldon Johnson's 1912 *The Autobiography of an Ex-Coloured Man* or Nella Larsen's 1929 *Passing*—in which the body refuses to be silenced even as it is made to disappear as a black body. These novels also give the appearance of reinforcing the idea of essential (or biological) racial differences even as they attempt to challenge such differences. In sum, during the decades after Reconstruction, the bodies that had been the visible sign of their ancestors' enslavement seem almost to have become an embarrassment to later generations of middle-class writers and their project of racial uplift and social advancement. Even so, it is possible—and, on my view, more productive—to argue that the late nineteenth- and early twentieth-century African American writers were, nonetheless, like their predecessors, using their narratives and the fact of their own racialized embodiment in order to *think being*—that is, to meditate on the meaning of human existence. Obviously, these postbellum writers meditated on the meaning of blackness in a white society, but at the same time they use the subjects of slavery and racism in order to reflect more fundamentally on the meaning and experience of human embodiment itself. That the founding impulse of African American narrative was itself grounded in the material experience of embodiment should come as no great surprise, since, on my view, our country's bitter history of institutionalized racism inspires, and even necessitates serious reflection on what philosophers have called "the problem of embodiment." It is no exaggeration to claim, therefore, that, perhaps uniquely among Western writers, African Americans have recognized the home truth that the problem of embodiment is the problem of human be-ing.[61]

Of course, the body of the African American was never completely absent from or entirely repressed in the postbellum novels, as is most evident from the fiction of the Harlem Renaissance (or what some have called the New Negro movement). What can be detected running from the mid-nineteenth century to the early twentieth century, then, are two parallel but competing strains of narrative, roughly corresponding to what eventually became known, during the Harlem Renaissance, as the Bohemian and Genteel Schools of African American literature. The Bohemian, represented by figures like Claude McKay, Zora Neale Hurston, and Langston Hughes, celebrated blackness and did not shy away from portraying African American bodies at work and at play. The Genteel School, represented by figures like W.E.B. Du Bois, Jessie Fauset, and Nella Larsen, were more inclined to celebrate the accomplishments and status of middle-class blacks, as part of the continuing project of uplifting the race.[62] Thus, even the early twentieth-century novels that are predicated on racial difference work to veil the bodies of their African American characters—a futile effort but one not without narrative consequences. It is my belief that these novels are the inheritors of a literary tradition that begins with writers like Harriet Jacobs, a tradition I will call the proto-Genteel School of slave narrators, that was built on the body's tacit (that is, unspoken) knowledge. But paralleling this tradition and providing a kind of corrective to it are those African American novels that are products of what I will call the proto-Bohemian School of writing, a tradition begun with Frederick Douglass and Harriet Wilson that is built on the body's express (that is, outspoken) recollection of *being*. But, whether the existence of a material self is highlighted or underplayed, these two competing strains of early African American narrative fiction are still informed by the philosophical problem of embodiment. Like the slave narratives before them, they, too, see the world otherwise.[63]

Thus the rest of my book is divided into three chapters and an epilogue. Chapter 1, "Thinking Through the Body," establishes the philosophical under-pinnings of the project. Chapter 2, "The Body's Recollection of Being," re-trieves the destructive hermeneutics of Frederick Douglass's first two narratives against a background of other male-authored slave narratives, beginning with a brief discussion of *The Life of Olaudah Equiano*. Chapter 3, "Disappearing Acts," retrieves the destructive hermeneutics of Harriet Wilson's *Our Nig* and Harriet Jacobs's *Incidents in the Life of a Slave Girl* against a background of other female-authored slave narratives, beginning with a brief discussion of *The History of Mary Prince*. This chapter opens with a discussion of how the prob-lem of embodiment manifested itself differently for African American women and how these differences led to differences in their narratives. The title, "Disappearing Acts," is meant to suggest how the material body, which plays such a major role in critiquing liberal humanism in the nineteenth-century male slave narratives, begins its slow descent into obscurity in the female narratives as early as the mid-nineteenth century.[64] The Epilogue, "Justice in the Flesh," explains how the racialized black body is further repressed in many postbellum and turn-of-the-century narratives—a repression that carries with it certain nar-rative restraints that eventually become formal markers in much African Ameri-can narrative.[65] But repressed or no, the perdurable fact of human embodiment marks these novels on virtually every page, as the authors make their impas-sioned, sentimental, and urgent pleas for a justice in the flesh that is both the gift and requirement of our human body-selves.

NOTES

1. Bryan S. Turner has argued that "our attitudes to the body are at least in part a reflection of the whole Christian tradition in the West. My body is flesh—it is the loca-tion of corrupting appetite, of sinful desire and of private irrationality. It is the negation of the true self, but also an instructive site of moral purpose and intention" (Turner 1984, 8). That is to say, if we wish to be saved we must "salve the body and . . . save the soul" (9).

2. Jaggar (1983, 46, 40, 41, 42). Jaggar maintains that "the liberal problematic would be transformed" if liberals were to include biology in their theorizing. Rather than treating "community and cooperation" as puzzling aberrations, "the existence of egoism, competitiveness and conflict . . . would themselves become puzzling and problematic" (41).

3. Though it probably can go without saying that we Westerners cannot escape the prison walls of our metaphysics, I will state it anyway. As Fredric Jameson observes of Jacques Derrida's work, his "thought denies itself the facile illusion of having passed be-yond the metaphysics of which it stands as a critique; of having emerged from the old models into some unexplored country whose existence such a critique had implied, if only by the negation of a negation. Instead, his philosophic language feels its way grop-ingly along the walls of its own conceptual prison, describing it from the inside as

though it were only one of the possible worlds of which the others are nonetheless inconceivable" (Jameson 1972, 186). As Derrida himself argues, "There is no sense in doing without the concepts of metaphysics in order to shake metaphysics. We have no language . . . which is foreign to this history; we can pronounce not a single destructive proposition which has not already had to slip into the form, the logic, and the implicit postulations of precisely what it seeks to contest" (Derrida 1978, 280–81). One might argue similarly of the slave narratives that they too offer a necessarily incomplete yet effective critique of metaphysics, and do so even as they also apparently conform to the formal and thematic expectations of their nineteenth-century liberal, Christian, abolitionist audience. One might also at least ask if the slaves did not bring with them memories of languages that were not metaphysical—at least in the Western sense. On this, see Paris (1995).

4. In his impassioned attack on the findings of nineteenth-century ethnologists, which he delivered on 12 July 1854, Frederick Douglass argued, for example, that debasing those whom they would enslave, slaveholders justify their own behavior and do so by overcoming "the *instinctive consciousness of the common brotherhood of man*" (Blassingame 1982, 507; emphasis added). Hoping to avoid any reified, nostalgic interpretation of Being in this project, which using an initial capital letter seems to permit if not invite, I have chosen *being* instead.

5. The term "body-self" is my own. Caught, like others before me, in the dualistic web of our language, I have coined this term to try to overcome the mind/body split that makes it possible to think that "I" can *have* a *body*, as though it were equally feasible to think there could be an "I" that did not have a body. "Body-self" is no doubt vulnerable to the charge that it, too, could engender its opposite, as in "nonbody-self," but the simple fact is that, given the way we think, I need the two terms to make my point: In English "body" does not imply a self, nor does "self" imply a body. And in my construction, neither term is an adjective. The term itself has the virtue of looking strange enough to get attention but not too strange—and of placing body before self, which, on my view, is just about right. I must confess I have not replaced the word "body" with "body-self" at every point in this project; I have tried to use it just often enough to keep my argument visible. Compare my use of "body-self" with Peter J. Hadreas's use of "body-subject" in his book on Merleau-Ponty (1986). Distinguishing his term from the more familiar and conventional ways of thinking about the body as either "objective" or an "idea," Hadreas defends his terminology by noting that for Merleau-Ponty, "the body always functions within a system and counts as a 'subject-side' of a subject/world system" and therefore, by this reasoning, "the expression, the 'body-subject,' counts as an appropriate general term for this fundamental notion" (Hadreas 1986, 63). As I am arguing that the slaves used their bodies to contest the notion of subject and subjectivity, I find "body-self" is more appropriate than Hadreas's term since it seems better able to refuse any prior liberal humanist claim.

6. For an essay that takes virtually the opposite position from mine, see Barrett 1995.

7. For a discussion of this concept see Chapter 1 (below).

8. For a discussion of Hegel's model as it applies to the slave-master relationship in American slavery, see Genovese (1978), in which he argues that "Hegel, who had studied classical political economy . . . , demonstrated that the deference, the degree of autonomy, and most strikingly, the irresistible compulsion driving the master to recognize the slave's existence as an independent being, all had roots in the labor process. The

master could not avoid knowing that his existence depended upon the slave" (34; see also pages 35 and 40). For a different angle on the same question, see Carter (1978, 89–91), and Blassingame (1978, 137–38). For an effective rebuttal to Hegel's notion of how a slave's subjectivity is formed, see Douglass (1855, 189). For a reading of Douglass that draws on Hegel, see Ziolkowski (1991). For a Hegelian reading of Du Bois, see Adell (1994).

9. For a comprehensive study of contemporary "racial formation," see Omi and Winant (1994). For a study of the development of scientific racism in Britain, see Stepan (1982). See also Foster (1994, 24–28) and Jordan (1968).

10. See also Clarke (1978).

11. As Winthrop D. Jordan puts it succinctly, "At the start of English settlement in America, no one had in mind to establish the institution of Negro slavery. Yet in less than a century the foundations of a peculiar institution had been laid" (Jordan 1968, 44). See also Giddings (1984).

12. Or, as Jordan puts it, "once the Negro became fully the slave it is not hard to see why white men looked down upon him" (Jordan 1968, 44).

13. Citing a 1664 statute in Maryland that attempted to assign perpetual enslavement through the father's lineage, Fields argues that "race" does not explain the language of this law. Instead, she argues, "the law shows society in the act of inventing race" (Fields 1990, 107). This law was intended to protect the property rights of the slave owners. Fields cites the preamble as reading: "'And forasmuch as divers freeborne English women forgetfull of their free Condicon and to the disgrace of our Nation doe intermarry with Negro slaues by which alsoe diuers suites may arise touching the Issue of such woemen and a great damage doth befall the Masters of such Negroes....'" (Fields 1990, 107). On her view, it is evident that race is not yet germane to the notion of perpetual enslavement because the law does not refer to "white women," but only "freeborne English women" (107).

14. See, for example, Fisher and Stepto's *Afro-American Literature: The Reconstruction of Instruction*, in which Stepto argues that what is needed is a study (like theirs) that "not only demonstrates the links between various critical approaches and course designs but also pursues this activity with considerable emphasis on what is literary (as opposed to sociological, ideological, etc.) in Afro-American written art" (Fisher and Stepto, 1979, 1).

15. Nancy Hartsock has argued similarly that "the creation of the Other is simultaneously the creation of the transcendent and omnipotent theorizer who can persuade himself that he exists outside time and space and power relations" (Hartsock 1987, 195). Peter Hohendahl has argued that "[i]n the Age of Enlightenment the concept of criticism cannot be separated from the institution of the public sphere. Every judgment is designed to be directed toward a public; communication with the reader is an integral part of the system. . . . Seen historically, the modern concept of literary criticism is closely tied to the rise of the liberal, bourgeois public sphere in the early eighteenth century. Literature served the emancipation movement of the middle class as an instrument to gain self-esteem and to articulate its human demands against the absolutist state and a hierarchical society" (Hohendahl 1982, 52).

16. On a similar topic, see Stephanie Smith (1994). For accounts of how reason becomes disembodied, see Bordo (1987), Leder (1990), and Barker (1995). Not all slaves were engaged in this critique, as is evident in Henry Bibb's *Narrative*, which he concludes by promising that he pledges himself forthwith "ever to contend for the natural

equality of the human family, without regard to color, which is but fading *matter*, while *mind* makes the man" (Bibb 1850, 204).

17. Rorty himself argues that "the vocabulary of Enlightenment rationalism, although it was essential to the beginnings of liberal democracy, has become an impediment to the preservation and progress of democratic societies" (Rorty 1989, 44). I take the phrase "end of history," of course, from the book by that name written by Francis Fukuyama (1992).

18. Compare my argument with that of Sidonie Smith, who says that Harriet Jacobs, in "trespass[ing] upon the grounds of the autobiographical 'I,'" like other nineteenth-century women who refused to be silenced, "challenges the very notions of American freedom, democracy, and equality, and in doing so contests the presence of the agency and autonomy associated with American notions of bourgeois individuality" (Smith 1993, 25, 45). While I agree with much of Smith's argument, I do not think she goes far enough in acknowledging what I am calling the anti-humanist critique (or the destructive hermeneutics) of the slave narratives. See also Stephanie Smith (1994).

19. Rorty's solution is to keep the spheres separate. On his view, "We need a redescription of liberalism as the hope that culture as a whole can be 'poeticized' rather than as the Enlightenment hope that it can be 'rationalized' or 'scientized'" (Rorty 1989, 53). Thus he argues on behalf of a culture in which citizens have "given up the attempt to unite one's private ways of dealing with one's finitude and one's sense of obligation to other human beings" (68). His model for achieving a better society is that of an ungrounded conversation (Rorty 1982, 160–75; see also Rorty 1985). Hartsock finds value in Rorty's conversational model of philosophizing but argues correctly that he "ignores power relations" and that he is "the inheritor of the disembodied, transcendent voice of reason" (Hartsock 1987, 199, 200). For another incisive critique of Rorty, see Fraser (1989, 93–110). Not everyone will agree with my assessment of the slave narratives; much critical energy has been expended, for example, in demonstrating the tension in Douglass's narratives between Douglass as racial exemplar (that is, a type) and Douglass as personal exemplar (that is, an individual). See the essays in Sundquist (1990), for example. Even though, in an 1852 address, Douglass insists on the singleness of men (Blassingame 1982, 352–53), elsewhere in his speeches he stresses the community of men and women, as he does in an 1849 address, "Too Much Religion, Too Little Humanity," in which he tells his listeners that just because he is black does not mean he does not love his friends and family. Furthermore, he says, if they were to assume the status of slave, they "would feel that we were your brothers and sisters"—a discovery that would soon result in the end of slavery (Blassingame 1982, 193).

20. As Thad Ziolkowski argues, Douglass, for example, "*writes the grain* of lived material circumstances" (Ziolkowski 1991, 149).

21. Readers should keep in mind that my project should in no way be construed as an attack on rationality but rather as an attempt to reconfigure it by re-placing it in the body. Levin rereads Heidegger's bodily metaphors and finds in their use evidence that Heidegger talked more about the body than he himself realized (Levin 1985).

22. I am not unmindful of the critical debates regarding the usefulness of European philosophy to a study of African American literature. For a defense of its applicability, see most recently Sandra Adell's book in which she "reflect[s] upon the extent to which twentieth-century black literature and criticism are implicated in the ensemble of Western literature and philosophy" (Adell 1994, 3). My project seeks to demonstrate the *critique* of Western philosophy that occurs in nineteenth-century African American literature.

23. For a fairly unfriendly critique of Spanos, see Lewandowski (1994).

24. Of Douglass's speeches, on the other hand, I would argue that he attempts the nearly impossible task of convincing the country to make good on its liberal humanistic contract with its citizens—including those it has enslaved for life. Thus he continues to rebuke America even as he argues that the mantle of liberty should protect all people. The reality is, he says in his farewell speech to the British people on 30 March 1847, that all of America "is one great falsehood, from beginning to end" (Blassingame 1982, 21; see also 27, 28). Or, as he puts it in an address delivered on 24 September 1847, he is no patriot, for how can he "love a country where the blood of my own blood, the flesh of my own flesh, is now toiling under the lash?" (Blassingame 1982, 103). Later, however, he will come to argue that the Constitution itself is anti-slavery (see Blassingame 1982, 349, 385).

25. Fields reminds us that "[t]he three-fifths clause does not distinguish between *blacks* and *whites*—not even, using more polite terms, between black and white *people*.... The three-fifths clause distinguishes between *free Persons*—who might be of European or African descent—and *other Persons*, a euphemism for *slaves*" (Fields 1990, 99).

26. See Memmi (1991).

27. Hortense Spillers describes the process of enslavement as reducing "the captive body . . . to a thing, becoming *being for* the captor"; as a consequence of "this absence *from* a subject position, the captured sexualities provide a physical and biological expression of 'otherness'" (Spillers 1987, 67).

28. For a recent attempt to reconcile the ideas of Heidegger and Merleau-Ponty, see Olafson (1995).

29. Borrowing from Foucault, Candace D. Lang characterizes what she calls "the advent of modernism" as being "marked by the emergence of the concept of the individual (favored by both socioeconomic and technological developments: the decline of the feudal system and concomitant increase in capitalist endeavor) and the invention of the printing press, which would enhance the notion of authorship by saving the text from the relative anonymity of oral tradition" (Lang 1988, 14). On this, see also Sidonie Smith (1993, 1–23) and Foucault (1979).

30. A major theme running through Douglass's speeches was an attempt to reclaim the principles of the Declaration of Independence for African Americans—most particularly the principle of liberty. In a resolution he submitted for approval to the Anti-Slavery Society of Canada in 1854, for example, Douglass urges the membership to condemn the expansion of slavery into Kansas and Nebraska and the consequent betrayal of the Declaration of Independence (Blassingame 1982, 495–96; see also 487). In respect to the notion of liberty, it must be acknowledged that Douglass considered it an indisputable, unchanging, and eternal truth. As he put it in an 1854 speech, one does not need to look for "new truths, till the old truths which have been uttered from the Declaration of Independence" are acknowledged and put into practice; "truth is from everlasting to everlasting. Such is the great truth of man's right to liberty. It entered into the very idea of man's creation" (Blassingame 1982, 454; see also 261). In the preface to his 1860 narrative, William Craft explains that he and his wife, Ellen, who even as slaves were familiar with the language of the Declaration of Independence, felt perfectly justified in escaping slavery "in order to obtain those rights which are so vividly set forth in the Declaration"; imbued with its principles of universal human rights, moreover, they "could not understand by what right [they] were held as 'chattels'" (Craft 1860, 270). See also Brown (1853, 181–83) and Sutton Griggs's little-known novel, *Imperium in Imperio: A Study of*

the Negro Race Problem (1899). For a discussion of how Jacobs modifies the notion of liberty, see Stephanie Smith (1994, 133–59).

31. As Sidonie Smith observes of this phenomenon, "the individual self could endure as a concept of human beingness only if, despite the specificities of individual experience, despite the multiplication of differences among people, the legend continued to bear universal marks" (Smith 1993, 9). James Olney reminds us that the words I have quoted from the Declaration of Independence were written by Jefferson, asserting that its call to resist oppression was exactly what "all the slave narratives [are] about, and Douglass's supremely so" (Olney 1989, 7).

32. For extended commentary on Foucault's anti-humanist discourse, see White (1979; 1987), Habermas (1981), and Fraser (1989). On Fraser's view, Habermas's attack on Foucault misses the point that Foucault is not rejecting modernity *tout court*, but that aspect of it we identify as humanism (Fraser 1989, 36). As Fraser succinctly summarizes the issue, the question is: On what grounds does Foucault reject humanism? Her argument is that "when Foucault is read as rejecting humanism exclusively on conceptual and philosophical grounds, Habermas's charge misses the mark"; on the other hand, when he is understood to be rejecting it on "strategic grounds, Habermas's charge is on target" because "Foucault has failed to establish that a pragmatic, de-Cartesianized humanism lacks critical force in the contemporary world" (52). "Finally, when Foucault is read as rejecting humanism on normative grounds, moral-philosophical considerations support Habermas's position. Without a non-humanist ethical paradigm, Foucault cannot make good his normative case against humanism" (53). On my view, the slave narratives offer just such a new paradigm and succeed where both Foucault and Heidegger fail. Clearly, as part of their own project of Enlightenment, the slave narrators struggled for emancipation (in the strong, modernist sense) and just as clearly they offered a dialectical form of critique (again, in the strong, modernist sense). But they did so from their particular and unique vantage point of embodied human be-ing—a vantage point that, by necessity, meant they also offered a negative critique, still in the strong sense, of liberal humanism itself. In grounding their critique on the principle of human embodiment, the slaves were, of course, paradoxically—and necessarily—still being metaphysical.

33. For a discussion of how pro-slavery Southerners rallied to defend themselves and their institution against the Abolitionists in the decades before the Civil War, see George M. Fredrickson's book, in which he argues that many Southerners, influenced by "Christian and humanitarian values," claimed that "the slave was not only unfit for freedom but was ideally suited to slavery; for the Negro found happiness and fulfillment only when he had a white master" (Fredrickson 1971, 52). "As long as the control of the master was firm and assured, the slave would be happy, loyal, and affectionate; but remove or weaken the authority of the master, and he would revert to type as a bloodthirsty savage" (54). See also Blassingame's *The Slave Community*, in which he argues that "the ministers not only denied that slavery in the abstract was immoral, they also insisted it was a divine institution which was a blessing to both master and slave" (Blassingame 1979, 82). For Douglass's views, see, for example, his 1847 speech, "Love of God, Love of Man, Love of Country" (Blassingame 1982, 93–106).

34. Althusser argues that "ideology 'acts' or 'functions' in such a way that it 'recruits' subjects among the individuals (it recruits them all), or 'transforms' the individuals into subjects (it transforms them all) by that very precise operation which [he calls] *interpellation* or hailing, and which can be imagined along the lines of the most commonplace everyday police (or other) hailing: 'Hey, you there!' " (Althusser 1970,

174). He distinguishes between (1) the (Repressive) State Apparatus and (2) the Ideological State Apparatuses (which can be schools, churches, families, etc.) by arguing that the first is singular and wholly public, while the second is plural, public, *and* private. He summarizes these differences by claiming that "the Repressive State Apparatus functions 'by violence', whereas the Ideological State Apparatuses *function 'by ideology'*" (145). For a critique of Althusser, see Thompson (1984).

35. In *My Bondage and My Freedom*, Douglass uses uncannily similar terms when he asserts that "[t]he slave is a subject, subjected by others; the slaveholder is a subject, but he is the author of his own subjection" (Douglass 1855, 189). For commentary on this, see Wald (1995, 101).

36. Of course, everybody can have it at birth and it can still be a made truth (such as a right to freedom). But the constructed nature of this truth is particularly evident when some human beings are said not to be born with the very characteristic that makes other human beings human.

37. This returns us, once again, to a paradox. For in claiming freedom for themselves, they were, of course, invoking a humanistic principle. In grounding their claim in the body-self, they were at once challenging both liberal humanism and metaphysics and, as I have already indicated, being metaphysical.

38. One might be tempted here to claim that there is a Western metaphysics from which a non-Westerner could indeed escape. At points in this book, I allude to this possibility but have been prevented from pursuing it by the limitations of my own epistemology. I recognize that, at times, I am trying to have it both ways—for, after all, from what conceivable uncorrupted position do I formulate and in what uncorrupted language do I articulate my own critique of metaphysics? Yet Levin's discussion of Merleau-Ponty convinces me that such a critique might be possible. Thus I find myself vacillating between his and Derrida's competing claims.

39. Again, I know I am hedging.

40. On this subject, see also Thompson (1984), when he remarks, in critiquing Chomsky, that "[o]ur competence to speak is a *practical* competence. It is also a competence which is differentiated socially and which is always manifested in actual instances of discourse" (7–8). On Douglass's ability to change the meaning of "nigger," see Baker (1980, 33–34). See also Kibbey and Stepto (1991). Pierre Macherey has argued that words are transformed as they are "woven" into a text—that is, "once the old bonds are broken there emerges a new 'reality'" (Macherey 1966, 44). See also Bakhtin (1987, especially 259–300).

41. For a pointed critique of Foucault's own unspoken reliance on the notion of subjectivity, see Balbus (1987.)

42. On the origins of this term "zero-degree," see Barthes (1953). For a discussion of the related phenomenon by which the ruling class (the bourgeoisie) ex-nominates itself, see Barthes (1957). As Barthes explains it, "the bourgeoisie is defined as *the social class which does not want to be named*. 'Bourgeois', 'petit-bourgeois', 'capitalism', 'proletariat' are the locus of an unceasing haemorrhage: meaning flows out of them until their very name becomes unnecessary" (1957, 138). Compare this with Lewis Gordon's claim that even though "the white body is regarded as Presence, it lives the mode of Absence, and it offers, instead, its perspective as Presence. In other words, the white body is expected to be seen by others without seeing itself being seen" (Gordon 1995, 103). For a discussion of how visual representations of black embodiment function in Western culture as a way to address the metaphysical problem of embodiment itself, see Dyer (1986,

67–139, but especially 138–39).

43. For more discussion of this essay, see Chapter 1 (below). Du Bois saw the dangers in this kind of thinking. In his attack on Booker T. Washington's call for African Americans to be given primarily (if not exclusively) a practical or industrial education, Du Bois anticipates Heidegger in asserting that there is a danger in "recent educational movements. The tendency is here, born of slavery and quickened to renewed life by the crazy imperialism of the day, to regard human beings as among the material resources of a land to be trained with an eye single to future dividends" (Du Bois 1903, 428). Fifty-five years earlier, in an address delivered in Rochester, Douglass argued that slavery's first task is to deform the very qualities "of its victims which distinguish *men* from *things*, and *persons* from *property*. Its first aim is to destroy all sense of high moral and religious responsibility. It reduces man to a mere machine" (Blassingame 1982, 255). And in her autobiography, Harriet Jacobs comments that these "God-breathing machines are no more, in the sight of their masters, than the cotton they plant, or the horses they tend" (Jacobs 1861, 8).

44. Following the practice of others, I have used the pagination of the German edition.

45. I am not the first to see a connection between Heidegger's concepts and the experience of slaves. Baker also makes this connection explicit in claiming that for the African American slave, "the white externality provided no ontological or ideological certainties; in fact, it explicitly denied slaves the grounds of being" (Baker 1980, 30). And, further, "[t]he white externality must have loomed like the Heideggerian 'nothingness,' the negative foundation of being" (31).

46. In Heidegger's terms, Being; in mine, *being*.

47. That this anxiety or dread did not disappear with slavery is evident in the use Richard Wright made of existential philosophy in his novels; on this see Fishburn (1977).

48. In using *ek-static*, I hope to echo Heidegger's sense that *Dasein* (literally, being-there, Heidegger's term for the being that is human) stands out in what David Krell describes as "the various moments of the temporality of care, being 'thrown' out of a past and 'projecting' itself toward a future by way of the present" (Heidegger 1947, 228, editor's note). In sum, it is what makes us human. In claiming presence for black slaves, I am challenging the white West's perception of them. In his own philosophical interrogation of racism, Lewis Gordon equates *Presence* with facticity and *Absence* with transcendence, arguing that in the Manichean world of anti-black racism, the two values are distributed differently between blacks and whites—with absence for the blacks becoming, as in the case of Ralph Ellison's hero, not transcendence at all but an invisibility which "fails to translate into . . . *human* presence" (Gordon 1995, 98). Conversely, presence is a problem for Frantz Fanon, who describes what it is like to be perceived as black. In "The Fact of Blackness," Fanon asserts that "[i]n the white world the man of colour encounters difficulties in the development of his bodily schema. Consciousness of the body is solely a negating activity" (Fanon 1952, 78). Once, after he has been called a "Negro" by a frightened child, he reports (79) of himself that having been "assailed at various points, the corporeal schema crumbled, its place taken by a racial epidermal schema. . . . I discovered my blackness, my ethnic characteristics; and I was battered down by tom-toms, cannibalism, intellectual deficiency, fetishism, racial defects, slave-ships, and above all else, above all: 'Sho' good eatin'.'" Fanon's impassioned response to the rejection and psychological abuse he encounters everywhere among whites is "to

assert myself as a BLACK MAN. Since the other hesitated to recognize me, there remained only one solution: to make myself known" (81)—much as I argue the slaves
made themselves known in their narratives. As Gordon remarks of Fanon's encounter,
"to see him as black is not to see *him* at all. His presence is a form of absence" (99).

49. In the introduction to *Being and Time*, Heidegger offers a critique of tradition,
arguing that both understanding and the past do not *"follow after"* but precede us; that is,
they go ahead of us (Heidegger 1927b, 63; this is a different translation of the introduction from that appearing in the full text of *Being and Time*, from which I also cite). As a
result, "Dasein not only has the inclination to be ensnared in the world in which it is and
to interpret itself in terms of that world by its reflected light; at the same time Dasein is
also ensnared in a tradition which it more or less explicitly grasps. This tradition deprives
Dasein of its own leadership in questioning and choosing" (65). Most particularly, tradition interferes with the understanding that makes us human at all, that is to say, "the ontological understanding" (65). Elsewhere Heidegger argues that "[m]etaphysics does not
ask about the truth of Being itself. Nor does it therefore ask in what way the essence of
man belongs to the truth of Being. Metaphysics has not only failed up to now to ask this
question, the question is inaccessible to metaphysics as such" (Heidegger 1947, 226–27).
It is my argument that the slave narratives ask—and answer—this question in terms of
the body-self. For a summary of the exclusionary attitudes toward those that are embodied differently, which the Western tradition has inherited from Plato and Aristotle, see
Spelman (1988), who shows how even the so-called inclusive discourse of American
feminism has been corrupted by this thinking. For a discussion of how we invent the
traditions we need to shore up our own contested claims to legitimacy, see Marilyn Butler (1985, especially 39–41).

50. Speaking in more general terms, Sidonie Smith also argues that, even taking the
editorial pressures of their Abolitionist sponsors into account, the antebellum African
American writer "had more latitude in the choice of narrative thrust and detail than his
successor, who would be bound to the whims of less sympathetic publishers and readers"
(Smith 1974, 9).

51. For additional discussion of Appiah's ideas, see Appiah (1992, especially chapters 1 and 2).

52. For an outsider's commentary on this debate, see Fuss (1989, 73–96).

53. Appiah's own quotation is from Thompson (1984, 62). The emphasis is
Thompson's.

54. Fields ends her essay by identifying those who continue to "create and re-create
race today" not just as white racists mobs but as those "academic 'liberals' and 'pro-
gressives'" in whose version of race the neutral shibboleths *difference* and *diversity* re-
place words like *slavery, injustice, oppression*, and *exploitation*, diverting attention from
the anything-but-neutral history these words denote" (Fields 1990, 117, 118).

55. See Appiah (1989, 56).

56. Raymond Williams and Thompson both remind us that no ideology, no matter
how powerful, is ever able to silence its critics completely; neither, for that matter, can
theorists themselves (especially if they are Marxist) even agree on what a correct definition of ideology might be (see Geuss 1981, 4–44; Williams 1977, 55–56 and 112–13).
For his part, Thompson argues that

the study of ideology may be conceived as the study of the ways in which meaning (signification)
serves to sustain relations of domination. Just as it cannot be assumed that dominant values or
norms are shared by all members of a society, so too it would be misguided to approach a society

on the assumption that its unity and stability were secured by a 'dominant ideology'. For ideology operates, not so much as a coherent system of statements imposed on a population from above, but rather through a complex series of mechanisms whereby meaning is mobilized, in the discursive practices of everyday life, for the maintenance of relations of domination. (Thompson 1984, 63)

Where Thompson urges theorists to investigate the "discursive forms" whereby ideology is "expressed," I am trying to theorize how the dominant ideology is discursively contested in nineteenth-century slave narratives (64). On this as it applies to Douglass, see Ziolkowski (1991) and Stephanie Smith (1994), who also discusses Jacobs.

57. See Jehlen (1981, 595). Jehlen is discussing the middle-class novel and its formal relationship to bourgeois ideology.

58. For more on this, see Tate (1992). On a related subject, see Grayson (1993).

59. For more on the subject of how prevailing conventions affected the composition of postbellum African American women's writing, see Tate (1992, especially 51–69).

60. For an exception, see Griggs (1899).

61. Another group of writers who seem capable of recognizing this human truth are those of the British working class, which, in part, will be the argument of Kevin Asman's Michigan State University doctoral dissertation.

62. The problem with this division, however, is the fact that a writer like Larsen does admit female sexual desire into her text, if only obliquely, thus aligning her with the Bohemians. But her upper middle-class African American women characters are light enough to pass for white: they are thus embodied as women but not as blacks. In her preface to *Contending Forces*, Hopkins issues a call to arms to her fellow African Americans, urging them to join her in portraying positive role models in their fiction, which can stand as both inspiration to other members of the race and as testimonials to their "*inmost thoughts and feelings,*" which have as yet gone unrecorded (Hopkins 1900, 14). See also Du Bois (1926).

63. I shall have to limit myself in the Epilogue to discussing those post-Reconstruction texts that were the precursors to the Genteel School and leave for another time discussion of how the meditation on embodiment has been conducted in twentieth-century African American narrative.

64. I take this title, of course, from Terry McMillan's 1989 novel of the same name. In her narrative, however, it is the men who disappear.

65. For an explanation of the changes that mark the shift from antebellum to postbellum slave narratives, see William Andrews (1989), in which he argues that most "postbellum ex-slave autobiographers . . . take pride in having endured slavery without having lost their sense of worth or purpose and without having given in to the despair that the antebellum narrator pictures as the lot of so many who languished in slavery" (Andrews 1989, 66). For a discussion of what he calls "the novelization of voice" in mid-nineteenth-century African American fictional narratives, see Andrews (1990). See also Claudia Tate's (1992) comprehensive history of early African American women's fiction.

1

Thinking Through the Body

Let me begin this chapter by unpacking some of Maurice Merleau-Ponty's concepts that are crucial to this project. I take my ideas whenever I can directly from Merleau-Ponty himself and have, in this effort, been strongly influenced by David Michael Levin's reading and adaptation of him in *The Body's Recollection of Being* (1985) and in a more recent essay, "Justice in the Flesh" (1990). What makes my work original is the application of these ideas to the slave narratives. It is my belief that these narratives offer us late twentieth-century readers a way to rethink thinking—a model, if you will, for thinking through the body (a phrase used by Levin in 1985 and by Adrienne Rich nearly ten years previously).[1] Levin, like Merleau-Ponty (and like Rich, whom he cites), is attempting to reshape thinking itself, which he argues is too implicated in the metaphysical tradition that hates the body. To correct this, he argues, thinking must repair its inborn relationship with our bodily sensations and sentiments and learn from "our bodily being" (Levin 1985, 61). My argument, following Levin and Heidegger, whom Levin quotes here, is that, contra metaphysics, "we 'are' bodily" (49).[2] We do not simply have or live in our bodies; we live as and through our bodies. As thinking beings, we therefore think through our bodies, even if metaphysics tells us otherwise. Our bodies have a tacit knowledge that we carry with us but often cannot speak (an idea also found in Michael Polanyi).[3] On one hand, because we use our bodies to attend to the world, they function as the nullpoint of our perceptual capacities. Our experience of the world is, in other words, a from-to phenomenon: We attend from our bodies to the world. As a result, our bodies can be (and often are) experienced as though they were absent to "us"—giving the false impression that the body-self can be split into a body and a self, an argument that underlies Drew Leder's (1990) meditation on Merleau-Ponty, Polanyi, and Descartes.[4] Because of metaphysics—which not only separates, divides, and alienates but also despises and humiliates the body—we see our bodies as distinct and self-contained material housing for our distinct and self-contained selves.[5] As I have suggested in the Introduction, liberal theory encourages us further to think of ourselves as separate entities, disembodied, rational beings who are dependent on one another for neither our identity nor our well-being. On my view, this conception of human beings as solitary, independent, disembodied creatures is both incorrect and harmful to our well-being, and is a political philosophy that must be undone. It is a view of human nature, for example, that in this country has historically helped to promote racial divisions wherein blacks, who were both identified with and known by their bodies, were said to be inferior to whites, who were identified by their bodies yet known by their rationality. Thus, one might argue that racial boundaries thematize the metaphysical perception and consequent practical experience that Westerners have of our separation and separability— just as the slave experience itself, wherein Africans were separated by law from Europeans and by bills of sale from one another, thematized the same dualism in Western political philosophy. In other words, the essence of slavery is a denial of human interconnectedness and a denial of what the body knows.

That the body "knows" is evident in virtually all our metaphors, as, for example, in our attempts to grasp an idea, hold a thought, turn a phrase.[6] That the body knows is also evident in the skill of our hands; the hands that have typed this manuscript, for example, know—as "I" do not—where the keys are.[7] Or, to overcome the mind/body dualism: The *I* of *me* that cannot verbalize its knowledge nonetheless knows where the keys are.[8] The same *I* of *me* also knows how to knead bread, knit sweaters, till the soil, form clay into statues, hug a friend, caress an animal. The *I* of *me* that speaks in words can tell someone else how to knead bread or knit a sweater, whereas the *I* of *me* that cannot speak in words can show someone else how to do these things—and probably do so more effectively, certainly more efficiently. But in all these cases of kneading, knitting, and so on, the *I* of *me* that speaks in words is dependent for its knowledge on the *I* of *me* that speaks in gestures. The hands of a skilled worker know how to plane the wood, how to bring out its grain and luster, how to form seamless joints. In working the wood (the clay, the metal, the cloth), the artisan expresses our primordial (and ongoing but hidden) relatedness-to-*being* (see also Levin 1985, 129). As Heidegger says, "the hand's gestures run everywhere through language, in their most perfect purity precisely when man speaks by being silent" (Heidegger 1954b, 16). And later, "We have called thinking the handicraft *par excellence. . . .* Thinking guides and sustains every gesture of the hand" (23). Not only does our language bespeak our gestures (as occurs in our metaphorical expressions); on Heidegger's view, "All the work of the hand is rooted in thinking" (16). Levin both accepts and reverses this truth, arguing that there exists "a maintaining of thought, which is rooted in the work of the hands" (Levin 1985, 123). It is only metaphysics that teaches us to overlook and even disparage what our hands know, that teaches us to regard the work of our hands (our handiwork) as somehow inferior to the work of the mind. It is metaphysics that also teaches us to separate hands and mind, associating the latter with subjectivity, that is, with the humanistic *I*, which is known in its opposition to the *not-I*. Thus, humanistically or metaphysically speaking, *I* is *not-my-body* and *I* is *not-you*. In short, the *I* is a disembodied individual. As a result, on Levin's view, the gift of our hands has not reached its full potential, which we could reach if only we could recognize what it is our hands already know (1985, 125).[9] To pursue his deconstruction of the subject/object, mind/body dualisms that characterize classical metaphysics—dualisms that must be overcome if we are to effectively resist the divisive, destructive nihilism of the age—Levin turns (as I turn) to Merleau-Ponty. But it is central to my argument that these same dualisms have already been overcome to a considerable degree in the composition of the slave narratives. The challenge to metaphysics is there; it is only that we have been prevented until now—by the thinking of metaphysics itself—from seeing it in its full radicalness. It is this challenge I hope to reveal more fully in the next two chapters when I reread selected slave narratives. What must be disclosed, brought back to light, is the slave body's primordial awareness of human interconnectedness through our common attunement to *being*.[10] What we are seeking here, in other words, is a genuine recollection of *being*, one embodied in the slaves and in their narratives.[11]

On Levin's view, we begin life able to understand *being* and our relation to it, an understanding that is ours by virtue of our embodiment. In other words, we know (of) *being* because we are embodied (Levin 1985, 8). It is Levin's argument that our bodies are designed and destined for movement, which he calls, following Merleau-Ponty, our capacity for "motility" (100). But he goes beyond Merleau-Ponty's phenomenology of the body to claim that this ability to move forms "a body of genuine understanding," which permits human beings to experience our innate place "in the field of Being as a whole" (Levin 1985, 99, 103).[12] In a baby's first gestures (gestures being a more limited expression of the entire body's potential for motility), however, Levin finds evidence of the inborn knowledge of our own relatedness-to-*being* and an unspoken understanding of the difference between *being* and being(s) (11). Offering his own challenge to the liberal humanist-metaphysical notion of the atomistic subject, Levin reads Merleau-Ponty as inviting him to argue that the body is "*inherently interactional*," inclined at birth to engage other human beings (Levin 1990, 40). It is only later, after the child's body has been thoroughly socialized, that it is marked by metaphysics and no longer able to see its inherent sociability.[13] Levin finds support for his argument that we all begin life as "*individuated* bodies, inhabited by intercorporeal synchronizations" (Levin 1990, 41) in "The Child's Relations With Others," where Merleau-Ponty describes a phase in early human development of "pre-communication, in which there is not one individual over against another but rather an anonymous collectivity, an undifferentiated group life" (Merleau-Ponty 1964a, 119). Levin uses these insights and his own observations to conclude that as infants, we are, in effect, predisposed "to acknowledge others and be responsive, to be touched and moved by their presence" (Levin 1990, 41). In sum, he is offering a reciprocal or social theory of subjectivity, one based, further, on Merleau-Ponty's (1968b) notion of the flesh introduced in his late and elliptical meditation, "The Intertwining—The Chiasm."

To understand Merleau-Ponty's difficult and widely contested concept of the flesh we must forgo our previous understanding of the term as synonymous with bodily matter or carnality. In Merleau-Ponty's usage, the flesh is neither mind nor matter.[14] Instead, one might think of it as similar to the ancient elements of earth, wind, and fire—that is, as "an 'element' of Being" (Merleau-Ponty 1968b, 139). It is not the body, though the body is needed to experience this manner of being. "Flesh" is the term Merleau-Ponty uses to designate what he calls "this Visibility, this generality of the Sensible in itself, this anonymity innate to My-self" (139). In other words, vision itself is inherently narcissistic, whereby we are intertwined with what we see in the outside world. In short, the seer and the seen engage one another in a binding, reciprocal relationship (139). It is this intertwining that helps explain the slave narratives and their composition. It is this universally experienced but historically denied knowledge of the reversibility of the flesh that the narrators themselves had to know in their own bodies—the profound and therapeutic gift of their (and our) human embodiment. Accepting this argument requires us, therefore, to give up those negative associations with the body that our Western religious and philosophical traditions have hammered into us. Accepting this argument also requires us, in Levin's terms, to renounce the overweening "authority" enjoyed by thinking itself during the reign of metaphysics (Levin 1985, 60). To achieve this requires us to "simply *give* our thought *to* the body" (61).[15] We must give up, that is, the subject-object dualism that underwrites our metaphysical systems. As Merleau-Ponty says, our manner of being in the world (that is, the flesh) is a "texture"—a tissue of visibility, whereby the world and the self intersect and adhere one to the other (Merleau-Ponty 1968b, 146). The flesh is "the coiling over of the visible upon the seeing body, of the tangible upon the touching body" (146).

In this context, the slaves knew (if only tacitly) that they were not the negative pole by which the whites could know themselves as different and superior. They knew they were not the object by which white subjectivity defined or distinguished itself. For how could they be? For them to be an object like any other object in the white man's world (Judge Taney's chattel principle notwithstanding) would mean that they themselves would have had to experience their own bodies as any other objects in the world—and this, I submit, is humanly impossible. As Harriet Jacobs says of herself, "I could not possibly regard myself as a piece of property" (Jacobs 1861, 187).[16] Jacobs knows intuitively what Frederick Olafson argues philosophically when he claims that "to the extent that we can be said to *observe* our own bodies at all, the position from which we do so appears to be the same one from which we observe everything, and that is the place where our bodies are" (1995, 203–204). To see ourselves as an object among other objects would be to evacuate our bodies, an event that only occurs imaginatively with psychosis or literally with death—when, indeed, our bodies do become object (as corpse or remains), but only to others, never to ourselves.[17] In sum, "'my body' is not something I come upon in my world, as it would be if it were an object. Instead, it is a condition of my coming upon anything at all" (Olafson 1995, 204). Thus while enslaved and emancipated African Americans might indeed have had a double-consciousness, even they could not achieve a fully objective perspective on their bodies. It is only the whites, trapped in and benefiting from the Western metaphysical tradition of liberal humanism, who thought they could see a black body as an object indistinguishable from a plowshare. The blacks knew better. Thomas Csordas, drawing on and citing from Merleau-Ponty (1964b, 18), argues similarly that "[i]f we do not perceive our own bodies as objects, neither do we perceive others as objects. Another person is perceived as another 'myself,' tearing itself away from being simply a phenomenon in my perceptual field, appropriating my phenomena and conferring on them the dimension of intersubjective being, and so offering 'the task of a true communication'" (Csordas 1990, 37).[18]

African American slaves knew, in their bodies and by their bodies, that black slave and white master were the two hands of the same knowing body, not exactly the same but not entirely different either—fleshy mirror images of one another, caught in the fold of the visible.[19] Slaves knew what Merleau-Ponty describes as the covenant between the things in the world, their movements and shape, and ourselves, whereby we let them borrow our bodies so that they might "inscribe" themselves upon us and give us "their resemblance"; in sum, "this *fold*, this central cavity of the visible which is [our] vision, these two mirror arrangements of the seeing and the visible, the touching and the touched," constitute our experience in the world (1968b, 146; emphasis added).[20] Earlier in the same essay, Merleau-Ponty urges us to accept not just the interrelatedness of the seer and the seen, but also that of the visible and the tangible, arguing that what can be seen is also tangible and what can be touched is also visible (134). Although here he invokes dualisms (the touched and the touching, the tangible and the visible), he too is trying to overcome them. He is, moreover, suggesting that what is true of the experience of one body (that it both touches and is touched, that it is sentient and sensed, that it sees because it is visible) is true of "the whole of the sensible of which it is a part, and to the world" (138). What he calls "this strange adhesion" (139), whereby there is "reciprocal insertion and intertwining" between seer and seen (138), can be thought of as "two mirrors facing one another where two indefinite series of images set in one another arise which belong really to neither of the two surfaces, since each is only the rejoinder of the other," a paired relationship that is "more real" than the surfaces themselves (139). But he cautions us to recognize that the reversibility he describes is "always imminent and never realized in fact" (147). That is, to use his example, our left hand cannot touch our right hand if the right is engaged in the act of touching another object: Either the right hand becomes the tool through which the left touches what the right had been touching by itself, or the right hand becomes the object of the left's touching, and the initial object of the right hand's touching is left behind, untouched. But this gap, he cautions us, is no "failure"; "it is spanned by the total being of my body, and by that of the world" (148).[21] He concludes this most difficult of essays by arguing, finally, that even "pure ideality" itself exists in the flesh—with the visibility of "the sensible world" having surrendered "the flesh of the body for that of language" (153).

This philosophically unprecedented concept of the flesh and its intertwining is the occasion for a series of debates published in *Ontology and Alterity in Merleau-Ponty* (Johnson and Smith, 1990). In his essay, M. C. Dillon argues, for example, that on Merleau-Ponty's view, "the body, as flesh, is the inside of the outside; that is, the Flesh of the world is the same as the flesh of the body, it is the outside of the inside: the circuit is closed within Flesh, within the relation of Flesh to itself, within its selfsameness. The one Flesh incorporates the duality of its fission, its dehiscence, its folding back upon itself" (Dillon 1990, 15). Gary Brent Madison reads Dillon as arguing—incorrectly—that Merleau-Ponty envisions otherness as "an encroachment from the outside" (Madison 1990, 33; see Dillon 1990, 21). On Madison's view, "when I begin to reflect, [the other] is already 'in' me, as a constitutive dimension of my flesh"; Madison (1990, 33) goes on to argue, contra Dillon, that "I do not 'project' the other; the other is what I discover when, in moments of reflexivity, I seek to lay hold of myself." "The flesh is the trace of the other, the inscription of the other, in the subject's own selfhood—in its very flesh. What 'flesh' 'means,'" Madison contends, therefore, "is that *the subject is for itself an other*" (Madison 1990, 31). Levin takes the view that questions of encroachment are irrelevant to Merleau-Ponty's theory of reversibility. The concepts of "encroachment" or "transgression," he claims, "come from and only make sense within, a discourse . . . that posits the metaphysical priority of the subject and conceptualizes it as a self-contained monad" (Levin 1990, 39).[22] On Levin's view, then, Merleau-Ponty teaches us that "*it is by grace of the flesh* that we are gathered with others into a primordial sociality" (Levin 1990, 40). Levin contends further that "a preliminary sense of justice [is] *already* schematized in and by the flesh: this sense is an original ideality, a *logos*, which gives the flesh its ethical and political axis" (43). It is this sense of justice, I believe, that Frederick Douglass, for example, knew in his own body (as I intend to demonstrate in Chapter 2).[23] On a deep intuitive level, this untutored slave knew the sociability of subjectivity; he knew, in Levin's terms, that "[w]e belong to a matrix of flesh; so much so that we can achieve an 'interior life' only by grace of our intercorporeality" (Levin 1990, 41). That Douglass knew this, I intend to argue, is manifest in his attention to the compassion he encounters in certain white people, a compassion that reaffirms his sense of self-worth and his relatedness-to-others and to *being* itself.

I have been attracted to these ideas from Levin and Merleau-Ponty because they allow me to argue from a philosophical standpoint for the notion of human connectedness, including our preconceptual attunement to *being*. I am thus not obliged to rely solely on historical record or a theory of cultural crossings to explain the presence of these ideas in the slave narratives,[24] although I do, at times, employ both in my efforts to understand what I consider to be some of the most remarkable documents ever produced that reveal how the concept of human community can survive and even be nourished throughout centuries of terrible human suffering. But even if I take into consideration the fact that their audience would be white and the demanding editorial pressures brought to bear

upon the ex-slaves by powerful and influential abolitionists who were employ-
ing these people in their own righteous yet somehow sublime—that is to say,
Transcendental—cause (see Elkins 1976),[25] I still cannot explain to myself why
their narratives convey so little anger and bitterness and virtually no desire for
revenge.[26] Why, I must then ask, when their body-selves had been so abused
and tormented by years of enslavement, why did these narrators—*how* did
they—achieve such a hopeful, believable vision of community and connectedness? Where did they get the courage to *bear* their thoughts in the body of their
texts?[27] How did they know that they belonged in a world that had largely rejected them and defined them in such negative terms? I can only conclude that
such knowledge is what makes us all human: that, in effect, they demonstrated
their own humanity—not in Hegelian terms by writing and thus proving their
own rationality but, in Levin's terms, by being able to "*listen* to the body's own
speech," a speech that recollected them (and can, by example, recollect us) to
being (Levin 1985, 61). It was the body, and its knowledge, that saved them.
Because so much of the world as they knew it had been constructed by whites
who defined them as virtually absent of those qualities that make us human (see
my discussion of Hegel below), they needed a powerful countermeasure if they
were to believe in their own humanity. They got this in part from the slave
community itself, which had not entirely forgotten its African ancestry and
which forged a complex, meaningful world sometimes complementary to but
other times counter to the hegemonic world of white people (see, for example,
Blassingame 1979, Genovese 1972, and Paris 1995). But they also carried with
them, in their own bodies, the knowledge that we all begin with, that we are all
attuned to *being*. Thus, even though on a surface level the narratives seem designed to convince skeptical white readers that the subjectivity of the slaves is
the same subjectivity as their own, I intend to argue that in their very composition, these narratives pose a challenge to the dualistic foundations of Western
subjectivity itself.[28]

Let there be no mistake. I am most assuredly not committing Hegel's fallacy
of considering Africans to be locked in a state of nature, unable to evolve or unprepared for the realm of freedom. To the contrary, I am proposing that, unlike
even the most sophisticated and highly educated whites of the time, these enslaved Africans, drawing on the gift of their bodies for thinking, achieved what
Levin calls a "deep ontological understanding," whereby they used the gestures
and motility of their bodies (in crafts, laboring, singing, dancing, and walking)
to recollect their own relatedness-to-*being* (Levin 1985, 11). Rather than suggesting that the African slaves were strangers to metaphysics and thus unfit for
freedom, I am proposing that they used the gift of their embodiment to redraw—
if not entirely to escape—the boundaries of Western metaphysics and, in the
process, to redefine what it means to be human. I am proposing, in other words,
that a philosophical challenge to metaphysics *informs* (all puns intended) the
slave narratives, a challenge that all too soon after their composition tragically
became lost (again) to conscious memory—but whose retrieval from the body of
these texts can help heal the body politic of today just as it helped to heal the

body politic of the nineteenth century. I am arguing, for the reasons I have already enumerated and to which I will return, that, unlike their white contemporaries who had been trained by metaphysics to deny the body and its truths, these Africans, who themselves to one degree or another had been denied a thoroughgoing indoctrination into Western metaphysical principles, retained, as their white contemporaries had not, access to an original (preconceptual) knowledge of our relatedness-to-*being*, a knowledge of reciprocity and community that is the gift of our human embodiment. They were able to do so, I argue further, because their bodies were so self-evidently important to their daily life. Unlike their white masters and mistresses, they did not have the luxury of forgetting the body and its needs; unable to forget the body, they did not forget its truths.

Just listen to one voice, that of Mary Prince, from whose account of slavery one could almost pick a passage at random to get a sense of how totally embodied she was: "My work was planting and hoeing sweet-potatoes, Indian corn, plantains, bananas, cabbages, pumpkins, onions, &c. I did all the household work, and attended upon a horse and cow besides—going also upon all errands" (Prince 1831, 13). But as bad as this work was, it still was not as bad, she says, as her time on Turk's Island, working in the salt ponds with boils on her bare feet. But did Mary Prince, embodied as she was, *think*? I contend she did, and did so through this suffering body by which she experienced the gift of *being* itself.[29] As Levin might argue, if we, who have not been enslaved, hope to have some success in "'[o]vercoming' metaphysics," we must find a way to overcome our historically mandated hostility toward the body (Levin 1985, 56):[30] "We must *retrieve* the ontological body" (56). It is this retrieval that I believe the slave narratives model for us. Though their narrators were definitionally not permitted to pass through the portals of liberal humanism by virtue of their enslaved state and African ancestry—and were thus discouraged from seeing themselves as rational beings who were part of the human community—these men and women could not have been completely unaware of the long-standing Western hatred of the body (be it black, white, or other). They had to know moreover—as James Pennington surely did—that they were despised because they were associated with and defined by their bodies (as chattel personal),[31] an awareness that helps to account for what I call the absent bodies of much subsequent African American narrative. But, paradoxically (and my argument is nothing if not paradoxical), being defined by and identified with their bodies had the philosophically productive outcome of allowing Africans to retrieve the ontological body. Not all slaves were capable of this retrieval, of course, as it was deeply counter-hegemonic. But I do believe we can find in many of the narratives evidence of this retrieval, evidence of a new kind of thinking, not independent of or hostile to the body but dependent on and respectful of the body. Venture Smith, for example, makes it abundantly clear that he both secures and retains his freedom—as well as that of his entire family and three other slaves—on the basis of the labors his durable and powerful body performs. He is, in fact, proud of his body, its African heritage, and its unusual capacities. Though he is old and frail when he relates his narrative, he describes himself as once being "straight and tall . . . and every way well proportioned" (like his African ancestors) and his strength as having been "equal if not superior to any man whom I have ever seen" (Smith 1897, 24). His portrait of himself is corroborated in an anecdotal addendum to his narrative that was compiled by H. M. Selden, in which it is clear that among his peers the now deceased Venture Smith has with his physical prowess entered the realm of the mythic.[32] Levin remarks of his discussion of Medard Boss's attempts to humanize medicine that for Boss the body should not be construed as either "the ontical body of 'common sense'" or as "the ontical body of science"; instead it is "the body of deepening experience always already inherent in Being as a whole" (Levin 1985, 61).[33] In my work, the body is all of these at once. It is the body we see in the mirror, the body by which we perceive (and know) others, the body that eats and sleeps and labors for a living, the body of biological science, *and* the ontological body. But, the flesh, in my usage, remains, as best I can manage it, a manner of being that inhabits the slave narratives and helps to explain their very existence.[34]

On the surface, the ex-slaves had to deny knowledge of our profoundly meaningful embodiment in order to (self)consciously argue their relatedness to whites as reasonable beings—and, of course, as a function of their entering the august temples of liberal humanism. Henry Louis Gates has most clearly articulated the Kantian, Humean, and Hegelian influence in the production of slave narratives, arguing that, by the nineteenth century, because the measure of humanity had become the ability to reason and because writing, after the invention of the printing press, had become the generally accepted "*visible* sign of reason," it became incumbent upon blacks to prove their ability to reason (and thus their humanity) by producing written texts (Gates 1985–86, 8; see also Gates 1989, 18–26; Appiah 1992, 52–53). On Gates's view, it fell to Hegel in *The Philosophy of History*[35] to define for the nineteenth century the prevailing views of Africa and Africans that effectively eliminated them from world history (at least in white eyes) but also inspired the production of slave narratives themselves. "[Africa] has no movement or development to exhibit," Hegel writes. "What we properly understand by Africa, is the Unhistorical, Undeveloped Spirit, still involved in the conditions of mere nature, and which had to be presented here only as on the threshold of the World's History" (Hegel 1956, 99). Having claimed that "Negroes" have a "perfect *contempt* for humanity" (95), that they are ignorant of "the immortality of the soul" (95), that "the devouring of human flesh is altogether consonant with the general principles" of their race (95), that Africans are brave in battle only because they have no "regard for life" (96), that they can best be characterized as absent of "self-control," Hegel can thus defend what he regards as their temporary enslavement to whites in the Americas as the Africans' mode of entry into "a higher morality and the culture connected with it" (99). Although Hegel acknowledges that, because "the essence of humanity is *Freedom*," slavery in all circumstances (whether found in the West or elsewhere, including Africa) constitutes itself as an "*injustice*," he is able to give comfort to Southern planters and their supporters by concluding that these undisciplined (and virtually inhuman) Africans must not be thrown into a freedom for which they are not prepared. Instead, he writes, they must be slowly raised ("matured") into recognizing the value of freedom. On his view, then, it was both humane and responsible to abolish slavery gradually, not suddenly while Africans were still unprepared to benefit from freedom (99). Given this hostile environment and what passed for "reasoning" in the early nineteenth century, Gates theorizes that if the formerly enslaved Africans "were to signify as full members of the Western human community, they would have to do so in their writings" (Gates 1989, 6; see also Gates, 1987a, 27–28).[36]

I want to accept Gates's premise but pursue it somewhat differently. As I have suggested, I argue that even as African Americans seemed to be attempting to carve out a realm of freedom for themselves within the tenets of liberal humanism (to all appearances by playing the game on its own terms), not only were they daily confronted with the brutal material consequences to their own well-being of living in a world that elevated the (white) mind at the expense of debasing the (black) body, they themselves knew intuitively that these despised and debased bodies held the secrets of their own relatedness-to-*being*. On some level, if only a tacit one, they knew *in* their bodies that they knew *with* their bodies—as everyone, black and white, slave and free, needs must do (though metaphysics teaches us otherwise). In the slave narratives, therefore, there are at least four challenges to liberal humanism and the normative dualism on which it relies. One is the challenge to its reliance on racial differences: that Africans are not fully human because they are without written history (Gates's argument). Second is the challenge to its association of Africans with the despised body. But the third and fourth, more fundamental, challenges are the implicit challenges to its metaphysical premises: (a) that bodies, being base matter, cannot and do not think; and (b) that individual subjectivity is a function of the subject-object division. In Gates's terms, then, we might even say that the slave narrators were signifying on Western humanism—seemingly agreeing with and honoring its principles while challenging its core.[37]

The books the ex-slaves wrote, therefore, speak the absent body. They give voice to the bodily felt experience of enslavement (the pain, deprivations, humiliations, sufferings, and so on), but they also give voice to the bodily knowledge of our relatedness-to-*being*. Furthermore, they stand in for the absent body of the slave whose work we hold in our hands when we read. Just as Booker T. Washington found it meaningful that white men shook his hand after his speeches (symbolizing, with the bodily contact, our relatedness),[38] the act of reading a slave narrative is an act of physical contact. Elaine Scarry has argued that human beings create what she calls artifacts in order to ease or prevent bodily pain. Thus, for example, one designs and makes a chair because bodies get tired from standing; within the very form of the chair, moreover, we see the desire to rid oneself of bodily discomfort (Scarry 1985, 290). Although the actual construction of the chair temporarily increases a person's sense of embodiment—since physical labor is required in the effort—the artifact has what Scarry calls a "lever" effect in that the payoff (in terms of pain avoided and pleasure assured) is greater than the original payment (the amount of work involved in the construction). What might take days to build, in other words, relieves the body of pain for years (310, 316). Just as chairs and coats are artifacts in Scarry's system, so, too, are works of literature. Thus we can argue (as I do elsewhere in a discussion of *Native Son*),[39] that we project ourselves into the world through literary artifacts, just as we project ourselves and our bodily needs in the more obviously material artifacts of chairs and coats. On Scarry's view, there are three stages in the act of creating artifacts. These stages involve converting "what is originally interior and private into something exterior and sharable," which, in turn, will be reabsorbed into the interior lives of others, in a process she calls "projection" (284). In other words, there is in this system what Scarry regards as "the reversal of inside and outside surfaces," a reversal that benefits "the sentient interior [which] gains some small share of the blissful immunity of inert inanimate objecthood" (285). At the same time, the exterior world, which is ignorant of and indifferent to our human pain, must give its attention to "the problem of sentience" (285). Thus, anticipating a cold winter I first imagine the pain that will bring me; to counteract this anticipated pain, I envision a sweater to keep me warm. Then, through hours of labor, I create a publicly visible artifact of the pain I hope to prevent—in short, I knit myself a sweater. This artifact functions as a material projection of my sentience—my desire to avoid pain—even as it protects me from this pain. My sweater, which is a product of bodily laboring, relieves me of painful embodiment in that, no longer forced to think about how cold I am, I can go about my other business virtually disembodied—that is to say, forgetful, for the nonce, of my body's physical needs. To this, I would add, however, that there is no actual disembodiment possible, no real "forgetting" of our bodies—since we know and experience the world by virtue of embodiment. If we know (or even remember) the world in our bodies, how can we, unless we are unconscious, forget (literally, fail to hold)[40] the body? That is to say, Scarry's system, while a useful model of pain, seems to be premised on what is ultimately a dualistic view of the mind/body question, one that, like other such models, values the mind over the body.[41]

Nonetheless her ideas about pain can be fruitfully applied to the slave narratives. The pain that inspired them, well-documented as it is, no doubt escapes our imaginings, for how can we, we who have never lived in slavery (though, indeed, we might be descendants of slaves), understand what it meant to be a slave for life?[42] Or, to repeat Alice Walker's famous question, "What did it mean for a black woman to be an artist in our grandmothers' time? In our great-grandmothers' day? It is a question," she observes darkly, "with an answer cruel enough to stop the blood" (Walker 1974, 233). Cruel it is, indeed, yet one function the slave narratives served, besides the one articulated by Gates, was to project their narrators' pain into the world. The unceasing interior pain the slaves knew in their body-selves was (and is) projected outwardly into their narrative artifacts, which became, upon their composition, part of the external world (both human and nonhuman), which could no longer ignore or pretend not to see the terrible human suffering engendered by the so-called "peculiar institution" of slavery. The actual composition of these narratives must have brought their authors some relief from the unbearable pain they had known throughout their lives, as they unburdened themselves in the pages of their texts. At the same time, these texts had a therapeutic effect on their nineteenth-century readers, as they continue to have an effect on us today. Just as the slaves lived in a world that would (or at least tried to) rend them from *being*, we, too, living in a racist society in the nihilistic and technology-mad twentieth century—in a country where a manager can earn more than 200 times the salary of the average worker—have lost touch with *being*. As Heidegger asked, who can ignore our dilemma? "Should we not safeguard and secure the existing bonds even if they hold human beings together ever so tenuously and merely for the present?" (Heidegger 1947, 255). Of course we must, he replies; but can doing so, he asks in another rhetorical question, ever relieve thinking of its deeper obligation to think "what still remains principally to be thought and, as Being, prior to all beings, is their guarantor and their truth?" (255). What we lack in this effort, on Heidegger's view, is the capacity to feel pain. We hide our needfulness from ourselves: "the fracture of his fragmentation does not yet reach down to man in his essence, despite all the unspeakable suffering, all the distress that all too many men endure. The pain that rises from the rift of that which is, does not yet reach man in his essence" (Heidegger 1954b, 84). In this estimation Heidegger is wrong, for it is this very pain that the nineteenth-century slave narratives bring to light. These narratives reveal to us what they revealed to their first readers: how we are divided against ourselves and alienated from *being*. As Levin argues more generally, it is precisely because the gift of our embodiment has been refused and the body itself despised that "a return of the long repressed" can today, at long last, bear with it an effective and thoughtful answer to the ravages of "nihilism"—and in so doing help to renew "our cultural tradition" (Levin 1985, 73, 74).

To make this argument clearer, I need to take a short side trip through one of Heidegger's late essays, "The Question Concerning Technology" (1954a). I am after a model for finding the solution to a problem within the depths of the problem itself. I want to argue, via Heidegger's essay, that the bodies in pain that were driven to write themselves into history are the same bodies—and their narratives the same artifacts—that can open us to the "healing dimension" (quoted in Levin 1985, 74). I will thus be arguing for perceiving the text as a kind of technology. But first we need to consider what the essence of technology is and why, on Heidegger's view, modern technology can be lethal to humanity.

Let me briefly repeat his argument. First, Heidegger disabuses us of the notion that the essence of technology has anything at all to do with the merely technological (1954a, 4), that is, with machines and their implementation. While it is certainly "correct" to say that modern technology, with which he is most concerned here, is, like former technologies, "a means to an end" and thus instrumental, "the merely correct," he cautions us, is not to be confused with the "true" (5, 6). For the essence of technology, therefore, we must seek further. The essence of technology, then, is a kind of "bringing-forth," that is, a *Her-vor-bringen*, which, according to the translator, is based on the verb *hervorbringen*, which means "to bring forth or produce, to generate or beget, to utter, to elicit"—all meanings Heidegger intended to convey (10; Note 9). "Technology [in its essence] is therefore no mere means," as common-sense might suggest; instead, it is more profoundly "a way of revealing" or disclosing (12). For all of its fearful powers and dangers, modern technology is also "a revealing," but the dominant revealing of this technology is "a challenging [*Herausfordern*], which puts to nature the unreasonable demand that it supply energy that can be extracted and stored as such" (14). Thus, for us, everything in nature becomes part of what Heidegger calls "the standing-reserve," waiting for our ordering (17). "As soon as what is unconcealed [brought forth, revealed] no longer concerns man even as object, but does so, rather, exclusively as standing-reserve, and man in the midst of objectlessness is nothing but the orderer of the standing-reserve," we find ourselves on a precipice, in danger of becoming part of the standing-reserve (26–27).[43] But the kind of commanding revealing that characterizes modern technology (what Heidegger calls its "Enframing") "does not simply endanger" us in our relationships among ourselves and to everything else. "As a destining, it banishes man into that kind of revealing which is an ordering"—one, in other words, that has the effect of eliminating "every other possibility of revealing" (27). Thus, while technology achieves a certain revealing (an achievement that is both desirable and positive), it achieves this at the expense of closing off other forms of revealing (which is in part what makes it so dangerous). Where, then, in an age of technology do we go to seek the "saving power"? We go, Heidegger suggests (in a move typical of his thinking) straight to the heart of the problem itself. We save ourselves from the brink of disaster by going into the essence of technology. (Bear with me; I am almost back to the slave narratives.) Having established an etymological relationship between *techne* and *episteme*, wherein both are "names for knowing in the widest sense" (13), and established that *techne* (from which we get our "technology") "reveals whatever does not bring itself forth" (13), Heidegger reminds us at the end of his essay that at one time the kind of "revealing that brings forth truth into the splendor of radiant appearing also was called *techne*" (34). Once even "the *poiesis* of the fine arts also was called *techne*" (34). In short, perhaps the realm of art, which is both related to and different from the essence of technology, can save us from the abyss. Thus, whereas the Enframing of modern technology can order us all into the standing-reserve, the essence of technology (its *poiesis*) can become our "saving grace."

In this same essay, Heidegger reminds us that the Greek language has "the word *aletheia* for revealing" which the Romans translated as *veritas* and which we, in turn, translate as truth (11, 12). Levin reminds us that "the bearing of thought must be understood in relation to our skillfulness (*techne*), and our capacity for practical activity in general (*phronesis*), but also, and more deeply, in relation to the primary experience of truth as an event of disclosing (*aletheia*)"

(Levin 1985, 91). I argue, following Heidegger and Levin (and echoing Scarry), that the pain-engendered texts that the ex-slaves wrote were and are *techne*—works of art, artifacts—engaged in revealing (bringing-forth) the truth of human community. Not only do the slave narratives reveal the pain of alienation and nihilism that is mostly kept hidden from us, especially in our official political philosophy, but their authors were able to find in this terrible pain "the saving power" of our relatedness-to-*being*, the knowledge of which inhered in their own pain-wracked bodies.[44] Additionally, these texts, modest as most of them were, sought to inspire compassion in their readers. They sought, that is, to inspire a bodily response, a response anticipated in the fact that we give books a hand when we begin to read (we reach out to the text, which is the stand-in for the author).[45] It is my argument that not only were the bodies of the ex-slaves implicated in the creation of their narratives (as subject matter and as laboring author, to name but two), but so too were the bodies of their readers. W. E. B. Du Bois was not unaware of this insight, as in a memorable passage from *The Souls of Black Folk*, he writes: "I *sit* with Shakespeare and he winces not. Across the color line I *move arm in arm* with Balzac and Dumas, where smiling men and welcoming women *glide* in gilded halls" (Du Bois 1903, 438; emphasis added).[46] Although one might be tempted to read this passage as "merely" metaphorical, I submit that these metaphors reveal an essential truth: that human community can be affirmed by holding the book of another in one's hands and attempting to understand it by, in effect, working or walking our way through it.[47] On my view, following Levin (1985) and Gadamer (1989), understanding is an act of compassion and communion—an act of human motility, in other words—that entails (depends upon) the reader's internalizing or incorporating the text.[48] It is the perfect integration.

Levin argues, and I concur, that when we open ourselves to "others in need, we *are* opening to Being" (1985, 97). Was (and is) this not the effect of the slave narratives on their reading audiences? Do they not call upon us to reach out in compassion to the authors and subjects of their narration? Is not reading, therefore, following Levin, a gesture: the profoundly human activity of reaching out to another, an affirmation of relatedness, thematizing—as do the Africans' ritualistic dances or the slaves' ring shouts—the intertwining that characterizes our connections to each other and to *being* itself? Do we not, in seeing the alterity in and of the text, also necessarily see ourselves? Is there not, moreover, in these texts, evidence of another's body? Do not their forewords, afterwords, and other amendments testify to the body of the author? Was it not important to both publisher and editor to affirm the fact that these narratives had been authored by African bodies, that the body of the text stands in for the (sentient) body of the author? Was this not their whole point, that even the despised Africans, enslaved because of their bodies, had the gift of reason?[49] Did they not have to assert embodiment only to deny it? Were not these texts often illustrated with the ex-slave's likeness? Had not many of these same books been written by the slaves themselves, that is to say, written down in the slaves' own hand? Did not these powerful little books often carry with them, therefore, a facsimile of their author's signature, the very mark of embodiment?[50] Levin describes the sacred origins of writing as "a ritualized gesture of piety, celebrating the presence, or the efficacy, of a divinity visible both in the grace and elegance of the gesture itself and also in the darkness of the inscription which that gesture makes, and leaves behind" (Levin 1985, 184). Did not the slaves regard writing in such a sacred fashion? Are not the words they left us, the words their hands so carefully and painstakingly transcribed, are not these words emblematic of the connection between their bodies and our own? In reading them, do we not submit our own bodies to the body of the text, the bodies of their authors? In their own time, in Du Bois's terms, did these books not function as a physical stand-in for the absent, proscribed bodies of their authors? Was it not deeply significant, as Washington noted of his own experience, that whites offered blacks their hands, by picking up their books, by holding them, and by interiorizing the pain and hope they projected? Were not—are not—bodies always the issue here?[51]

Although my project is not an anthropological one, most contemporary scholars have come to agree that "the world the slaves made"[52] was crafted with skill, originality, and intelligence out of the materials at hand: materials originating in the colonies (and later the states) and in the various African customs that survived the middle passage. As I have suggested before, it is neither my intention nor my place to unravel the knotty question of how much of current (or historical) African American culture is African and how much is American. To do so, on one hand, would assume, against Appiah's argument, an ability to summarize Africa and, on the other, an ability to characterize an American culture absent of Africans and their influences.[53] To do so, further, would be to undermine my own project—that of arguing for a preconceptual relatedness-to-*being* through which all humans are brought together. If not an anthropological exercise, my project is also not one that traces philosophical connections between the free Africans of Africa and the enslaved Africans of the Americas.[54] It does bear repeating, however, that I am not claiming we are all alike, as my earlier invocation of Merleau-Ponty's concept of the flesh (especially as it pertains to questions of alterity and ontology) is meant to suggest. What I wish to do in the pages that follow, instead, is trace the outline (the torso, if you will) of the challenge to liberal humanism that informs the texts by which the slave narrators hoped to enter the civil discourse of their time. It is the gift of embodiment that these texts reveal and remember for us; it is the gift of the slaves' own embodiment that to all appearances author(iz)ed their entry into metaphysics even as they undermined many of its tenets from within. It is a gift, a new—or should I say, *old*, as in primal, original, inborn?—way of thinking that thinking itself conceals from us. It is a way of thinking through the body. I am not making a racial argument here but an ontological one. The truth of our relatedness-to-*being* that the slave narratives recollect for us was not born in or even of slavery, on my view. Instead, it was unconcealed by slavery, the institution that strove mightily to hide it from view. By virtue of the fact that a diverse group of people were assigned a race and thus legally consigned to enslavement for life as human chattel, concepts of "race" necessarily inform my project, but my argument, unlike that of the slave-holders and their supporters, does not depend on any notions of racial difference. Race, for all its enduring material, political, and psychological consequences to those said to be raced,[55] is but an illusion. On Appiah's view, race is an invention, on Fields's view, it is an ideology, and on Gates's view it is a trope (Gates 1985–86, 5). It is perhaps because race was invented as it was in the Americas that we have this particular form of unconcealment (that is, the slave narrative); or, to put it differently, what we in the West might mistakenly regard as the overly-embodied experience of the slaves for life helped make possible this unconcealment. That the slaves suffered bodily harm, bodily pain, bodily discomfort, and bodily disfigurement, I do not contest for a minute. I do contest the view that such bodily suffering did not have its own "saving grace." Neither was the slaves' embodiment necessarily always one of suffering. But unlike their white owners, whose bodies were shaped—that is, misinformed, deformed—by the habitus of Western humanism, the slaves as a group never lost touch with the body's recollection of *being*. Out of what a liberal humanist could not but see as a wholly negative experience, these African slaves, who could see otherwise, crafted for themselves (and for us) a therapeutic anti-humanism (a destructive hermeneutics), one that redefines what it means to be human, one that is not based on the dualisms of mind and body, subject and object, self and other—but on their necessary intertwining. In sum, it is my argument that the slaves' dis-covered within their own bodies the truth of our relatedness-to-*being* and our relatedness-to-each-other. As inevitable as I hope to make the slaves' dis-covery seem in the pages that follow, I would misrepresent my argument if I did not caution readers that, on my view, *being* did not require slavery and its attendant racism to unconceal itself. Neither do I mean by focusing only on African American literature to suggest that *being* has not unconcealed itself elsewhere.[56] It is, however, our rare privilege and responsibility today to understand (again) this particular, historically specific, phenomenon of unconcealment that we know as the nineteenth-century American slave narratives.

NOTES

1. In her classic feminist manifesto, *Of Woman Born*, Rich calls for women "to *think through the body*, to connect what has been so cruelly disorganized—our great mental capacities, hardly used; our highly developed tactile sense; our genius for close observation; our complicated, pain-enduring, multipleasured physicality" (Rich 1977, 290). It is her conviction that woman are finally poised to transform "our physicality into both knowledge and power" (290). This transformation will entail, furthermore, "far more essential change to human society than the seizing of the means of production by workers" (292). Levin envisions a similarly sweeping change to society.

2. Heidegger's statement appears in "Rapture as Aesthetic State" (in his *The Will to Power as Art*, "Nietzsche," Vol. 1). Let me briefly contextualize Heidegger's claim, which he adapts from Nietzsche's position on art. On Heidegger's reading of Nietzsche, art is "to be the countermovement to nihilism" *and* (what seems at first glance to be a

nonsensical position) art is also "to be properly grasped by way of physiology and with its means" (Heidegger 1961, 92). If art is merely "processes in the nerve cells," Heidegger inquires, where can we possibly "find something that could of itself determine meaning, posit values, and erect standards?" (92–93). It is this conflict that Heidegger attempts to reconcile in his understanding of Nietzsche's inquiry into aesthetics. Heidegger reads Nietzsche as arguing that "states of feeling, taken to be purely psychical, are to be traced back to the bodily condition proper to them" (96). Quoting from a lengthy statement in *Twilight of the Idols* (1888), Heidegger reminds us that for Nietzsche "rapture is the basic aesthetic state, a rapture which for its part is variously conditioned, released, and increased" (97). In sum, the "'physiological precondition' of art . . . is feeling" (98). For its part, feeling "means the way we find ourselves to be with ourselves, and thereby at the same time with things, with beings that we ourselves are not. Rapture is always rapturous feeling." Then Heidegger asks of Nietzsche's claim, where is the body in all of this? He answers, on behalf of Nietzsche, that we should not even be posing the question in this way, "as though there were a bodily state housed in the basement with feelings dwelling upstairs. Feeling, as feeling oneself to be, is precisely the way we are corporeally" (98). (On a related issue, see Patton 1991.) It is then he goes on to assert what Levin quotes, "We do not 'have' a body; rather, we 'are' bodily" (99). On this subject, see also Olafson (1995) who says of his own project that it is "an attempt to show how a human body differs from a physical object without reintroducing any of the dualistic apparatus that has dominated our thought about the body for so long. In this way, [he tries] to develop the concept of the human body to the point at which what 'it' does is more appropriately described as what 'I' do and, in so doing, to give a defensible import to the thesis that *my* body is what *I* am" (200). For a feminist critique and appropriation of some of these ideas, see Grosz (1994). See also Gordon (1995).

3. Polanyi argues, for example, that "[a]ll thought is incarnate; it lives by the body and by the favour of society" (Polanyi 1961, 134) and "[t]he way the body participates in the act of perception can be generalized . . . to include the bodily roots of all knowledge and thought. Our body is the only assembly of things known almost exclusively by relying on our awareness of them for attending to something else. . . . Every time we make sense of the world, we rely on our tacit knowledge of impacts made by the world on our body and the complex responses of our body to these impacts" (Polanyi 1964, 147–48).

4. As a philosopher who has also been trained in human medicine, Leder is more interested in the physiology of the body than is Merleau-Ponty, in whose work on embodiment Leder finds "a distinct resemblance to its Cartesian predecessor, never fully fleshed out with bone and guts" (Leder 1990, 36). In tracing the role of the body in philosophical systems (most particularly, the missing body in Descartes), Leder distinguishes among differing kinds of bodily absence. One is the form of "self-concealment" that he identifies as "focal *disappearance*," the disappearance of the organs that are engaged in perception (the eye does not see itself when it sees) (26). Another is "*background disappearance*," the disappearance of "bodily regions" which are temporarily "relegated to a supportive role, involved in irrelevant movement, or simply put out of play" (26). A third is *depth disappearance*," the (always already) disappearance of our internal organs and their functioning (53). In sum, except for moments of pain or discomfort or sexual pleasure, we tend not to be consciously aware of our bodies—a generalization I would amend by suggesting it applies less to a universal bodily experience (or lack thereof) than to the experience of financially secure, white, heterosexual men. Those of us who are embodied differently (from them) have our bodies brought to our

attention on a more regular basis. For yet another discussion of Descartes as a thinker who both inherited and formalized the Western dualisms found in Plato, Aristotle, and Augustine, see Susan Bordo's *The Flight to Objectivity*, in which she argues that with Descartes, "nature became *defined* by its lack of affiliation with divinity, with spirit. All that which is God-like or spiritual—freedom, will, and sentience—belong entirely and exclusively to *res cogitans*. All else—the earth, the heavens, animals, the human body— is merely mechanically interacting matter" (Bordo 1987, 102).

5. For a discussion and effective critique of this dualistic view of our bodies, see Olafson (1995).

6. On this see Mark Johnson (1987) who claims that *"any adequate account of meaning and rationality must give a central place to embodied and imaginative structures of understanding by which we grasp our world"* (Johnson 1987, xiii).

7. In *Phenomenology of Perception*, Merleau-Ponty observes that

To get used to a hat, a car or a stick is to be transplanted into them, or conversely, to incorporate them into the bulk of our own body. Habit expresses our power of dilating our being-in-the-world, or changing our existence by appropriating fresh instruments. It is possible to know how to type without being able to say where the letters which make the words are to be found on the banks of keys. To know how to type is not, then, to know the place of each letter among the keys, nor even to have acquired a conditioned reflex for each one, which is set in motion by the letter as it comes before our eye. If habit is neither a form of knowledge nor an involuntary action, what then is it? It is knowledge in the hands, which is forthcoming only when bodily effort is made, and cannot be formulated in detachment from that effort. (Merleau-Ponty 1981, 143–44)

8. The phrase *"I of me"* is yet another way of saying the body-self.

9. These are all ideas that I will return to in an attempt to theorize the acts of writing and reading as complementary gestures, dependent upon the hands of author and reader—gestures that literally bring the two together in an act of understanding. In urging free blacks to learn trades, Douglass argued in 1853 that "the education of the hands must precede that of the head. We can never have an educated class until we have more men of means amongst us" (Foner 1950b, 237).

10. Blassingame finds a similar theme of reunion in the spirituals, claiming that "one of the most striking characteristics of the spirituals was the frequent reference to meeting fathers, mothers, relatives, and friends in Heaven. Although possibly related to ancestor worship in Africa, songs of this nature probably grew out of the slaves' longing to be reunited with loved ones torn away from them by cruel masters" (Blassingame 1979, 140). See also Paris (1995).

11. This notion of recollection is Heideggerian, though I have taken my usage from Levin, for whom it means not merely recalling and retrieving what we have lost, in losing touch with *being*, but transforming the gifts of the past so they might serve us well in our efforts to recover our relatedness-to-*being*. Heidegger argues that "when recollection of the history of Being names thinkers and pursues their thoughts, this thinking is the listening response which belongs to the claim of Being, as determination attuned by the voice of that claim. . . . Recollection of the history of Being returns to the claim of the soundless voice of Being and to the manner of its attuning" (Heidegger 1973, 77; originally printed in 1961 as a part of vol. 2 of his *Nietzsche*; see also Levin 1985, 156).

12. The concept of "Being" in this system—transcribed as *being* in mine—is "the dimensionality within which all beings are to be encountered"; that is to say, although being rises up within *being*, *being* is not an individual being (Levin 1985, 11).

13. See also Jaggar (1983). That bodies are marked by their society I do not contest. The question I cannot answer satisfactorily is: To what degree can the body evade being marked? Pierre Bourdieu has addressed this question in *Outline of a Theory of Practice* (1972), where he describes what he calls "*the socially informed body*, with its tastes and distastes, its compulsions and repulsions, with, in a word, all its *senses*, that is to say, not only the traditional five senses—which never escape the structuring action of social determinations—but also the sense of necessity and the sense of duty, the sense of direction and the sense of reality, the sense of balance and the sense of beauty . . . , and so on" (Bourdieu 1972, 124). Drawing on Bourdieu's work, John B. Thompson describes how "the body is literally moulded into certain forms, so that the habitus is reflected in the whole way that one carries oneself in the world, the way that one walks, speaks, acts, eats" (Thompson 1984, 53). On Bourdieu's view, the habitus, "the product of history, produces individual and collective practices, and hence history, in accordance with the schemes engendered by history" (Bourdieu 1972, 82). "This does not mean," Thompson assures us, "that actors are to be regarded as mere dupes of the social structures which determine their every action." Instead, individuals have choices and "they often act in reflective and deliberative ways; but their action and reflection always [take] place within a structured space of possibilities that defines a certain *style of life*" (Thompson 1984, 53). On this subject, see also Csordas (1990) and Grosz (1994).

14. Hortense Spillers makes a different distinction between body and flesh, claiming that "before the 'body' there is the 'flesh,' that zero degree of social conceptualization that does not escape concealment under the brush of discourse, or the reflexes of iconography" (Spillers 1987, 67). Of his usage of flesh, Merleau-Ponty says, "there is no name in traditional philosophy to designate it" (1968b, 139; see also 147)—an assessment with which Gary Brent Madison concurs (Madison 1990, 31).

15. There is a danger, evident in Levin's choice of words, of reinstituting the mind/body dualism when he says we must give our thought to the body, as though, somehow, the mind had contained it before and now the body can contain it. If the body contains our thought, we are back where we started from, with the body being the material covering for the immaterial thought that occurs in our incorporeal minds. But this would be to misunderstand Levin, who, I think, is speaking in historical terms here. Reversing his reversal of Heidegger, we might argue that if thought owns the body, then thought has the body—literally, thought holds the body in hand. That is to say, thought has body. Or, to borrow from Olafson, "a human body is oriented to its world and, as so oriented, 'it' is an 'I'" (1995, 248).

16. Or as Douglass asserts, even though the slave has been denied "communion with the human race, and compelled to find companionship" among the farm animals, nonetheless the slave "*knows* he is not a beast, but is as truly a man as his master" (Blassingame 1982, 327). See also Douglass's 1857 speech, "The Dred Scott Decision," in Foner (1950b, 407–24).

17. On this, see also Gordon (1995, 35).

18. For more on Csordas, see my use of him in Chapter 2 (below). See also Merleau-Ponty (1982–83, 33–63) and Grosz (1994, 86–111).

19. Compare my argument to Leder's. "To speak of forming one body," he writes, "is thus never meant to deny difference but, rather, to assert the truth of relation. Through compassion we actualize a 'oneness' in the sense of Merleau-Pontian chiasm, a coiling circuit of connection between divergent terms" (Leder 1990, 162). For a comprehensive discussion of compassion as it pertains to the slave narratives, see Chapter 2 (below).

20. In *Phenomenology of Perception*, Merleau-Ponty anticipates this later idea when he writes, "I am not . . . , in Hegel's phrase, 'a hole in being', but a hollow, a fold, which has been made and which can be unmade" (Merleau-Ponty 1981, 215). Levin remarks that this passage is an instance of Merleau-Ponty's ability to conquer the metaphysical subject-object division (Levin 1985, 65).

21. For commentary on these ideas, see Leder (1990) and Grosz (1994).

22. Compare this with Jaggar's argument that liberal philosophy conceives of rationality "as a property of individuals rather than of groups," a conception, which she critiques, that relies upon the "metaphysical assumption . . . that human individuals are ontologically prior to society" (Jaggar 1983, 28). This liberal humanist view of subjectivity underlies the slave narratives and must have had something to do with an individual slave's decision to run off, no matter the cost to those left behind. It is challenged, I will argue, by a contrary, communitarian or social view in which the slaves recognized the importance of family and community in the formation of themselves (see Stephanie Smith 1994 and Paris 1995).

23. See also the Epilogue.

24. On this subject, see, for example, Herskovits (1990), Levine (1977), Joseph Holloway (1990), Gilroy (1993), and Paris (1995).

25. Elkins, arguing for an institutional understanding of slavery, claims that this interpretation would have been anathema to many abolitionists because of their ties to Transcendentalism. "Not only did these men fail to analyze slavery itself as an institution," Elkins asserts, "but they failed equally to consider and exploit institutional means for subverting it" (Elkins 1976, 168). More to the point: "The Transcendentalists were preoccupied with the natural essence of the slave, when they considered him at all. The question was not so much what the institution had made of him but what it prevented him from being—his naked inviolate self" (169). For a critique of Elkins's other arguments, especially his questionable claims about the personality of slaves, see the essays in Gilmore (1978).

26. Not all slaves were as sanguine as Lunsford Lane, who describes his condition of servitude, terrible as it was, nonetheless as "comparatively a happy, indeed a highly favored one" (Lane 1842, iii). But even James W. C. Pennington, who almost seems to have written his narrative in response to Lane's more cheerful account of a kind master and who says he can never forgive slavery for robbing him of an education ("the injury is irreparable"), nonetheless can wish only a single "harm" on slaveholders, "that they may be speedily delivered from the guilt of a sin, which, if not repented of, must bring down the judgment of Almighty God upon their devoted heads" (Pennington 1849, 56, 57). I do not want to understate the terrible suffering the slave narrators recounted, suffering to themselves and suffering to their families and friends; neither do I find an absence of outrage in their accounts. But what I find most remarkable in these narratives are men and women whose spirits were not irredeemably scarred or even deformed by enslavement. Others might explain their contemplative manner as evidence of their having found religion—an explanation proffered by some and endorsed by their editors and patrons, themselves of the Christian faith. I have chosen to explain the almost meditative quality of their narratives less as evidence of their authors' Christianity and more as evidence of their primordial attunement to *being*. The virtue of my explanation is that it helps explain how these slaves for life maintained a sense of community and self-worth even if they had not been introduced to the gospel. I see in these narratives an astonishing capacity to contest the negative representations of themselves that circulated among the white power

structure of the time. I contend that this capacity, paradoxically enough, was the gift of their bodies. Paris contends it is in their African heritage (1995).

27. Levin reminds us that "to bear" means many things, including "to hold," "to possess," "to give birth," "to bring forth," "to support," "to call for," " to carry," "to supply," "to tolerate," and so on (*Webster's New World Dictionary*, Third College Edition, 1988, 121).

28. Various feminist readings of the male-written slave narratives, most particularly Deborah McDowell's reading of Douglass, have convinced me that as much as the narrators were able to challenge the mind/body division by re-embodying reason, they were much less successful in challenging the male-female division. See McDowell (1991).

29. This is an idea I return to in my discussion of *Our Nig*. That slaves saw themselves through—if not *as*—their own working bodies is evident in many narratives. William Grimes's narrative, for all its attention to the many beatings he received while enslaved, is equally memorable for its account of the dozens of jobs he did, both as a slave and as a free man (Grimes 1855). So vast was the range of his work experiences, his narrative could serve as a compendium of mid-nineteenth-century labor practices. Douglass himself often exhorted free blacks to "learn trades, or die," claiming further that it is pointless to "talk about being men, if we do not the work of men" (Foner 1950b, 223, 224; see also 225–38).

30. On this, see Bordo (1987) and Griffin (1981). See also Stallybrass and White (1986).

31. Pennington argues eloquently that "[t]he being of slavery, its soul and body, lives and moves in the chattel principle, the property principle, the bill of sale principle; the cart-whip, starvation, and nakedness, are its inevitable consequences to a greater or less extent, warring with the dispositions of men" (1849, iv–v).

32. Although in life Smith is denied the full assimilation into society that he craves, he does discover, according to Andrews, "that he could yet find consolation in his love for his wife, his conviction of his own integrity, and above all, his freedom." In making this discovery he helped to establish in the slave narratives "a concept of Afro-American fulfillment independent of the myths of integration and success popularized by the predominant culture" (Andrews 1982, 16).

33. Boss, who has been deeply influenced by Heidegger and Merleau-Ponty, argues that "[h]uman presence is in no way confined to the point in space at which the human body (as a self-contained physical object) is to be found" (Boss 1979, 89). The being of a human "is fundamentally openness in the sense of a capacity to perceive something *as* something. Human existence does not *possess* this openness in the form of one of a number of discrete properties. Rather, it *is* nothing other than being open for perceiving and understanding the things it encounters for what they are, and not for anything else" (89).

34. Levin's usage seems to undergo slippage, as I am sure mine does, too; since we are both intent on retrieving the knowledge of the body, it is hard not to slip between "body" and "flesh."

35. This book was first presented as a series of lectures in 1822–23, again in 1824–25, and finally in 1830–31, shortly before Hegel's death in 1831; my citations are from the 1956 Dover republication of the 1899 edition.

36. For more on the influence of Hegelian and other European thought on the development of racism in the United States, see Fredrickson (1971).

37. Not willing to go as far as I do in making a claim for the anti-humanistic impulse behind the slave narratives, Raymond Hedin nonetheless has argued that "black writers'

deviations from conventional form are often as strategic as their acceptance and use of those forms" (Hedin 1982b, 34).

38. Significantly enough, after his Atlanta Exposition speech (1895), Washington recalls in *Up from Slavery,*

The first thing that I remember, after I had finished speaking, was that Governor Bullock rushed across the platform and took me by the hand, and that others did the same. . . . I did not appreciate to any degree, however, the impression which my address seemed to have made, until the next morning, when I went into the business part of the city. As soon as I was recognized, I was surprised to find myself pointed out and surrounded by a crowd of men who wished to shake hands with me. (Washington 1901, 225)

Two decades earlier William Wells Brown ended his historical reportage, *My Southern Home: or, The South and Its People,* with a call for racial amalgamation that is accompanied by a drawing of an interracial handshake (1880, 252).

39. In an unpublished manuscript.

40. *Webster's New World Dictionary* (Third College Edition, 1988, 529).

41. Scarry seems to make explicit this division in describing torture as being able "to split the human being into two, to make emphatic the ever present but, except in the extremity of sickness and death, only latent distinction between a self and a body" (Scarry 1985, 48). In discussing pain, Leder also uses dualistic terms to describe the experience, arguing that the "cleavage between body and self [reported by patients and researchers] is not only initiated by the pain but may also serve as an adaptive response to it" (Leder 1990, 77). See more on these ideas in Chapter 2 (below).

42. That this is a potentially impossible task has not discouraged others from pursuing it, with varying degrees of success. See, for example, Charles Johnson (1982), Sherley Anne Williams (1986), and Morrison (1987). For a discussion of the relative absence of passages that attempt to describe pain in literature, see Scarry (1985, especially the Introduction).

43. See my use of this in the text of the Introduction and in Note 43, in which I argue that Du Bois anticipated Heidegger's worries by claiming that African Americans were, in effect, in danger of becoming part of the standing-reserve (Du Bois 1903, 428).

44. In treating these narratives as both *techne* and *poiesis,* I am not unaware that the narratives themselves were constructed to deny their own status as literary constructions, as Olney reminds us when he claims that

the very intention and premise of [a slave narrative] is to give a picture of 'slavery *as it is.*' Thus it is the writer's claim, it *must* be his claim, that he is not emplotting, he is not fictionalizing, and he is not performing any act of *poiesis* (= shaping, making). To give a true picture of slavery as it really is, he must maintain that he exercises a clear-glass, neutral memory that is neither creative nor faulty—indeed, if it were creative it would be *eo ipso* faulty for 'creative' would be understood by skeptical readers as a synonym for 'lying.' (Olney 1985, 150)

45. Drawing on Nina Baym's work (1984), Robyn Warhol attempts to rehabilitate the sentimental novels of the nineteenth century by reminding us that "sentimental passages in a text were part of the text's machinery for 'working an effect' in a reader's body, and if that effect were one of 'pathos,' the result would be to the benefit of the reader" (Warhol 1992, 105–106). For more on this, see Chapter 3 (below).

46. Although Du Bois has for good reason titled his book *The Souls of Black Folk,* he concludes its "Forethought" by reaffirming his connections with other African Ameri-

cans in the following bodily terms: "need I add that I who speak here am bone of the bone and flesh of the flesh of them that live within the Veil?" (Du Bois 1903, 360). For a reading of this book that traces its debts to German metaphysics and therefore treats this passage quite differently, see Adell (1994, 11–28).

47. As Andrews asseverates in his own study of slave narratives, metaphors, in the best of circumstances, are not simply decorative appurtenances to argumentation; rather, they "*are* arguments" (Andrews 1986, 11). In his "Forethought" Du Bois directly addresses his readers, asking them to "receive my little book in all charity, studying my words with me, forgiving mistake and foible for sake of the faith and passion that is in me, and seeking the grain of truth hidden there" (Du Bois 1903, 359). In the "After-Thought," he changes his metaphor by imploring "God the Reader" not to allow his book to "fall still-born into the world-wilderness," but to permit to spring "from out its leaves vigor of thought and thoughtful deed. . . . Thus in Thy good time may infinite reason turn the tangle straight, and these crooked marks on fragile leaf be not indeed THE END" (Du Bois 1903, 547). For more on Du Bois's metaphors, see Rampersad (1989, 116–18, 120).

48. Although Gadamer, in *Truth and Method*, does not thematize the role of bodies in understanding, his notion that understanding, interpretation, and application all imply one another leads me to argue that for him, too, the act of understanding a text involves the body. If, as he argues, all understanding is an interpretation and if application "co-determines [understanding] as a whole from the beginning" (Gadamer 1989, 324), where else but in our bodies is this application to manifest itself? For further discussion of Gadamer's view of the relationship among understanding, interpretation, and application, see Chapter 3 (below) and Fishburn (1995). Leder describes the phenomenon of understanding in similar terms, referring to "communicative sociality" as a form of "*mutual incorporation*"; that is to say, by a process of "natural empathy, one body takes up the affective responses of another" (Leder 1990, 94). Surely this was the communicative goal ex-slaves had in mind as they worked the lecture circuit and composed their narratives.

49. Appiah reminds us that in the case of sonnets, for example, the formal constraints of this poetic genre "can be seen as part of its subjective structure" (1989, 53). Similarly, on his view, "Slave narratives . . . clearly constitute not merely an objective class but a subjective genre, articulated very early in the history of their production. We are *meant* to recognize Harriet Jacobs' *Incidents in the Life of a Slave Girl* as a slave narrative" (53). To this I would append the argument that we are meant to recognize *Incidents* and other narratives as having been written (that is, crafted) by the *hands* of a slave. Likewise, Douglass is forever reminding us that he is writing the narrative we are reading. Thus it is crucial to their meaning and their significance that these texts be understood to have come from the pens of black bodies. To Appiah's remarks about the narratives' subjective status, I would only repeat that I read these narratives as challenging the prevailing notion of subjectivity—a concept that, in the nineteenth century at least, by definition left out the slaves.

50. Henry Bibb's narrative is introduced by a white man who says of his own knowledge, "the writer of this introduction is well acquainted with [Bibb's] handwriting and style. . . . Many of the closing pages of it were written by Mr. Bibb in my office" (Bibb 1850, ii). Compare my reading of these signs to Olney's claim that the "portrait and the signature . . . , like the prefatory and appended letters, the titular tag 'Written by Himself,' and the standard opening 'I was born,' are intended to attest to the real existence of

a narrator, the sense being that the status of the narrative will be continually called into doubt, and so it cannot even begin, until the narrator's real existence is firmly established." Olney considers the content of the narratives to be "a second-stage argument; prior to [their] claim of truthfulness is the simple, existential claim: 'I exist'" (Olney 1985, 155). What concerns me is how this "real existence" is embodied and how this embodiment informs the texts themselves.

51. As stand-ins for their authors, books are not entirely analogous to bodies, since a person, having written a book, can (presumably) see it as a free-standing object in the world. But in their very visibility, their materiality, they remind us of the embodied basis of our thinking. It is no accident that we speak of the *body* of the text. A book is solid evidence that we think as bodies.

52. I take this phrase, of course, from the subtitle of Eugene D. Genovese's sweeping study (first published in 1972 and reprinted in 1976), *Roll, Jordan, Roll: The World the Slaves Made*.

53. Such an effort also seems to presuppose some kind of pure African presence in the United States. As Ralph D. Carter puts it, "The issue is not that there were African survivals in the slave culture but that there are large amounts of Africanisms in the entire society" (Carter 1978, 75).

54. The thorny question of African philosophy (that is, philosophies) is one I have no intention of addressing here as it would take me entirely out of the province of my own project. On this matter, see, for example, Appiah (1992), Serequeberhan (1991), Soyinka (1990), Jahn (1990), and Masolo (1994). I am also not unmindful of the fact that the claims I make for Levin, Merleau-Ponty, and Heidegger sound like they are intended to be understood as both universal and foundational ones. In my own defense, let me say, first, it is axiomatic that we need foundations if we are ever to build an argument. But this is not to say that these foundations are not made themselves. Who is to say whether the body really knows? What does it mean even to ask that question? Let me also say that, for me, the virtue of these particular Western philosophers (notwithstanding Heidegger's terrible use by and collaboration with the Nazis, including his postwar unwillingness to condemn them by name) is that all three, while writing within the Western philosophical tradition, are themselves, like the slave narrators, challenging its most basic foundations. And they have allowed me, as no critics before, to rethink my ideas about African American literature. For discussion of the relationship between Heidegger and Nazism, see the critical essays in Rockmore and Margolis (1992) and a more sympathetic approach found in Spanos (1993).

55. Clearly, if we accept the fact that there are different races, even those who claim to be zero-degree raced (that is, the whites) must be assigned a race and studied through this lens.

56. For a study of how the eighteenth-century British notion of self and subjectivity was contested in print, see Nussbaum (1989), who argues that "autobiographical writing, published and private, serves as a location where residual and emergent notions of gender and class clash to replicate and challenge reigning notions of identity" (xiv).

2

The Body's Recollection of Being

I have argued in the preceding chapter that slave narrators carried in their very bodies the memory or knowledge of human connectedness denied them by the ideology—and professional European philosophy—of the time. To repeat, it is my argument that, however influential the principles and politics of normative dualism were in eighteenth- and nineteenth-century Euro-American thought (and however influential they remain today), not everyone in the West was equally convinced of their truth.[1] Neither, of course, were those ideas universally accepted outside the West. Among those best positioned to resist the deep-seated hatred of the body within Western culture, paradoxically enough, were those persons most identified with their bodies—that is, the African American slaves.[2] Unlike the European philosophers and their white American counterparts, the transplanted Africans and their enslaved descendants certainly did not define themselves as naturally of an inferior race or devalue the body as a matter of course. In fact, what many travelers to both Africa and the American South reported as savage or barbaric dancing among the Africans—that is, what whites saw as unrestrained and sexual dancing[3]—was, I believe, evidence that these people, unmarked as yet by Western metaphysics, valued the body and used its motility to recollect their own relatedness-to-*being*.[4] John Blassingame notes, for example, that "[i]n traditional African dances there was little separation of sacred and secular performances" (Blassingame 1979, 23).[5] As I shall suggest below, we need look no further than the eighteenth-century narrative of Olaudah Equiano (or Gustavus Vassa) for evidence of how important dancing was to Igbo culture and how cultural and/or ancestral memory is instilled in the body. For Blassingame, in fact, "[t]he most remarkable aspect of the whole process of enslavement is the extent to which the American-born slaves were able to retain their ancestors' culture" (47).[6] Appiah believes similarly that, whether in the Americas or in Africa, the Euro-Americans never colonized the Africans to nearly the extent they thought they had. Invoking Zora Neale Hurston's classic 1937 novel *Their Eyes Were Watching God* as his example, Appiah argues that there are "many moments of cultural autonomy in black America that achieve, against far greater ideological odds than ever faced the majority of Africa's colonized peoples, an equally resilient sense of their own worth" (Appiah 1992, 9). G. W. F. Hegel, however, locked within his own disenabling prejudices,[7] is apparently completely disinclined to ascribe to the physical activity of Africans any worth or positive motivation, convinced as he is of the Africans' absolute "contempt for humanity" (Hegel 1956, 95, 96). Drawing on anecdotal (and severely limited) accounts of European travelers, Hegel describes all Africans (an entire continent of differing peoples, languages, and customs)[8] as remaining for the most part "passive" until they are stimulated into action, "and then they are quite beside themselves. The destruction which is the consequence of their excitement, is caused by the fact that it is no positive idea, no thought which produces these commotions;—a physical rather than a spiritual enthusiasm" (Hegel 1956, 98). For us to fully overcome Hegel's judgment, we must not content ourselves by countering that the enthusiasm of Africans is, of course, both spiritual and produced by thinking. Although it is tempting simply to assert the obvious—that just because Hegel fails to understand the Africans' spirituality and thinking does not mean they do not exist—and then move on, I believe we must also challenge his deeper claim that the body does not think. In fine, he seems to be arguing that the behavior of Africans is inexplicable because it is unmotivated by thought (that is, reason). Nineteenth-century European metaphysician that he is, Hegel is incapable of seeing, as Levin puts it, that "[u]nderstanding *begins* in, and begins *as*, a bodily granted feeling" (Levin 1985, 266). It is this (to us) mostly unexpressed understanding of understanding that informs the earliest slave narratives. It is this understanding we need, now more than ever perhaps, to reveal.

In 1789,[9] thirty-three years before Hegel's lectures, the former slave Olaudah Equiano, retracing the course of his life from his early days in Western Africa to his capture, enslavement, conversion to Christianity, and eventual freedom in England, attempts to forestall what will become the prevailing attitudes of the nineteenth century: that African and white are irremediably different races, implicated in each other's lives only insofar as the latter can save the former from savagery and damnation. In the first few pages of Equiano's narrative, nay, in the very title itself—*The Interesting Narrative of the Life of Olaudah Equiano, or Gustavus Vassa, the African. Written by Himself*—lie the tensions my study addresses and the truths it hopes to reveal. On one hand, Equiano's narrative purports to be a documentary account of how an African slave became Christianized and civilized, an account designed to convince his readers of the fact that slavery ought everywhere to be abolished because Africans belonged within the human family, as equal, reasonable beings. Equiano is thus first in the tradition of slave narrators engaged in what Gates calls an indictment of "the metaphysical system" that had been used to defend the institution of slavery (Gates 1987b, ix). On the other hand, this indictment is a reworking of Western metaphysics, one that on the surface accepts its premises and argues for the inclusion of Africans in its definition of what it means to be human—but one that also challenges (or signifies on) metaphysical premises by reinstating the body at the heart of the human experience.

Equiano opens his narrative with a fairly standard apologia for having the impertinence to write a memoir of such an unexceptional life, acknowledging that he is able to give readers an account "of neither a saint, a hero, nor a tyrant" (Equiano 1814, 11). It is only because he is African and not European, he assures us, that he considers himself "as a *particular favourite of Heaven*" (12). But had he been European, he tells us, he might be tempted to complain of his vast suffering. Having established his spiritual election and warned us he will not dwell too long on the extraordinary sufferings that he (needs must have) endured as a slave, he turns to a brief account of his Igbo heritage. The role of the body in memorializing and transmitting cultural heritage is clear in the Igbo tradition Equiano describes by which the elders of his people achieve the distinction of what he terms Embrenche, or literally the "mark of grandeur." This honor, he informs us, "is conferred on the person . . . by cutting the skin across at the top of the forehead, and drawing it down to the eyebrows; and applying a warm hand to it, . . . and rubbing it until it shrinks up into a thick wale across the forehead" (12–13).[10] As his father and brother had been marked, so was he to have been awarded this "badge" of distinction (13) had he not been kidnapped into slavery. A Christian now at the composition of his manuscript and absent the visible mark of distinction for which his natal culture had destined him, he nonetheless bears the remains of Igbo tradition in his physical body and in the body of the text he delivers to us, his readers, who, in turn, by understanding it internalize and transmit these traditions forward into the future. Fondly and proudly, Equiano thus recollects that his people are virtually "a nation of dancers, musicians, and poets," and all their important public occasions are "accompanied with songs and music" (Equiano 1814, 14).[11] The clothing of both sexes is similar, he recalls, and dyed a shade of blue that makes it superior to any European cloth he has yet seen (14). Content with plain fare, his people have not yet been corrupted by those culinary practices that "debauch the taste" (15). Before eating, moreover, they "always wash [their] hands: indeed [their] cleanliness on all occasions is extreme; but on this it is an indisputable ceremony"—in other words, it is a cultural value that is ritualistically inscribed upon the body (15). Noting that their chief form of labor is simply increasing the abundance with which their land is already blessed, Equiano takes pride in the fact that the slaves from his region are known for their "hardiness, intelligence, integrity and zeal" (17). Those who have remained in Africa benefit from their living conditions in their attractiveness, health, and strength (17). This is, in short, clearly a man who remembers his West African heritage in his body—just as subsequent generations of slaves and ex-slaves would remember it in theirs, in their dances, songs, and religious services (as I am asserting philosophically, but as Blassingame and others document anecdotally).[12] Although his forehead has not been marked, he has apparently, in conformity with the customs of his culture, been circumcised (23). I am arguing, therefore, that through the rituals of "sacrifices and burnt-offerings," through "washings and purifications" and as a result of daily living among the Igbo people, Equiano's body—like that of everyone else—functions as a living memorial of his natal culture (23).[13] I am also arguing that his body-self remembers how important all bodies are to any people and their culture, whether the importance is understated (if not denied), as it is in the West, or foregrounded, as it is among the Igbo. But writing as he is at the close of the eighteenth century, Equiano knows he cannot reach his British audience except on the level of disembodied reason. He thus concludes his account of his early life by apologizing for lingering so long on these "manners and customs" and explains the details by asserting that they "had made an *impression* on my *mind* which time could not erase" (25; emphasis added). Writing 200 years later, I can argue that these manners and customs made a lasting impression on his body, which has become a kind of living palimpsest. In other words, where the Christian faith and Western metaphysics that he has embraced have attempted to erase or rub out what Equiano first learned among his African people, these new systems have merely written over the knowledge his body-self first learned. The original knowledge, while supplemented by a competing system, has been neither eradicated nor completely obscured by the new ways of thinking he has learned in the West.[14]

Although his title page reminds us that his *Life* (the "visible sign" of his reason) has been "written by himself"—that is to say, in his own hand, by his own body—his dedication page, addressed "To the Lords Spiritual and Temporal, and the Commons of the Parliament of Great Britain," tries at once to deflect attention away from and toward the fact of human embodiment (his own and that of his esteemed audience). He begins in "deference and respect," suggesting by his choice of words that his is the body of a supplicant, lowering itself before authority; he then confesses that he wishes "to lay at [their] feet the following genuine narrative" (again suggesting servility but also embodying his audience, with feet if nothing else)[15] in order to "*excite* in [their] august assemblies a sense of *compassion* for the miseries" that have been inflicted upon his fellow enslaved Africans (Equiano 1814, 3; emphasis added). He is, in short, asking for action: He wants his narrative to move the body of government to end the slave trade, and he hopes to accomplish this by exciting their compassion, literally, by calling forth a shared agony[16] that will stir up their emotions and get their feet marching. In the narrative itself he clearly seeks their compassion in his description of the middle passage, an account that must entail graphic description of bodily suffering, his own and that of other recently enslaved Africans (35–36).[17] Even so, he is attuned to the Western audience he addresses and fully cognizant of their cultural prejudices (having recently learned them himself), and so concludes the opening paragraph of his dedication with the following sentence, the first clause not nearly as ambiguous in its claims as the second. The first clause reads: "By the horrors of that trade was I first torn away from all the tender connections that were naturally dear to my heart" (3). By this he apparently seems to be establishing himself as worthy of their attention on two counts: In presenting the history of his life to this august assembly he has already demonstrated that like themselves he too is a man of reason, and with this clause he further informs them that, even as an untutored African pagan, he, again like themselves, already had "natural" connections to those he loved.[18] This claim of common humanity is followed immediately by the second, more ambiguous clause, which reads in its entirety: "but these [horrors of the slave trade], through the mysterious ways of Providence, *I ought* to regard as infinitely more than compensated by the introduction I have thence obtained to the knowledge of the Christian religion, and of a nation which, by its liberal sentiments, its humanity, the glorious freedom of its government, and its proficiency in arts and sciences, has *exalted the dignity of human nature*" (3; emphasis added). Let me attend to the italicized passages. In the first ("I ought") Equiano tells them it is his duty, his moral obligation to consider the horrors of the slave trade to have been more than compensated by his introduction to Christianity. But he does not say, "I regard" them as having been compensated, only that "I *ought* to regard them." While his narrative seems to bear out the interpretation that he is sincere in this passage, I am not entirely sure he has convinced himself to the extent he wishes to convince his audience.[19] For evidence of his occasional slippage, we can turn to a passage on page 31, for example, in which he blames "fortune" for his ups and downs—a statement for which the eighteenth-century editor chastises him but cautions readers not to assume it in any way reflects "atheistical motives." What I find of further interest in this footnote is the editor's claim that Equiano has made here "a slip of his *pen*"; I read this as the ability of the body to surface even among the hostile waters of Western thought (31). The body may be at fault here, but at least it seems to exist: A slip of the pen seems not to be metaphorical phrasing but a literal explanation of what could have happened to make Equiano so forget himself and what he has learned. Having "heard the term thus misapplied by others, and from an imitative habit, he thoughtlessly gave it the same appellation" (31). Clearly his editor believes that Equiano's body made him err. In the second passage I have italicized, Equiano, having allowed the body in at the beginning of his dedication, hastily ushers it out again at the end, in his reference to exalting the dignity of human nature. No bodies need apply here. But as I have suggested in my reading of his brief history of the Guinea coast (which follows a mere handful of pages after his dedication), he lets the body back in and does so joyfully. But, there, of course, he is talking about African bodies in Africa, a far safer topic of conversation, one that in the late eighteenth century would have had a predictable and conventional response. It is only if he himself or his learned audience were to be embodied that red flags would go up.

But as my project is one that focuses on African *American* literature,[20] let us turn to the experiences of the enslaved Africans in the United States, particularly the experience of Frederick Douglass.

❧

Frederick Douglass

Narrative of the Life of Frederick Douglass, an American Slave. Written by Himself (1845) and *My Bondage and My Freedom* (1855)

There is no better place to look for what the body-selves of the slaves knew than in two of the greatest slave narratives ever written—*Narrative of the Life of Frederick Douglass* and *My Bondage and My Freedom*. Everyone, it seems, regards Douglass's texts as paradigmatic examples of early African American narrative, as, indeed, for my purposes I shall regard them also.[21] But in treating his texts as paradigmatic meditations on the problem of embodiment, I do not mean to suggest they attain a mastery of these themes that other texts are incapable of achieving. My next chapter, which focuses on women's narratives, should make this sufficiently clear. I do mean to suggest, however, that all the themes this project addresses are evident in his first two autobiographies: the suffering of the body-self, the demonstration of sweet reason, the re-embodiment of reason, the desire for and expression of compassion, the need for justice in the flesh, and the body's recollection of *being*. It is not my goal, as it has been that of others,[22] to trace the significant changes in Douglass's writing that occur between his first two narratives. Rather, I wish to unconceal what these two texts collectively have to say about the problem of embodiment. I will, however, concede that, in general, by the time he composed *My Bondage and My Freedom* in 1855, Douglass seems better able to give voice to his body's tacit recollection of *being*. He thematizes this most clearly in the attention he gives to the compassionate treatment he receives at the hands of black and white alike. But even though Douglass begins his 1845 *Narrative* with a litany of what he, as a slave, does not or cannot know,[23] what is remarkable is how much he already does know about what it means for all of us to be related, not just to each other, but to *being* itself. It is clear to me that he also knows we experience this interconnectedness through our bodies—that his has been the intertwining with others that Merleau-Ponty calls the *flesh*.[24] Although Douglass is clearly concerned in this, the first of his life histories, to give adequate proof of both his prior enslavement and his superior reason, the body is not about to absent itself in his accounts. In fact, as I argue more fully below, he makes good use of his handsome, powerful body in his speeches and narratives alike. But his body is not the only one to make an appearance in his texts.

Not insignificantly, one of the first events Douglass recalls in his *Narrative* is that of a beating he witnessed. The person being beaten is his Aunt Hester,[25] who has been caught spending time with a slave man from another plantation. The beating comes as a shock to the young boy because it is so brutal and because having until only recently lived "on the outskirts of the plantation" with his grandmother and several other young slave children, Douglass had been protected from such graphic evidence of the violence that distinguishes life on the plantation for its adult slaves (Douglass 1845, 19).[26] Watching his aunt plead for mercy as their master strips her to the waist, hangs her from a hook screwed to a ceiling joist, and beats her unremittingly until "the warm, red blood . . . came dripping to the floor," Douglass learns in his body-self, perhaps for the first time but certainly for all time, what being another man's slave entails (18).[27] Although he subsequently will witness many such atrocities, it is this one that seems to leave the most lasting impression, as it begins the shaping of his own body into that of a slave's body. "It struck me with awful force" (18), he recalls, as though he himself had been the recipient of the whipping he witnesses—thus supporting my reading that his body is learning its vulnerability and debasement at the hands of these other, more powerful, embodied beings and that his body is recognizing, for the first time, his connectedness to the other plantation slaves.

Examining the often subtle differences between Douglass's first and second narratives, Priscilla Wald finds it significant that in *My Bondage and My Freedom*, Douglass describes his introduction to "the realities of slavery" (Douglass 1855, 150) as having occurred not with the beating but when his grandmother gave him over to his master (Wald 1995, 83, 96). I read this 1855 passage as evidence of Douglass's calling attention to the sudden loss of compassion, the loss of human connectedness he had known in his grandmother's household.[28] He makes the significance of this loss quite explicit when he describes his brothers and sisters as being literal strangers to him, since "slavery had robbed these terms of their true meaning" (Douglass 1855, 149). Although his siblings regard him "with a certain degree of compassion," it is his grandmother for whom he longs (149). The loss of human sympathy he feels at her betrayal and departure is one that is further confirmed in his accounts of plantation violence. For later in the same text he avers that witnessing his aunt's flogging called to his attention, more effectively than any reported accounts of beatings, "the gross features of slavery" (179)—and that such beatings made him "inquire into the nature and history of slavery" (178). Thus his witnessing against slavery seems, in part, dependent upon his witnessing of it—a witnessing that he, paradoxically enough, can only report to his readers.[29] "It was the blood-stained gate," he continues graphically in the *Narrative*, "the entrance to the hell of slavery, through which I was about to pass. It was a most terrible spectacle" (Douglass 1845, 18). So frightened is he of the economics of violence that effectively separate master from slave, he hides himself in "a closet, and dared not venture out till long after the bloody transaction was over" (19). In sum, he has learned (at his aunt's expense) not to entrust his body to the hands of his master, as he had once entrusted it to the hands of his loving grandmother. But it is, in part, because he was protected initially by his grandmother's care from the physical and psychological horrors of slavery that I believe he is able to rise above them and assert himself as a man[30]—and assert, if sometimes only indirectly, the relatedness of all human beings through *being*. Although his sufferings are great, his body-self never forgets the original compassion he experienced in his grandmother's humble dwelling. Before making this argument, however, I first want to attend to what besides floggings his body-self learns of slavery on the Lloyd plantation.

Food and clothing were always in short supply, as was sleep. Once a month, slaves were given their rations, which amounted to no more than eight pounds of meat or fish and four pecks of corn meal (21). Living on these meager portions they were expected to work all day in the field and, before collapsing in utter exhaustion, take care of their own domestic needs, such as preparing their meals and washing and mending the few clothes that they were allowed to own (21). A slave's "bed" consisted of a single rough blanket which had to serve as mattress and cover on a hard, cold, dirt floor (21).[31] By these deprivations slaves learned in their bodies not only what it means to be the property of another person, but they also learned, I argue, to attend to their bodies in ways most white people (and certainly most plantation owners) never had to do. On one hand, such attention to our embodiment is both uncommon and unnatural. As I mentioned in the preceding chapter, Drew Leder (1990) has argued that, because our bodies are the means by which we perceive the world, we largely attend from our bodies to phenomena outside them. Because much of what goes on with our bodies goes on inside them, many of the most important processes of our bodies—circulation of the blood and its oxygenation in the lungs, digestion of food and absorption of nutrients, attacks on foreign invaders and cell repair—are hidden from ordinary view. As a result, our bodies are, generally speaking, absent to us.[32] But for an entire group of people to be poorly clothed and fed and deprived of sufficient rest for generation upon generation surely puts into question the applicability of Leder's rule of thumb to the relationship between slaves and their bodies—as, of course, does the commonplace fact of flogging and other forms of physical torture and humiliation by which the "peculiar institution's" reign of terror inscribed itself for hundreds of years upon the body-selves of the oppressed. That slavery marked the bodies of the enslaved is perhaps too obvious to need repeating here, but I find it significant that Douglass and other nineteenth-century slave narrators, in contrast to their immediate successors, did not choose to "white out" their bodies when they composed their narratives. In fact, the body is very much at the heart of these documents. Douglass records, moreover, the process by which the body of the enslaved learns its debased status—and how the body overcomes this status.

In his *Narrative*, for example, Douglass anticipates an argument made by Elaine Scarry 140 years later in *The Body in Pain* (1985), when she argues that under conditions of extraordinary pain, an individual's entire world and very self are destroyed, a phenomenon that is "experienced spatially as either the contraction of the universe down to the immediate vicinity of the body or as the body swelling to fill the entire universe" (Scarry 1985, 35). In situations of total domination, moreover, the tormented becomes virtually all body while the tormentor becomes all voice (57). Summarizing her argument, Scarry claims that "[w]orld, self, and voice are lost, or nearly lost, through the intense pain of torture" (35). Does this not seem to describe what happens to Hester—and even Douglass himself, as he watches his aunt's punishment? Having seen that Hester's words carry no effect with her all-powerful tormentor, the young boy, fearing he too will become all body, hides himself from view. The thrust of Scarry's argument also seems to lie behind Douglass's account of a master who will not permit contradiction, a master who with his sons "enjoyed the luxury of whipping the servants" whenever they wished, no matter the reason, no matter the age, sex, or status of the slave being tormented (Douglass 1845, 26). Of Colonel Lloyd, Douglass writes further that he could not tolerate being challenged by a slave. "When he spoke," very literally, "a slave must stand, listen, and tremble" (26).

As I suggested earlier, Scarry's system seems to be premised on a dualistic view of mind and body. But one way of getting around this problem would be to treat the act of torture as thematizing the metaphysical split between mind and body. That is, believing in the mind/body split, the torturer sets out in the mistaken conviction that it is possible to convert another human being into pure matter—much as Susan Griffin (1981) argues that certain men, formed themselves by the pornographic imagination, set out with the equally impossible goal of denying their own embodiment by converting woman (as the Other) into a debased, all-sexualized body. For slave owners who believed that Africans were their personal property, it must have seemed a small step to think it was possible to beat them into a state of pure objectivity, where, in metaphysical terms, the slaves would lose all claim to subjectivity (if they had any to begin with). As I have argued in Chapter 1, in reality this state of pure objectivity can only occur in death when we are no longer body but merely corpse—when we are, in effect, no longer human be-ings.[33] But that the body-self, during torture, has no words to speak does not imply it has lost its intentional presence in the world. It may mean it is not in a position to attend *to* the world except in painful revulsion from it, but this does not mean it is without thought or presence. Compare my argument with Thomas Csordas's claims about speaking in tongues. Csordas argues, after Merleau-Ponty, that "speech is an act or phonetic *gesture* in which one takes up an existential position in the world" (Csordas 1990, 25; emphasis added). He then goes on to argue that "glossolalia by its formal characteristic of eliminating the semantic level of linguistic structure highlights precisely the existential reality of intelligent bodies inhabiting a meaningful world. . . . The stripping away of the semantic dimension in glossolalia is not an absence, but rather the drawing back of a discursive curtain to reveal the grounding of language in natural life, as a bodily act" (25). In sum, he is using Merleau-Ponty to claim that "[g]lossolalia reveals language as incarnate, and this existential fact is homologous with the religious significance of the Word made Flesh, the unity of human and divine" (25). Is it not possible to adapt this argument to my own and reason, not that pain is language-destroying but, contra Scarry, that pain is the body-self speaking? Or, to put it in Csordas's terms, might we not see pain as "the embodiment of nonverbal thought" (26)?[34]

For Douglass, what seems most capable of recalling in him the abyss and despair—the pain—of perpetual enslavement are the slave songs he first encountered on the plantation. So effective are the songs at expressing the meaning of slavery, Douglass is inclined to believe, "that the *mere hearing* of those songs would do more to impress some minds with the horrible character of slavery, than the *reading* of whole volumes of philosophy on the subject could do" (1845, 24; emphasis added). Although, for purposes of comparison, Douglass temporarily seems to be relying on a distinction between hearing as a merely physical activity and reading as a more respectable (because disembodied) mental activity, he is, in effect, overcoming this division, just as his comparison elevates the slave songs over learned texts.[35] He achieves this reconciliation by recalling us to our bodies and what they know by using himself as example. While he was still a slave, he tells us, he did not "understand the deep meaning of those rude and apparently incoherent songs." Encircled by slavery, he "neither saw nor heard as those without might see and hear" (24). What strikes me about this passage is, first, how he equates the activities of seeing and hearing—the former being the mode of perception most privileged in Enlightenment thought—and then treats both modes as the equivalent of *understanding*. Clearly, he is telling us in this passage that it is with his body he comes to understand (that is, internalize) the meaning of these songs. Second, what strikes me is how this understanding remained tacit while he was enslaved; it is only after he is removed from slavery that he can articulate the meaning of the songs—and the meaning literally brings him to tears. The tones themselves were "loud, long, and deep; they breathed the prayer and complaint of souls boiling over with the bitterest anguish" (24). Each was a call to end slavery. "The hearing of those wild notes," he continues, "always depressed my spirit, and filled me with ineffable sadness," so much so that his body-self responds by weeping (24). "The mere recurrence to those songs, even now, afflicts me; and *while I am writing these lines, an expression of feeling* has already found its way down my cheek" (24; emphasis added).[36] What a remarkable passage this is in a narrative apparently designed to pave the way for the author to enter liberal humanism as a manly subject among subjects, when the narrator candidly admits, in a self-revealing and self-conscious moment, that it is his body the songs speak to—that it is in and through his body that he knew slavery and, moreover, that it is in and through his body that he is *revealing* its terrors to us. "To those songs," he goes on, "I trace my first glimmering *conception* of the dehumanizing character of slavery. I can never get rid of that conception. Those songs still follow me, to deepen my hatred of slavery, and quicken my *sympathies* for my brethren in bonds" (24; emphasis added).[37] This is no mere sentimentalism. An *idea* is being described as originating in the act of aural perception—that is, in the body-self. Thus what Douglass's body tacitly learns from witnessing his aunt's flogging is later brought to conceptual presence by the hearing of these songs. If anyone else wishes to understand "the soul-killing effects of slavery," Douglass therefore advises that person to listen to the songs on Colonel Lloyd's plantation and, on the day the slave's pitiful portion is meted out, "analyze the sounds"— not the words—"that shall pass through the chambers of his soul,—and if he is not thus impressed, it will only be because 'there is no flesh in his obdurate heart'" (24).[38] Has the capacity of the body (that is, the body-self) to respond to an emotional appeal and understand its conceptual content ever been stated more powerfully?

On my view, then, Douglass's great accomplishment is that he takes the nonverbal but meaningful suffering of his body—combined with the nonverbal suffering of other powerless bodies—and translates it into language, the powerful self-conscious and self-affirming language of his *Narrative*, whereby he labors to end the suffering of all slaves by recollecting our common relatedness-to-*being*.[39] That is, he translates the immanent, ineffable, *gestural* language of his suffering body into the public domain of what Csordas calls "vernacular speech" (1990, 26).[40] Or, to put it in Leder's terms, Douglass collapses the "*hermeneutical* and [the] *pragmatic* moment" of his pain's "telic demand" and converts them into a narrative through which he simultaneously *interprets* his pain and *acts* to end it (Leder 1990, 78).[41] In so doing, he transforms his body-self into a text, by which he reaches out to others and in so doing makes possible their reciprocal compassionate response. By this assertion I do not mean to invoke a sentimental reading or the conventional (though now contested)[42] sentimental response—that of crying for the self-indulgent sake of crying. Neither do I mean that Douglass is doing here what he despised the abolitionists for trying to do in treating the visible scars on his back as the text of his former enslavement.[43] I am making the more radical claim that the text of his body has become, quite literally, the body of his text—which, further, we embodied readers hold in our hands when we read. The success of his endeavor lay in what those hands would do once they put down the body of the text. That is, would these hands work to make real the justice in the flesh his narratives envision? Would the bodies of these readers incorporate his message of human relatedness? Where the slave songs, as Douglass himself comes to realize, also speak the body-self in pain and envision an alternative time and place when its pain will end, they are, for him, almost too full of the pain they speak. Although Douglass is brought to unwelcome tears by the slave songs, perhaps their greatest accomplishment is their enduring ability to give voice to bodies in pain—and in so doing recall us to the fact of our own embodiment, by which, like Douglass himself, we too might rediscover the truths that lie within but are too seldom spoken of or for. As Douglass puts it, in a speech delivered on 1 December 1850, "ask the slave—*what* is his condition?—*what* his state of mind?—*what* he thinks of his enslavement? and you had as well address your inquiries to the *silent dead*. There comes no *voice* from the enslaved" (Blassingame 1982, 259). Yet, conflating hearing and reading myself here, it is the voice[44] of the formerly enslaved we hear in the *Narrative*, a voice that calls out to be heard by our body-selves as Douglass heard the slave songs, a voice that is at once emotion and idea, engaging us in the common telic demand to end the pain it expresses.[45]

But if Douglass's body had been marked by slavery, his body, as he thematizes in an oft-cited passage, is also the means by which he finally becomes a man—this, of course, being his famous fight with Covey, which Douglass cites as "the turning-point of my career as a slave. It rekindled the few expiring embers of freedom, and revived within me a sense of my own manhood" (1845,

65). What I want to note about this passage is how important physical strength and physical resistance—that is, the capacities of the body itself—are to Douglass's claim to achieving manhood (in a reversal of how weak and helpless he felt in the face of the whipping he witnessed as a child). If Gates is correct in his assertion that the ex-slaves began writing to prove their humanity, it is even more striking that a central passage in a text purporting to be the visible sign of reason involves the capacities of the body to free the spirit of the man. "My long-crushed spirit rose," Douglass writes, "cowardice departed, bold defiance took its place; and I now resolved that, however long I might remain a slave in *form*, the day had passed forever when I could be a slave in *fact*" (65; emphasis added).[46] I want to argue that while Douglass's body (his form) still appeared to be enslaved (as in truth it did remain, legally speaking), this body, in successfully resisting one who literally embodied the slavocracy, brought to light what his body-self had forgotten how to say but already knew—that, *in fact*, he was no slave. In sum, the fight unleashed his own body's recollection of *being*. In this passage Douglass also claims, significantly, to have "repelled by force the bloody arm of slavery" (65), re-embodying through his telling synecdoche the institution that is composed of men, guilty but weak physical beings very like the one he has just defeated.[47]

In *My Bondage and My Freedom*, Douglass retains many of the same phrases he uses in his *Narrative*, adding to them the assertion that he "was a changed *being* after that fight" (Douglass 1855, 286; emphasis added). "I was nothing before; I WAS A MAN NOW. It recalled to life my crushed self-respect and my self-confidence, and inspired me with a renewed determination to be A FREE-MAN. A man, without force, is without the essential dignity of humanity" (286). Neither are these passages simple manly bravado, as many have found them. In a true Heideggerian moment, Douglass has found the "saving grace" at the heart of his problem. If the essence of slavery is to deny—on the basis of purported bodily differences—the interconnectedness of human beings (or, in Pontian terms, the alterity in ontology) and if slavery maintains itself through violence, Douglass will overcome its metaphysics and its regime through force (a bodily attribute that he equates with dignity—with subjecthood) by bringing down the man who stands for such separation (1845, 64; 1855, 284). Quite literally, in grounding Covey in (the fact of) his own vulnerable corporeality, Douglass gives the lie to bodily difference—as he does in his speeches, when he is arguing for the oneness of all human beings. Thus he who would keep Douglass, as body and as body-self, separate from other bodies and body-selves is himself defeated by Douglass's own body(-self), a defeat that has the dual effect of freeing "self" from the parenthetical imprisonment of my previous clause and of freeing this body-self to recollect the inborn knowledge of its connection to other body-selves. On my view this passage is a reinstatement of the body's importance even to a subject, a man of reason.[48] A similar expression of the importance of the body occurs in Douglass's repeated avowals in speeches and published essays that "the colored men must learn trades" if they are to gain the respect of their fellow Americans (Foner 1950b, 234). "We must show that we can *do* as well as *be*" (224). In short, he is calling upon his people to learn to work with their hands and thus begin to advance the race.

Whereas Douglass did take a chance, writing about his own embodiment as he did, that, as an ex-slave, he might be perceived by his contemporary liberal humanist readers as more debased body than rational being, as a male he had a certain cultural permission to talk about his body-self and enjoyed a certain narrative advantage in choosing to do so. In making this choice to speak his body and the bodies of other slaves, he thus helped to found what I have called the proto-Bohemian School of African American writing. To function as an effective spokesman for the abolitionist cause, in his speeches and his autobiographies, he had to strike just the right balance between demonstrating his superior intelligence (his rationality) and exploiting his physical suffering. He needed to inspire in listeners and readers a sense of pity and outrage that such a splendid specimen of manhood as himself could ever be treated as mere chattel and thus be deserving of perpetual enslavement.[49] As orator and writer, he could use his body's suffering to deepen the pity and outrage his audience would feel on his behalf as they came to realize how undeserving of his fate this brilliant, eloquent man had been.[50] He could, if he were skillful enough, even use the fact of his embodiment to symbolize the common humanity he shared with listeners and readers alike.[51] For how could his New England audience not recoil in sympathetic horror from his accounts of going hungry and being beaten? How, after hearing these accounts of bodily suffering, could they not work themselves to end it? How could an already sympathetic Northern man not find common cause with Douglass's account of besting Covey by the strength of his own body?[52] And how could an already sympathetic Northern woman not find it in her heart to wish it was she who had ministered to his head wounds as we shall soon see Miss Lucretia Auld did? That Douglass successfully translated his narrative accounts of human compassion into effective political action on the part of his readers there is no doubt. That Douglass was, by definition and, on my argument, by design, also questioning the metaphysical system of his time there is equally no doubt, though such questioning most probably was undetected by his audience—as much of it has gone undetected by his twentieth-century readers, for we in the West remain as much as ever enthralled by its dualistic thinking.[53] But whether or not his nineteenth-century readers could fully understand the role that Douglass's body-self played in his narratives, they could respond to what his body-self knew of human connectedness and our common relatedness-to-*being*. And, I dare say, rather than remaining a liability as they had been in Maryland, his handsome black visage and upright figure must have been a decided advantage to him on the abolitionist lecture circuit in New England. Although white men achieved the status of subject and citizen by virtue of their superior reason, because it was widely believed in the nineteenth century that a man's character and intelligence could be read in his appearance,[54] it did not hurt—and often helped—if he were literally seen to be a manly subject by the additional virtue of his countenance, cranial capacity, and aristocratic bearing. In this regard, at least among the abolitionists, Frederick Douglass's noble appearance could easily be seen as symbolic of his noble character.[55]

The fight with Covey, when considered in conjunction with the uses Douglass made of his body in his speeches, helps us find additional examples in Douglass's first two autobiographies of what the body knows and how this knowledge can be the salvation, not just of the slaves, but of us all. Before continuing with Douglass's texts, however, it is helpful to my argument to note that similar kinds of insights inform a lesser-known slave narrative, *The Fugitive Blacksmith; or, Events in the History of James W. C. Pennington*, written about the same time (1849) as Douglass's first autobiography. It will be recalled that I invoked Pennington's name earlier in his assertion that slavery relied upon and was defined by "the chattel principle" (Pennington 1849, vii). Not one to mince words, this ordained Presbyterian minister and former slave speaks bluntly about young slave women being forced into prostitution and sets out to debunk the myth that there could ever be any truth in the descriptive phrase, the "'mildest form of slavery'" (x). Although he too suffers, like Douglass, from severe deprivations, he does live with both of his parents and is trained, as his title reveals, as a blacksmith. But once he witnesses his father wronged and beaten unfairly by his master and is himself beaten, he loses what has been heretofore a great comfort to him, that is, his "mechanic's pleasure and pride" (9). It is as though these two overt attacks—the one on the body of his family, the other on his own body—put into perspective for the first time that the members of the Pennington family, however loving and skilled they might have been, are nonetheless human chattel. Once Pennington discovers this truth, he can no longer live as a slave. Most of his narrative, in fact, is the account of his escape, as he lingers over details of his family life only briefly.

At the end of his short narrative, as he wraps up his story, he reveals that his purpose had been to show "the *hand* of God with a slave; and to elicit your *sympathy* in behalf of the fugitive slave" so readers will remember how much the fugitive slave "needs friends on free soil" (1849, 56; emphasis added). As I have argued before, I find metaphors like the *hand* of God pregnant with meaning. I thus read this passage to mean that if God himself (a being, as Scarry argues, without a body if ever there was one)[56] has been willing to reach out a hand to a fugitive slave, it should not be asking too much to ask for similar acts of (bodily) compassion from mere mortals, those who encounter fleeing slaves on the road and those who encounter them in the pages of a narrative. Before Pennington closes his narrative, however, he bitterly attacks slavery for denying him an education. "It cost me two years' hard labour, after I fled," he reports, "to unshackle my mind; it was three years before I had purged my language of slavery's idioms; it was *four years* before I had thrown off the crouching aspect of slavery" (56; emphasis added). These distinctions are germane to my argument as they demonstrate that we carry our culture with us in our bodies, an imprint that is virtually impossible to erase. What Pennington says he most regrets "is a great lack of that general information" which he should have learned as a youth instead of being left in ignorance as a slave (56). What perhaps he does not recognize, because his culture fails to recognize it either, is that he carries within his body the memory of a loving family and the skill of his hands, both forms of knowledge that not only helped him survive slavery and his harrowing escape but also helped turn him into a good and decent human being, one who is so honest that he can barely stand to lie to his would-be captors in order to save himself from being returned to slavery (22).[57] That he did value his skilled hands is evident in the title he chose, *The Fugitive Blacksmith*, which calls attention to his craft as a skilled worker and not just his status as a runaway slave. That his family connections are also important to him is clear from his admission that the day he left was a "heartaching" one, forcing him to ask himself, "shall I hide my purpose from them? moreover, how will my flight affect them when I am gone?" (12). This is the voice of a man connected in love and by blood to other human beings. When he learns for the first time the sheer number of men and women who are enslaved, for example, his mind is "completely staggered" by the sum, which has the effect of filling him with physical agony and leaving him convinced of his own sins against God (52). What he thematizes, in short, is what his time and religion would expect him to thematize: his sufferings as a slave and his conversion to Christianity. Underneath it all, unthematized but evident to us today, is the role of the body in slavery and the role of the body in overcoming slavery and recollecting us to *being*—which, for Pennington, was God himself.

Family is also important to Douglass for the human connections it implies and makes real. Although in his first autobiography he could not see what his mother had done for him, he did have the memory of his grandmother's love, confined as the love itself was to the first few years of his life. But he also had other human connections as well that I am arguing left their mark on his young body, marks that worked to counter those equally memorable ones of oppression and domination—though Douglass cautions us to remember that all kindness was relative when it came to the actions of slave masters (Douglass 1845, 28). Nevertheless, shortly after being taken to Colonel Lloyd's plantation, Douglass strikes up a "connection" with one of Lloyd's sons, a relationship that, while legally imposed on him as a slave, was nonetheless advantageous to him in that Daniel Lloyd grew fond of him and became his protector (33). Moreover, though his elation is short-lived, Douglass is delighted to move to Baltimore, where he is on loan to the Aulds and, even as an adult, considers it to have been a mark of his election by "divine Providence" that he alone, of all the slaves, was chosen (36). His new mistress, Mrs. Sophia Auld, had never had a slave before and as a consequence had yet to learn how to treat them. Before she has learned her new role (and learned it only too well), she, too, gives the young slave lessons in human compassion. She is so different from the whites he has known on the plantation that he scarcely knows how to "approach her" (36). What he had learned is useless. "The crouching servility, usually so acceptable a quality in a slave, did not answer when manifested toward her" (37). Not only must his body learn to stand tall, but Douglass also has the unusual opportunity, if only briefly, of being taught to read by Mrs. Auld. But the kindness of this woman, whose face inspires "rapture" in young Douglass's soul when he first sets eyes upon her (35), is soon undone by slavery, which, on his account, caused her as much harm as it did himself. When he first arrived, Douglass reports, "she was a pious, warm, and tender-hearted woman. There was no sorrow or suffering for which she had not a tear. She had bread for the hungry, clothes for the naked, and comfort for every mourner that came within her reach" (40). Even the young white boys who live near the Aulds show Douglass the face of human kindness by reassuring him that something would happen so he would not always remain enslaved (41). This sentiment is shared by an Irish dockworker who tells him it is a shame that someone as "fine" as he "should be a slave for life" (43). By these few examples, I do not mean to overstate the good that accrued to Douglass as a slave. I am seeking evidence of human compassion that he encountered, moments in which other human beings reached out (their hands) to him and reaffirmed their common humanity. It is this compassion, I believe, that helped make it possible for him to listen to what his body already knew of our human relatedness-to-*being*.[58]

For further evidence of this, we need only turn to the second rendition of his autobiography, *My Bondage and My Freedom*, written ten years after the *Narrative* and no longer under the watchful eyes of William Lloyd Garrison. Significantly, his second autobiography is introduced, not by a white man who will authorize what an ex-slave has authored, but by another black man, who remarks how encouraging it is to see "the ease with which black men, scarce one remove from barbarism . . . vault into the high places of the most advanced and painfully acquired civilization" (Douglass 1855, 125). James M'Cune Smith goes on to describe Douglass's virtues, which include (but are not limited to) "a majestic self-hood; determined courage; a deep and agonizing sympathy with his embruted, crushed and bleeding fellow slaves, and an extraordinary depth of passion, together with that rare alliance between passion and intellect, which enables the former, when deeply roused, to excite, develop and sustain the latter" (126). Key among these virtues, on my view, is the "sympathy" or compassion that Douglass is said to have for other slaves.[59] In explaining Douglass's success, Smith also draws upon the fact that the young slave's body was "well trained" as it was permitted to "[run] wild until advanced into boyhood" (127). He finds it significant, moreover, that "[w]hat his hand found to do, he did with his might; even while conscious that he was wronged out of his daily earnings, he worked, and worked hard" (127). Remarkable as Douglass is, however, Smith is compelled to note that his early education did not include more than a minimal amount of "a mother's care" (127). That he sorely missed a mother's love is clear enough from Douglass's own statements, but that he nonetheless still experienced the healing powers of human compassion is equally evident. It will be recalled from the previous chapter that Levin, drawing on Heidegger, claims that whenever we open ourselves to those in need we are at the same time "opening to Being."[60] He thus contends that when we feel compassion for others, we are expressing "an awareness of universality and wholeness" (Levin 1985, 97). Surely this, too, is what Smith means when he speaks of Douglass's sympathy for his fellow slaves. We express this compassion quite literally when we *are moved* to help others (Levin 1985, 98). This is why compassion is central to my understanding of Douglass, as it is central to my understanding of the other slave narrators.[61] In opening a slave narrative, readers ideally open themselves to the experience of their narrators and in so doing acknowledge our relatedness-to-*being* itself.[62] It is this same relatedness that Douglass experienced in those moments of compassion when white people reached out to him in kindness and charity—from Colonel Lloyd's son to his new master's wife to Garrison himself. It is this compassion that left Douglass open to others, even though he knew such openness could be dangerous and would not always be reciprocated; it is this compassion, moreover, that left him open to *being* and eventually helped make possible the composition of the very texts we read. That Douglass himself knew this is clear from what he says in his first two autobiographies, but where the knowledge remains somewhat tacit in his *Narrative*, it is more openly thematized in *My Bondage and My Freedom*.

It is not irrelevant to my argument that by the time he composed his second autobiography, he had become more charitable to his own mother, more open to understanding what she did for him and at what physical cost she did it. In his *Narrative*, Douglass can write dispassionately that since he never experienced, to any degree, his mother's loving attention, he learns of her death "with much the same emotions I should have probably felt at the death of a stranger" (1845, 16). But ten years later, he can recognize the extent of her love for him, absent though she was, having been rented out to work on another plantation. "The pains she took, and the toil she endured, to see me," he finally admits, "tells [sic] me that a true mother's heart was hers, and that slavery had difficulty in paralyzing it with unmotherly indifference" (1855, 152–53). Although it is a continuing sorrow to him to have been denied knowledge of and counsel from his mother, in his second autobiography he takes pride in her appearance, likening it to an illustration he has seen in Prichard's *Natural History of Man* (1843),[63] and in the remarkable fact that she, alone of all the slaves in Tuckahoe, had learned how to read (Douglass 1855, 152, 155). Whereas in 1845 he is still too bitter at being deprived of his mother's love to see what she was able to offer him,[64] by 1855 he attributes his own love of learning to "the native genius of my sable, unprotected, and uncultivated *mother*—a woman, who belonged to a race whose mental endowments it is, at present, fashionable to hold in disparagement and contempt" (156). In *My Bondage and My Freedom*, moreover, he takes pains to describe the accomplishments of his maternal grandmother, remarking on her skill at nursing, fishing, making nets, and growing sweet potatoes (141).[65] In short, Douglass is praising the fully realized gifts of his grandmother's hands—or to put it in my terms, he praises the capacity of her body to think. That this is an appropriate gloss on the text is clear from Douglass's choice of words, when he states that his grandmother was "a *capital hand* at making nets" (141; emphasis added). If we recall that "capital" derives from *caput* or head, we can see clearly that Douglass has intuited that nursing, fishing, making nets, and growing potatoes are thoughtful gestures, an insight that anticipates Heidegger's, Levin's, and my arguments, and one that works to challenge metaphysics on its own grounds. This is the same woman, Betsey Bailey, who with her husband, Isaac, not only lovingly cares for Douglass as an infant and young child but also cares for the many children born to her other daughters. Living with his grandparents on Holme Hill Farm, Douglass is protected for years from the knowledge that he is a slave. During this time, before the knowledge of "Old Master" poisons the dream of childhood, Douglass's character is set (1855, 143). Although he remains justifiably embittered by what slavery denied him and what slavery tried to teach him, he is not merely the product of this negative influence, as the narratives themselves attest. His grandmother helps form a different kind of person, one who was able to listen to and heed what his body had always known. His memory and assessment of his grandmother reveal that he recognized the capacity of his body (all bodies) for ontological thinking, the inborn predisposition to reach out to others and assert our relatedness-to-*being*.

"The germs of *affection* with which the Almighty . . . *arms* the helpless infant against the ills and vicissitudes of his lot," he writes, "had been directed in their growth toward that loving old grandmother, whose *gentle hand* and *kind deportment* it was the first effort of my infantile understanding to comprehend and appreciate" (152; emphasis added).[66] Although Douglass invokes God to explain the natural affection with which he began life, his claim differs little from those made by Levin and Merleau-Ponty, who argue, it will be recalled, that while we must learn to differentiate ourselves from one another, we are, as infants, predisposed to sociability.[67] The grandmother who loved and cared for him in his helplessness, he describes, moreover, as having a gentle hand and a kind deportment. In sum, she literally bears love for him in her body. In Levin's terms, she is compassionate; in Heidegger's terms, she cares. Both of Douglass's terms that I have italicized—her *"gentle hand"* and *"kind deportment"*— seem intended to carry the same weight of meaning as Levin's compassion and Heidegger's care. That is to say, they are meant to suggest what it means to be human. By calling attention to Douglass's choice of words, I hope to support my argument that Douglass himself, intent as he has been on demonstrating his own individuality and asserting his own will—individuality and will being necessary in the struggle to free himself from enslavement and assert himself as an equal among other Western individuals—has nevertheless come to recognize by 1855 that what makes us truly human is less our individuality than our ability to care for others.[68] These passages, like so many others in Douglass's narratives, function therefore to remind us of the gift of embodiment, the gift by which we recollect our relatedness-to-*being*.

Although twentieth-century critics continue to debate whether Douglass believes in the root that he is given by Sandy Jenkins (a debate fostered, I believe, by the texts' ambiguities on the subject),[69] it is clear that Douglass is grateful to Sandy and appreciates his act of human kindness. If anything, in the ten-year interval between his two autobiographies, Douglass's appreciation of Jenkins's gift seems to have increased. On his account, having been brutally beaten by Covey and sought refuge in the woods, Douglass is discovered there by Jenkins, who, in the 1845 version, "very kindly invited me to go home with him" albeit the two were only casually acquainted (63). By 1855, Douglass describes him as a "*friend* not an enemy" (279). And once Douglass explains his dilemma to this "good-hearted" person, he is gratified to see that "he deeply *compassioned* my distress" (279; emphasis added). Even though it is dangerous, Jenkins nonetheless invites Douglass to accompany him home—because, Douglass explains, Jenkins was "too generous to permit the fear of punishment to prevent his relieving a brother bondman from hunger and exposure" (279). Jenkins's wife, who is herself free, is equally kind. They wish to help him, Douglass says, because he was "loved by the colored people," believing as they do that he "was hated for [his] knowledge, and persecuted because [he] was feared" (279–80). Whatever their motives, these people nonetheless put their own bodies in danger by reaching out to succor him. Douglass is not unaware of this, as what he remembers of the evening is the supper of "ash cake and cold water," which is, of all the meals he has ever eaten, the one "most sweet to my taste, and now most vivid in my memory" (280). Although he may have bragged about how his literacy is seen by his fellow slaves, his body remembers the gift of human compassion he has been given that night. An inverse kind of compassion occurs when Covey tries to beat Douglass and calls upon two other slaves—Bill, the hired hand, and Caroline, Covey's own slave woman—to help him. Both refuse to lend their hands to such an activity (285). For his part, once he has finished his year at Covey's and gone to St. Michael's to work for Mr. Freeland, Douglass establishes a Sunday School for his fellow slaves, a venture that united them in deep and lasting brotherhood. Although it is possible that Jenkins betrays the group when they plan their escape, Douglass reports that they "loved him too well" to think him guilty (321).

It is thus crucial to our understanding of his narrative to attend closely to those passages in which he also describes the compassionate acts of white persons toward himself, for it is in these that he most clearly articulates his understanding of our openness-for-*being*. Douglass may hope to pull the wool over the eyes of the Garrisonians by claiming in his narrative only to "relate and describe," but it is clear to me that he has not, after all, "let others philosophize" (189).[70] One lengthy example of his philosophizing on the role of compassion and how it is expressed in gestures of the human body opens Chapter 9 of *My Bondage and My Freedom*, in which Douglass describes in detail the kindness of Miss Lucretia Auld. As he says, in a domestic environment marked by its severity and bleak indifference, "the slightest word or look of kindness passed, with me, for its full value" (Douglass 1855, 206). Not only does Miss Lucretia speak kindly to the young slave, giving him to believe that at the very least she pities him, she also secures extra portions of bread and butter for him. One time, moreover, after he has been bested by another boy during a fight and left with a nasty gash on his forehead, she "quietly acted the good Samaritan. With her own soft *hand* she washed the blood from my head and face, fetched her own balsam bottle, and with the balsam wetted a nice piece of white linen, and bound up my head" (207; emphasis added). His spirit was as much healed by her solicitude, he reports, as his head was healed by the balsam. Even though his memories of slavery contain much bitterness, the friendship and compassion of white persons like Miss Lucretia gave him reason to be thankful, and he enjoys remembering "any instances of kindness, any sunbeams of humane treatment, which found [their] way to my soul through the iron grating of my house of bondage" (208). It is, in part, because of his grandmother's initial care and Miss Lucretia's compassion that Douglass retains his inborn openness-for-*being*, an openness to other human beings and to the world around him. Once he is forced to leave his grandmother's hut, he tells us, the "little tendrils of affection" by which he first bound himself to the world began to seek new attachments "and to entwine about the new objects" in his environment (161). Secure in himself because of his grandmother's influence and Miss Lucretia's solicitous attention, he thus opens himself to the world in his strange new surroundings. Replacing the objects of his early childhood affection are a windmill, a creek, and "a large sloop" (161). To the young boy, these new objects "were wondrous things, full of thoughts and ideas. A child cannot well look at such objects without *thinking*" (161). Detailing the vast and well-cared-for estate of Colonel Lloyd, Douglass is not so much judgmental as appreciative, remarking that gazing upon "this elaborate exhibition of wealth, power, and vanity" was "a treat to my young and gradually opening mind" (162).[71] As I have noted, young Douglass's mind, however, is also stimulated into further thought by the beatings and violence he witnesses, and, as a consequence, he begins to question why he is a slave, why some are masters and others must be slaves, and when slavery originated. Thus begins what he will come to call "this everlasting thinking which distressed and tormented me" (227).

It is critical to my argument that Douglass describes the onset of his thinking as occurring while he wanders throughout the plantation (see also his account of thinking while driving an ox cart; Douglass 1855, 183). It will be recalled from Chapter 1 (above) that Levin, drawing on the work of Merleau-Ponty, stresses the fact that human motility forms "a body of genuine understanding" that permits human beings to experience our innate place "in the field of Being as a whole" (Levin 1985, 103). Just as I have stressed the importance of gestures and compassion in my reading of Douglass's autobiographies, here, too, I want to follow Levin and stress the more basic phenomenon of bodily motility in the slave narratives, using the concept of motility, as Levin does, to subsume the concepts of both gesture and compassion.[72] For Levin, as for me, it is a fact of deep philosophical import that human beings move out into the world, that they are attuned to *being* in the movements of their bodies. For my purposes, it is of particular significance that, ordinarily, the motility of the slave's body was severely restricted. Not only were most slaves forbidden from leaving the plantation and required to sleep, awake, and labor on command,[73] but, as Douglass has reminded us, the very posture of their bodies was determined for them.[74] It was no small privilege, then, for someone like the young Frederick Douglass to have had the physical freedom to wander around the "woods and fields" and along the banks of the river seemingly at will (179).[75] Neither was it insignificant that once he moved to Baltimore, he was expected to return his body to an upright position. And it is important, as Douglass notes of his relatively "benign child-hood," that unlike the little white boys, a slave boy does not have "to listen to lectures on propriety of behavior" and is not "chided for handling his little knife and fork improperly or awkwardly, for he has none" (144).[76] Lacking the dis-cipline and parental attention to which most little boys are subjected, the slave boy is for much of "the first eight years of his life, a spirited, joyous, uproarious, and happy boy" (145).[77] Where some might find irony in this passage (espe-cially as it documents real privations, such as insufficient medication), I believe that Douglass is establishing here as elsewhere that, at the beginning of his life, his body remained unmarked by the white plantation culture of nineteenth-century Maryland. As he says later, contrasting his experience with that of his fellow slaves, "[t]he overseer had written his character on the living parchment of most of their backs, and left them callous; my back . . . was yet tender" (239).[78]

Originally unshaped by white society and its metaphysical thinking, Doug-lass is free, as few white youth ever would be, to open himself to *being* by thinking through his body. Although some might doubt Douglass's claim that he was only seven or eight when he first began to think about slavery and how he might free himself of its shackles, my reading of the narratives makes it virtually impossible for this brilliant youth to have done anything else.[79] It is my argu-ment that, even though as a child he had heard rumors of "Old Master" and sub-sequently witnessed the beating of his aunt, the care of his grandmother and the compassionate treatment of Miss Lucretia helped him retain—in his body—the preconceptual attunement to *being* with which we all begin life but which is trained out of us by the reign of metaphysics and the habitus of liberal human-ism.[80] Unclaimed as yet by metaphysics, unhabituated by the strictures of West-ern civilization, and free to wander in the woods, Douglass was able to listen to the truths that inhered in his body. Thus it is that an eight-year-old boy, "quite ignorant of the existence of the free states," could nonetheless conceive of him-self as one day being free (179). "This cheering assurance was," in his words, "an *inborn dream of my human nature*—a constant menace to slavery—and one which all the powers of slavery were unable to silence or extinguish" (179; em-phasis added). He puts this knowledge in a negative frame a few pages later, when he states that the physical suffering he experiences and witnesses led him to wish that he had "never been born" (209). "I was just as well aware of the unjust, unnatural and murderous character of slavery," he continues, "when nine years old, as I am now" (209). But he ends this chapter by repeating once more his conviction that one day he would be free. Even though he learns much of human compassion and openness-for-*being* on the plantation, he is only too happy to be sent to Baltimore to live with the Aulds. Looking back on the change in his circumstances, he considers it the pivotal event of his young life. If he had not at such a tender age been spared "the rigors of slavery," if he had not left the plantation before his "spirit had been crushed," he thinks it certain he would never have become a free man (212).

It is therefore important to consider carefully what Douglass says of his new life in Baltimore, especially since these passages thematize most of the strands of my argument. His initial impression of his new mistress, Sophia Auld, as we have seen from his *Narrative*, is entirely positive, her abundant kindness seeming to surpass even that of Miss Lucretia (Douglass 1855, 212). Her appearance is so welcoming and her actions so benevolent, in fact, that the young slave begins to think of her almost as his mother rather than his mistress, fondly recalling that little "Freddie" was a particular favorite of hers: "Nor did he lack the caressing strokes of her gentle hand, to convince him that, though *motherless*, he was not *friendless*" (215). What Douglass stresses in these passages is Miss Sophia's countenance and behavior, that is to say, the bearing of her body toward her new slave, a bearing that communicates love and compassion to such an extent that Douglass's own body reciprocates by abandoning its "crouching servility" (215). The adult Douglass attributes her unusual behavior to the fact that, unlike most women who own slaves, Sophia Auld had been a professional weaver before her marriage and had "depended almost entirely upon her own industry for a living" (215). Douglass apparently believes that his mistress had retained an openness-for-*being* in the skillful use of her hands. As he earlier observes in his *Narrative*, "by constant application to her business, she had been in a good degree preserved from the blighting and dehumanizing effects of slavery" (Douglass 1845, 36). And it is her hands—her "tender hands"—that he stresses in *My Bondage and My Freedom* (Douglass 1855, 216).[81] He also explains Sophia Auld's compassionate behavior toward him as exemplary of a "natural love in our fellow creatures" with which nature equips us, an explanation that resonates with Levin's position that as humans we are predisposed in our very embodiment to reach out to others (222). At first Douglass's body is not made to suffer in the Auld household as it has suffered on the Lloyd plantation. In Baltimore he has a bed, sufficient food, and decent clothing. Douglass feels so safe and secure with Mrs. Auld that he does not hesitate to ask her to teach him how to read—a task she begins willingly before she is accosted by her husband and berated, in front of Douglass, for ruining the boy for slavery by educating him. Listening carefully to Auld's unwitting "anti-slavery lecture," Douglass learns for the first time that it is "knowledge" that will free him and vows to seek such knowledge at any cost (Douglass 1855, 217, 218). Although he is sorry to have lost the help of Mrs. Auld, he is grateful for what Mr. Auld has, quite unknowingly, taught him about the value of an education. It is a lesson that immediately explains to Douglass a mystery he has been pondering all his life: how it is that the whites have been able to enslave the blacks.

I will attend shortly to some of the stratagems by which the young boy teaches himself to read and write. I want to focus first on Levin's argument that "writing is a gestural process" (Levin 1985, 184). Although writing was once considered to be what Levin calls "a sacred gesture," a ritual performance through which divinity made itself known to humans and by which (in sacred texts) it inscribed its will upon their bodies, we no longer think much about the act of writing, except perhaps instrumentally (184). The art of penmanship, moreover, seems no longer to be taught or valued. What have we come to? Or, to reverse the question, what have we lost? To answer that, we need only turn to the slave narratives. There we will discover the ritual meaning of reading and writing.[82] There it will be revealed to us the power of writing to gather us together in our shared relatedness-to-*being*. Douglass himself eloquently thematizes the unifying and equalizing capacities of literacy.[83] When he hears Hugh Auld warn his wife about the momentous consequences that would occur in society should a slave be educated, Douglass reports that these admonitions reawakened his own thinking process, describing the event as a "new and special revelation" capable as no other of explaining the world to him (218). Is there any wonder that he thus sets out, by any means possible, no matter how unpalatable to him, to complete the education that Sophia Auld had so compassionately begun? It is highly significant, on my view, that Douglass learns the first few letters of the alphabet from a woman whose own demeanor has taught the young slave boy his true value as a human being. Although Douglass, writing in the mid-nineteenth century, cannot thematize his insight—cannot, perhaps, even articulate what his insight is—it is clear to me that Douglass's account of this extraordinary exchange between a young slave and his not-yet-corrupted slave mistress is one that relies upon the body's recollection of *being*. Theirs is, in sum, a bodily exchange, whereby he, in the conventional way expected of his time, gives his body to her as labor, but she, in violation of convention if not, strictly speaking, of law,[84] reciprocates by giving the gifts of her body to him. Her first gift is compassion, when, in love and respect, she reaches out to her new charge and attends to his emotional and physical needs.[85] Her second gift is instruction, when, motivated by the same love and respect, she teaches his hands how to form letters.[86]

It is thus with a discussion of Douglass's writing that I wish to gather together the various strands of my interpretation of his first two narratives. It is a discussion that the texts seem to invite, as more than once in both the *Narrative* and *My Bondage and My Freedom*, Douglass self-consciously calls attention to the fact of his writing—and does so in ways that call attention to the additional fact of human embodiment.[87] In some passages he focuses on himself as the person doing the writing, such as when he says that but for being sent to Baltimore he would still be in chains rather than "seated" at his own table, engaged in "writing this Narrative" (Douglass 1845, 35); in others he admits to sparing his readers from too numerous or overly graphic accounts of the violence inflicted on the bodies of slaves, such as when he says bluntly that he will protect the "kind reader" from any more "heart-sickening details" (Douglass 1855, 205). In still others he admits that language is hardly adequate to describe what he experienced, such as when, in Chapter 8, he wants to describe the overseer, Austin Gore (Douglass 1855, 199). Having described in Chapter 15 Covey's unremitting brutality and depravity, Douglass opens chapter 16 by confessing that he simply does not have the "heart to repeat each separate transaction" between the two of them; those readers wishing to know what life was like throughout his yearlong stay with Covey will simply have to imagine it themselves (Douglass 1855, 270).[88] As he sums up his experiences with Covey, which had left him "a *living embodiment* of mental and physical wretchedness," Douglass admits bitterly that he will "never be able to narrate" the mental anguish caused him by this man's ill-treatment (Douglass 1855, 269; emphasis added). But in what is perhaps the most famous example of his self-conscious narration, he conflates the suffering of his body with the act of writing itself. "My feet have been so cracked with the frost," he writes, "that the pen with which I am writing might be laid in the gashes" (Douglass 1845, 33; 1855, 208). In this vivid image, which unites his suffering body with his writing body, Douglass shrewdly reminds his readers of the advancements he has made from untutored slave to literate narrator, but, more important to my purposes, he also uncannily directs our attention to the bodily basis of writing and, by extrapolation, the bodily basis of thinking itself.[89]

Let us now consider the relationship between Douglass and other persons as they occur within and through the body of his text. I have argued that the slave narratives stand in for the absent bodies of the slaves, a point I will return to momentarily. But first, I want to argue that Douglass realizes (if only tacitly) that the bodies of Sophia Auld and the little white boys from whom he gains additional instruction (paying them with the biscuits he carries in his pockets) have joined with his own in composing these narratives. Their bodies teach his body what it needs to know if he is to reach out successfully to other bodies. Levin describes writing as "an act of submission" wherein the writer conforms to "the visibility of a grammatical virtue" (Levin 1985, 185). It is this virtue, of course, in which Douglass first seeks instruction. For his gestures to convey meaning, and for him to understand the gestures of others, his body must be schooled in the mysteries of literacy. Paradoxically, to gain the freedom he desires, Douglass must surrender his body to the bodies of others and to the system of language through which he will assert his full humanity.[90] Having achieved literacy, he then must write his narratives in such a way as to maximize the understanding of his readers. In other words, he needs to ensure that his readers are willing to submit their bodies to the authority of his text (see Levin 1985, 215).[91] In "The Experience of Others," Merleau-Ponty (1982–83) finds that the relationship between a writer and a reader is analogous to the relationship between actor and audience—and both relationships thematize what happens in ordinary living. When two bodies (that is, two persons) encounter one another, on Merleau-Ponty's view, it is as though "the other person's intuitions and motor realizations existed in a sort of relation of internal encroachment, as if my body and the body of the other person together formed a system" (Merleau-Ponty 1982–83, 52). So it is in the theater. Merleau-Ponty writes: "What I learn to view as the body of another person is the possibility of movements for me. The actor's art is therefore only an extension of the art which we all possess. My bodily schema directs itself to the perceived world and to the imaginary as well" (1982–83, 53). During the drama, "only behaviour is seen, and all thoughts are behavior" (53). Because of the magic that occurs in the theater when the actor's gestures "make objects emerge from the world's surface," however, the feelings "between the actor and his audience" are "ambiguous" ones, "particularly admiration and hatred" (53). So it is with writers and their readers: "The reader will value the writer to the extent that the writer expresses the reader. Yet he will detest the writer, for the writer always takes the initiative" (53–54). Thus Douglass, the man who was a slave, must project himself in his text as a man who is no longer a slave and as one who never should have been enslaved in the first place (see Niemtzow 1982). He must assume the "imaginary role" of narrator—of literate, reasonable, and embodied human being (Merleau-Ponty 1982–83, 54). "If it is true that all consciousness of the world is at the same time imagination of the world," Merleau-Ponty argues, "it is impossible not to encounter something of the imaginary within consciousness. One would therefore have to say that all life is the invention of a role which exists only through the expression that I give to it" (54). In considering how this expressiveness functions, however, we must never forget that other persons must be taken "into account" (55). For as he has established elsewhere and repeats again here, "[t]here is already a kind of presence of other people in me" (56). What takes this experience outside the realm of art is the fact that "life unfolds for real whereas relations between writer and audience are characterized by the 'as if'" (56).

I want to utilize this insight and modify it. I would agree with Merleau-Ponty that in the theater and in most reading situations the relationship between writer and audience is indeed hypothetical, permitting a sympathetic identification during one performance (or reading) and a stubborn resistance during another with no permanent consequences necessarily attending either outcome. In the case of the slave narratives, however, I believe that more than a hypothetical relationship is at stake. For the slave narrators who fail in their chosen task, there may be no going back for another performance, another reading, on the part of the audience. The first reading may very well be not just the only one but the *real* one, the one with very real consequences for all involved. It was therefore of the utmost importance that these narrators get it right.[92] They had to know their readers and know how to persuade them to surrender their own bodies to the authority of the text. On my terms, if they wished to be understood, they had to convince readers to submit to the ex-slave's (textual) body and its superior knowledge, a dicey prospect at best. This helps explain, of course, why the abolitionists and the white editors needed to establish the authenticity of the accounts—and to do so, whether they were aware of the fact or not, by invoking the *body* of the narrator.[93] This also helps to explain, I believe, why Douglass is unwilling to burden his readers with too many details about Gore's and Covey's depraved indifference to the suffering of slaves. Having suffered in his own body seemingly endless physical abuse, and having suffered from simply witnessing the abuse with which the other slaves were subjected, he is not about to inflict on his readers (that is, their bodies) a detailed account of the suffering he has known. He knows if he is to obtain the readers' compassion, he must himself show compassion to them as it was shown to him in the bodies of Miss Lucretia and Miss Sophia. Even as he asserts his own suffering in order to inspire the compassion of his readers and excite them to action, he must understate this suffering, else he risks losing them. Either he will not be believed or his account will literally turn them away, unwilling to suffer any more.[94]

Let me conclude this section by returning to the question of motility. It will be recalled that I emphasized the importance of Douglass's wandering about the Lloyd plantation as a youth, arguing that such wandering allowed the young slave boy to hear—and heed—his body's recollection of *being*. Very like his contemporary, Henry David Thoreau, Douglass seems to have found new depths in himself by opening himself to nature during his wanderings. In "A Winter Walk" (1843), Thoreau remarks, for example, "With so little effort does nature reassert her rule and blot out the traces of men" (Thoreau 1982, 73). Douglass, similarly, seems as a very young child to have forgotten his enslaved status as he ran "wild" (Douglass 1855, 144). Later he would use his wandering to think, to consider the meaning of his life as a slave.[95] It is as though, in these wanderings, he is literally tracing out on the soil of the Lloyd plantation what his relationship to the world is going to be. The tracks of these walks are reproduced (that is, represented) in the narratives he later composed; they remain in the body of the text in the type the narratives are set in. Douglass did not find a slave at the end of his journeys; he found a free man—as shall we if we take the journey with him.[96] Not only will we find Frederick Douglass a man, but we will find ourselves and renew our own relatedness-to-*being*.

Walter Benjamin has compared the experience of flying over a road in an airplane with the more immediate experience of walking down it. "Only he who walks the road on foot," Benjamin argues, "learns of the power it commands, and of how, from the very scenery that for the flier is only the unfurled plain, it calls forth distances, belvederes, clearings, prospects at each of its turns" (Benjamin 1986, 66). Benjamin then compares the differential between these two kinds of experience to that between reading and transcribing a text. "Only the copied text thus commands the soul of him who is occupied with it," he argues, "whereas the mere reader never discovers the new aspects of his inner self that are opened by the text, that road cut through the interior jungle forever closing behind it: because the reader follows the movement of his mind in the free flight of daydreaming, whereas the copier submits it to command" (66). Having myself experienced the power of copying out a text, even if only in the fragmentary pieces that constitute my note-taking, I can attest to the accuracy of Benjamin's distinction. But let us continue our own journey a bit further here and imagine what happens if we consider ourselves as readers to be as fully embodied as we are as writers or copiers. Is it such a great leap, after all, to imagine, approaching the problem from one direction, that in reading and following the argument of a text, we are, indeed, quite literally, finding our way through it—walking ourselves through it? Or, to approach it from another direction, can we not say, as both Gadamer (1989) and Levin invite us to, that in understanding a text we have, again quite literally, internalized it, incorporated it, made it a part of us, a part of our body? If authors have bodies (*pace* Barthes), and texts have bodies, why not readers also? Why are we the only disembodied member of the triumvirate? As I suggested in the previous chapter, the traces of the slave's body inform the body of the slave narrative. In holding such a book in our hands, we are acknowledging our common embodied humanity. In reading these narratives—narratives that speak of the body, to the body, and with the body—we can, if only we permit ourselves, rethink thinking. It is clear to me that Douglass is addressing not just an abstract, "fictionalized" audience, but the very bodies of his readers. If he did not have to deny or relinquish his body to assert his humanity, why must we?[97] As ambitious as his slave narratives have been said to be, I find that previous readers have not yet begun to imagine just how ambitious they really were. Frederick Douglass was not only entering liberal humanism but re*forming* it.[98] Is it any wonder, then, that Douglass thematizes the act of writing? Does he not recognize, as I have argued previously, that his narratives stand in for his own absent body? Does he not further recognize that it is only by and in our embodiment that we are truly human?

Although Douglass has been regarded by generations of readers as the most important and influential of all the slave narrators, his insights about the body's recollection of *being* are not unique to him, as becomes evident when we examine Harriet Wilson's 1859 autobiographical novel, *Our Nig*, and Harriet Jacobs's 1861 pseudonymous narrative, *Incidents in the Life of a Slave Girl*—two texts that exemplify the differences between the proto-Bohemian and proto-Genteel Schools of writers.

NOTES

1. Robyn Warhol, for example, cites Joseph Roach's studies on acting, in which he argues that "this mind/body split was not current in the nineteenth-century psychology and physiology. The dominant idea of the dynamics of mind and body during the Victorian period in Europe and America was a version of monism, elaborated by George Henry Lewes," which considered "the mind and body not as a duality, but a continuum" (Warhol 1992, 112). Of these ideas Roach himself says that "Lewes believed that mind and body constitute one entity, not two. Every experience presents a double aspect—objective and subjective. The body is merely the objective aspect of a subjective process called mind" (Roach 1985, 182). See Lewes (1875, 146). For a late-twentieth-century attempt to see the body-mind whole, see Olafson (1995).

2. In a Freudian interpretation of American slavery, Earl Thorpe has written that "[c]ompelled to be repressed around white people and 'turned off' by the version of reality that oppression and exploitation molded for them, black slaves became unusually biased against the world of the reality principle. This bias also was characteristic of much of the original 'posture' of blacks in Africa" (Thorpe 1978, 54–55).

3. Melville J. Herskovits lends some insight into how cultural differences affect interpretations such as these: "What is most European in the dancing of Negroes in the United States . . . is when a man and a woman dance with their arms about each other. In Africa . . . this is regarded as nothing short of immoral. This reaction . . . is exactly similar to that of Europeans who witness for the first time the manipulation of the muscles of hips and buttocks that are marks of good African dancing" (Herskovits 1990, 271).

4. Thorpe argues, in fact, that it is conceivable that African Americans' "most important gifts are laughter, song, rhythm, dance, happiness, joy and the health and dedication to life, justice, and freedom, which are related to these. Eros and life and love are the

voice of the untrammeled id and the body" (Thorpe 1978, 59).

5. For critical response to and contextualizing of the 1972 edition of Blassingame's book, see Gilmore (1978).

6. Blassingame gives several accounts of dancing among the slaves, some reported by former slaves themselves. One of his major theses is that many features of "West African culture are so distinctive that it is relatively easy to discover their presence or absence among Southern slaves." For example, "[d]ances, folk tales, music, magic, and language patterns" all lend themselves to such investigations (Blassingame 1979, 22). Others have contested the extent of these connections, especially as they seem to rely on the problematic notion of *an* African (or *a* West African) cultural tradition. Responding to his critics in a later essay (one that predates the revised edition of his book from which I cite), Blassingame admits that "the specific areas of [African] impact are difficult to locate with any degree of certainty." Even so, he continues, he did not earlier fully appreciate the Ashanti proverb, "Ancient things remain in the ears." If he had, he tells us, he would have argued in 1972 for even more African influences in "the slaves' proverbs, folktales [sic], sexual attitudes, material culture, and religious practices" (Blassingame 1978, 150). While I find the African influences such as those Blassingame documents quite compatible with my claims, I remind readers that my analysis is not dependent on them. Neither do I intend here to imply myself that the many hundreds of African cultures form a monocultural system. Appiah reminds us of these differences in his pointed critique of Wole Soyinka's *Myth, Literature and the African World* (1990), a text that takes as its task introducing Western readers to so-called African myth and literature. Rather than taking the route Soyinka has taken in this series of lectures—that Yoruba philosophy is somehow a typical manifestation of African philosophies—Appiah asserts that Africa "is a plenum richly populated with the metaphysical thought worlds of . . . 'myriad races and cultures'" (Appiah 1992, 81). In her historical study of slave narratives, Frances Foster detects a pattern suggesting that those "narrators who began their lives in Africa maintained a strong sense of who they were . . . throughout their enslavement" (Foster 1994, 9–10).

7. I take this notion of disenabling prejudices from Gadamer (1989); for more on this concept see Chapter 3 (below).

8. In making such a gross and unfounded generalization, Hegel was not alone. According to Nancy Stepan, it was not at all uncommon in scientific literature to see that "an abstracted 'Negro' or 'Hottentot', with one kind of physical form, language or customs, would be made to stand as an image of all 'Africans', and to stand comparison with an abstracted and idealised European, a 'Newton', for example" (Stepan 1982, xviii). For Douglass's response to such ethnological comparisons, see his scathing 1854 address, "The Claims of the Negro Ethnologically Considered," in Blassingame (1982, 497–525).

9. I cite from the standard 1814 edition reprinted in Gates (1987b).

10. Even so, Equiano (1814, 32) takes pride in distinguishing his people from those who disfigure their bodies by "ornament[ing] themselves with scars, and likewise fil[ing] their teeth very sharp." For further discussion of this practice, see Allison (1995) and Acholonu (1989). More generally, see also Grosz (1994, 138–59).

11. Valerie Smith also stresses the importance of his African heritage to the mature, Westernized Equiano, but does so without relying on the notion of embodiment that I introduce here. See Smith (1987, 16–18).

12. Blassingame argues that while the cultural transmission was at its height in the

eighteenth century, by the nineteenth there still remained "overwhelming evidence of the survival of African song and dance forms" in America (Blassingame 1979, 36). See also Joseph Holloway (1990), Herskovits (1990), and Genovese (1972). For a more literary approach to this question, see Karla Holloway (1992) and Wilentz (1992).

13. Compare my argument about Equiano to Levin's argument that circumcision is not simply a ritual violation of the body but one that "initiates the ancestral body into a spiritual process which Jews call 'remembrance'" (Levin 1985, 203). For an anthropological study of Equiano's likely ancestry among the Isseke Igbo people, see Acholonu (1989). For an illustrated study of the various ways cultures leave their marks on the bodies of their people, see Polhemus (1978).

14. Bourdieu finds it significant that when societies, especially repressive ones, want to create a new person "through a process of 'deculturation' and 'reculturation,'" they effect change by attending to "the seemingly most insignificant details of *dress, bearing,* physical and verbal *manners*." They do so because they consider the body to be "a memory"—that is, "they entrust to it in abbreviated and practical, i.e. mnemonic, form the fundamental principles of the arbitrary content of the culture. The principles em-bodied in this way are placed beyond the grasp of consciousness, and hence cannot be touched by voluntary, deliberate transformation, cannot even be made explicit" (Bourdieu 1972, 94; see also 218, Note 44). On this subject, see also Patterson (1982). In contrast to my reading, Andrews reads this narrative as "an analysis of the *process* of acculturation, the process by which the African was divested . . . of his native cultural values and identity and assumed his new role in the white world order" (Andrews 1982, 20).

15. I wonder how surprised Equiano might have been to hear Levin's assertion that "[t]hinking begins, fundamentally, in the feet. Its roots are there" (Levin 1985, 55). Not nearly as surprised, I would wager, as those at whose feet he lay his *Life*.

16. "To excite" comes from Latin *excitare*, to call forth, which is the frequentative of "*ex-*, out + pp. of *ciere*, to call, summon" (*Webster's New World Dictionary*, Third College Edition, 1988, 474). This is a felicitous choice of words since it also invokes the verb "to cite" which is from the Latin "*citare*, to arouse, summon," which is based on *ciere*, "to put into motion" (256). "Compassion" is from the Latin "*com-*, together + *pati*, to suffer" (284).

17. In reading this account, one cannot help but be struck by how brief it is. Having experienced in those few weeks in the hold a lifetime of suffering, he reduces it in his *Life* to a mere two paragraphs (or three, if one counts the lead-in paragraph of the section) .

18. He continues this theme later by drawing connections between the customs of his people and those of the Jews. How effective a gesture of relatedness this might have been is questionable, however, given the anti-Semitism of the English (on this subject, as it pertains to the body of the Jew in the nineteenth century, see Gilman 1985–86, 1990, 1991). In any event, the burden of Equiano's manuscript is to demonstrate the blessings of his conversion to Christianity.

19. Reading Equiano's *Life* as a modified version of a conversion narrative, Valerie Smith argues that "[i]nscribed throughout his narrative . . . is a simultaneous adoption of and withdrawal from the assumptions that inform the conventions of his genre" (Smith 1987, 13). "No doubt he reveres the European's Christianity," she continues, "but he presents it as his way of recovering a lost ideal and shows how it suits a system of values and priorities conditioned by African cultural practice" (19). This argument is in line with Andrews's claim that, in the absence of a controlling, agenda-driven editor, Equiano

was better able than his contemporaries to integrate his Western and his African experiences into a complex vision of his life. He thus includes in his narrative "the memory (improved by research) of an African pastoral way of life that he pictured as the moral superior of the West in virtually every respect except in religion" (Andrews 1986, 57). On the question of what Equiano remembered and what he gleaned from other sources, see Allison (1995) and Acholonu (1989).

20. In making this distinction, I am following the lead of Andrews, who notes that careful attention to Equiano's narrative will show that throughout his lifetime his sojourn in North America was limited to approximately two years (Andrews 1986, 56). For a contrasting point of view, see Allison (1995).

21. For a discussion of how, in the nineteenth century, Phillis Wheatley was replaced by Douglass as the exemplary figure of their race, see Gates (1990). For a concise history of the critical treatments Douglass's *Narrative* and his subsequent autobiographies have received over the years, see Andrews (1991). For a more critical investigation of "Douglass's function in literary history and interpretation" from a feminist perspective, see McDowell (1991, 193).

22. Most recently, see, for example, Stephanie Smith (1994) and Wald (1995).

23. For a discussion of the gaps in slave narratives, see Hedin (1982b) and Wald (1995).

24. Addressing what they call "The Antilanguage of Slavery," Kibbey and Stepto read the first paragraph of Douglass's 1845 *Narrative* as suggesting, rather mysteriously, "the slave's total lack of language as either an epistemological or an expressive instrument" (Kibbey and Stepto 1991, 171). Ziolkowski reads it as privileging, if only in the negative, "the main members of the Enlightenment family of concepts"—those of "sight and empiricism," as well as "the system of verification"—and thus as a "catalog of the dominant discourse's fundamental concepts" (Ziolkowski 1991, 152). But if the dominant discourse ensnares Douglass, on Ziolkowski's view (which is similar to mine), Douglass, by virtue of his own reasonable discourse, is from the start positioned "to cast the net himself"; in other words, the "discourse, though treacherous, is . . . capable of being redirected from within" (152). For a discussion of how Douglass manipulates sentimental discourse to his own ends, see Stephanie Smith (1994, 111–33).

25. In *My Bondage and My Freedom*, she is called Esther (Douglass 1855, 175–77). On this shift, see Stephanie Smith (1994, 119–24) and Wald (1995, 82–83).

26. My citations are from the Library of America edition of Douglass's autobiographies, in which his *Narrative* is reprinted pages 1–102, and *My Bondage and My Freedom* 103–452.

27. For readings of this scene that unpack the significance of its gender differences, see Van Leer (1990), Franchot (1990), McDowell (1991), and Stephanie Smith (1994). McDowell argues, for example, that there is a significant difference between male and female victims in whipping scenes. "While the women are tied up—the classic stance of women in pornography—and unable to resist, the men are 'free,' if you like, to struggle" (McDowell 1991, 204). Tracing the changes in this account from Douglass's first autobiography to his third, Smith reads them as progressively revealing "the potentially signifying defiance of wounded (feminized) flesh" (Smith 1994, 118).

28. For more discussion of this, see below in this chapter. For discussion of the African roots of community, care, and compassion in the slave culture, see Paris (1995).

29. Yet, on my view, such reporting is sufficient to work the change Douglass desires in the bodies of his readers. For more on this see below in this chapter.

30. He as much as says this when he describes the anxiety he suffered after his master has died, claiming that, he, in comparison with the other slaves, "had known what it was to be kindly treated" (1845, 46).

31. For an account of similar deprivations on a Virginia plantation, see James L. Smith's narrative (1881, 151–53).

32. Olafson would probably challenge much of Leder's argument as it tends to portray the lived experience of being human in a dualistic framework, implying as it does that an *I* (the immaterial mind) uses an *it* (the material body) as an instrument for perceiving the world. Of this way of conceptualizing what it means to be human, Olafson remarks on our ability to put instruments down after we have used them—something we cannot do with our own bodies. He then echoes Leder in arguing that if bodies were indeed instruments, we ought to be able to see them "from all sides"—again, something we cannot do. Finally he suggests that "the reason each of us can observe his own body only to a limited degree is that my body is not as separate from me, as an observer, as one would expect it to be when it is described as an instrument and an object" (Olafson 1995, 202). I do not, however, wish to make Olafson's argument for him; furthermore, as a corrective to myself, I do think we can become so obsessed with detecting the residual dualism in many of these studies that we overlook where they can be useful to us.

33. Similarly Judith Butler argues that

if women are only their bodies, if their consciousness and freedom are only so many disguised permutations of bodily need and necessity, then women have, in effect, exclusively monopolized the bodily sphere of life. By defining women as 'Other', men are able through the shortcut of definition to dispose of their bodies, to make themselves other than their bodies . . . and to make their bodies other than themselves. From this belief that the body is Other, it is not a far leap to the conclusion that others *are* their bodies, while the masculine 'I' is a noncorporeal soul." (Butler 1987, 133)

For more on the conflicted relationship between women and their bodies in the nineteenth century, see Chapter 3 (below).

34. Compare these arguments with Leder's claim that pain "is ultimately a manner of being-in-the-world. As such, pain reorganizes our lived space and time, our relations with others and with ourselves" (Leder 1990, 73). Thus, "the painful body emerges" in its disruptiveness "as an *alien presence*" that requires us to act to free ourselves of pain (73; see also 76–78).

35. In the 1855 text, Douglass claims that hearing the songs would be more effective in conveying the horrors of slavery than reading "whole volumes of its mere physical cruelties. They speak to the heart and to the soul of the thoughtful" (184). He then includes a lengthy extract from the *Narrative* that describes the effect of the songs on himself.

36. Gates reads this passage to mean that understanding "came only with a certain aesthetic distance and an acceptance of the critical imperative" (Gates 1979, 230). When Douglass describes himself as being no longer "within the circle," he is reminding his readers, on Gates's view, that "[n]ot only is meaning culture-bound and the referents of all signs an assigned relation . . . but *how* we read determines *what* we read, in the truest sense of the hermeneutic circle" (230; see also Gates 1989). Ziolkowski counters that although Douglass's "interpretation of the songs is shaped by the cognitive and physical distance literacy permits, this shape is neither simple nor simply the somehow liberating one Gates seems to imply" (Ziolkowski 1991, 156). Instead, Ziolkowski reads this pas-

sage in tandem with the passage that describes Hester's beating to argue that Douglass's "pained self-consciousness takes its rise in part from the gulf created between Douglass and his community by his acquisition of literacy and its class-specific mobility" (156).

37. For a different take on these passages, see Stuckey's argument that Douglass's meditation on slave music is perhaps his "most lasting theoretical contribution" in that it "contains language that comes as close to suggesting an African *approach* to music as one might find" (Stuckey 1990, 41).

38. Some of the tension that others have remarked in Douglass's *Narrative* is evident here, as he directs his readers outside his text to the songs themselves. Yet what they will learn from the songs are "the soul-killing effects of slavery," and Douglass would not have us think that his soul has been killed by slavery. Douglass's quotation is from Book 2 ("The Time-Piece") of William Cowper's satirical poem, *The Task*, which opens with the poet expressing a desire for sanctuary in the wilderness, where he will be protected from the evils of the world, including racial division and hatred. The line Douglass found useful for his purposes is followed by one useful for mine: "There is no flesh in man's obdurate heart,/ It does not feel for man. The nat'ral bond/ Of brotherhood is fever'd as the flax/ That falls asunder at the touch of fire" (Cowper 1785, 35).

39. But even Douglass admits defeat in the face of having to put into words the severity of the beating his aunt received. In *My Bondage and My Freedom*, for example, he says that everything about the event "was revolting and shocking . . . to the last degree; and when the motives of this brutal castigation are considered, language has no power to convey a just sense of its awful criminality" (Douglass 1855, 177). Cynthia Davis offers a less charitable interpretation of his "impotence" in this scene, as she follows McDowell (1991) in claiming that "[t]hrough the very act of looking, Douglass is able to derive not only pleasure but power from his identification with the (over)seer" (Davis 1993, 399). For a similar argument, see Foster (1994, xxx). Jenny Franchot has also argued that "Douglass's description of Esther's whipping serves finally to make visible his heroic attainment of control, irony, and distance in the narrative voice. As his interpolated references to the struggles of writing subordinate her punishment to his authoring, so Esther's punishment provides him a temporary membership in the suffering body whose final function is to afford him a permanent escape from it" (Franchot 1990, 148; see also 155–56). For critical commentary on Franchot's reading, see Stephanie Smith (1994, 111–33). See also Ziolkowski (1991) and Barrett (1995).

40. For a different approach to the question of "voice" in slave narratives, see Stepto (1979 and 1991), O'Meally (1979), and Cobb (1982).

41. This adapts Leder's argument. On his view the "pragmatic" desire to rid ourselves of pain is accompanied by what he calls a *"hermeneutical . . . moment"*—that is, the desire to understand the pain and its causes, a desire that sends us to other texts (1990, 78).

42. For more on this, see, for example, Warhol (1992) and my discussion in Chapter 3 (below).

43. Douglass also complains about being introduced as a "'chattel'—a 'thing'" (Douglass 1855, 366).

44. For more on this, see my discussion of the metaphysics of presence in Chapter 3 (below).

45. Wald, attending to the slightly modified citational use Douglass makes of this passage in his second autobiography, argues of his *Narrative* that it "is itself a slave song, a haunting melody that says more through form than its author can express di-

rectly" (Wald 1995, 99).

46. In his second autobiography Douglass himself italicizes these words (1855, 286).

47. Ziolkowski reads the fight as a "victorious oedipal struggle" when Douglass "'touches the Father' of slavery's patriarchal violence and overcomes it" (Ziolkowski 1991, 159). Gibson cautions us to remember that "Douglass's victory is won not because he beats Covey but because he thwarts Covey's intention to beat him" (1985, 562).

48. As Gibson remarks of this passage, "[j]ust as Douglass carried to the grave the scars of slavery, he also carried kinesthetically the significance of his victory over Covey" (1990, 90). Russell Reising reads it as an example of Douglass "insisting that only a consolidation of human powers—intellectual, spiritual, and physical—can represent the fullest in human experience" (Reising 1986, 265). Less sweepingly than Douglass, but just as significantly, Elizabeth Keckley reports that after she physically resisted the beatings she received from her master and his friend, her master eventually begs her forgiveness "and afterwards was an altered man. He was never known to strike one of his servants from that day forward" (Keckley 1868, 37). Contrary to my reading of Douglass, Valerie Smith has argued that, generally speaking, in "mythologizing rugged individuality, physical strength, and geographic mobility, the [male-authored] narratives enshrine cultural definitions of masculinity. The plot of the standard narrative may thus be seen as not only the journey from slavery to freedom but also the journey from slavehood to manhood" (Smith 1987, 34). See also Stephanie Smith (1994, 114–17).

49. That is, Douglass had to demonstrate his qualifications as a specific body-self to be included in the unified, unspecified body politic. In this effort, his maleness was an advantage but his race a distinct disadvantage. As Moira Gatens reminds us, "[f]rom its classical articulation in Greek philosophy, only a body deemed capable of reason and sacrifice can be admitted into the political body as an active member" (Gatens 1991, 81). She continues: "At different times, different kinds of beings have been excluded from the pact, often simply by virtue of their corporeal specificity. Slaves, foreigners, women, the conquered, children, the working classes, have all been excluded from political participation, at one time or another, by their bodily specificity" (82). Sánchez-Eppler reminds us that "[f]eminists and abolitionists were acutely aware of the dependence of personhood on the condition of the human body, since the political and legal subordination of both women and slaves was predicated on biology" (Sánchez-Eppler 1993, 17). On this, see also Spelman (1988) and Sidonie Smith (1993). For a discussion of the limits Douglass faced in discussing his own sexuality, see Moses (1990).

50. William Lloyd Garrison's Preface to the *Narrative* makes this advantage quite clear, when Garrison describes his own impassioned response to hearing the first speech by "one in physical proportion and stature commanding and exact—in intellect richly endowed—in natural eloquence a prodigy—in soul manifestly 'created but a little lower than the angels'—yet a slave, ay, a fugitive slave" (Douglass 1845, 4). As Baker observes of this passage, such "a talented, heroic, and richly endowed figure . . . was of inestimable 'public usefulness' to the abolitionist crusade" (Baker 1980, 42). Philip S. Foner quotes the editor of the Concord *Herald of Freedom* as reporting that Douglass "was cut out for a hero. . . . He has the 'heart to conceive, the head to contrive, and the hand to execute.' A commanding person over six feet, we should say, in height, and of most manly proportions. His head would strike a phrenologist amid a sea of them in Exeter Hall, and his voice would ring like a trumpet in the field" (Foner 1950a, 48).

51. In a famous exchange, Douglass does just this as he responds to the ethnological claims of a "Mr. Grant" that black persons were not fully human: "look at me—look the

negro in the face, examine his woolly head, his entire physical conformation; I invite you
to the examination, and ask this audience to judge between me and that gentleman. . . .
Am I a man?" (Blassingame 1982, 238). For an account of the simultaneous commodifi-
cation, appropriation, and fear of black male bodies that characterized the attitude toward
minstrelsy among antebellum Northerners, see Lott (1993, 149), in which he claims that
"the repellent elements repressed from white consciousness and projected onto black
people were far from securely alienated; they are always already 'inside,' part of 'us.'
Hence the threat of this projected material, and the occasional pleasure of its threat." See
also Stallybrass and White (1986, 201).

52. I am, perhaps, assuming too much here when I make the claim for ease of identification between Douglass and his white male audience. For what is perhaps a more realistic view, see Yarborough (1990, 174).

53. Fox-Genovese argues, for example, that Douglass "firmly identified himself with
the triumph of manliness and individuality that slavery suppressed." In making this
move, he openly invited "his northern readers to recognize that the sufferings and ineq-
uities to which he had been subjected by the very condition of enslavement directly con-
travened their deepest principles of individualism. He assumed that the most effective
way to reach his readers was to remind them that he was a man like themselves" (Fox-
Genovese 1988, 375.). On this, see also McDowell (1991). Niemtzow has argued, similarly, that Douglass, writing in an era in which most African Americans were illiterate,
"has offered a move of assent toward structuring a self for white readers. Indeed, by
agreeing to face the page at all, by agreeing to the primacy of the definition of a self as
someone who reads and writes, Douglass has adopted a white definition of selfhood, and
tries to attain it" (Niemtzow 1982, 101). While I agree with Fox-Genovese that Douglass
wishes to be seen as a man, I am also convinced that in identifying himself as a man he
was simultaneously redefining his century's notion of (male) subjectivity—not by making it more feminine but by making it less dependent on the mind/body split of Western
metaphysics. I am arguing, against positions like that taken by Niemtzow, that Douglass
is contesting the prevailing metaphysical definition of subjectivity, and that he does so
on the basis of his body-self's recollection of *being*, an anti-liberal humanist critique that
Niemtzow, her own vision of self bounded by Western metaphysics, apparently cannot
see. For a different understanding of Douglass's motives, see Byerman (1982).

54. On this, see Gilman (1985–86; 1990); Goldberg (1990; 1993); Gould (1981);
Sánchez-Eppler (1993); and Stepan (1982). Stepan reminds us, for example, that "phrenology depended on the belief that, just as the face was an outward sign of the inner soul,
a belief on which the earlier science of physiognomy had rested, so the bony head was an
outward reflection of the structure of the different organs of the brain. Here phrenology
came very close to Cuvier's belief that one could use the shape of the head as a physical
sign of underlying nervous organisation" (Stepan 1982, 20–21). For a discussion of how
physiognomy came to be crucial to the descriptions of heroines in mid-nineteenth-
century British novels, see Fahnestock (1981). See also Michie (1987, especially 79–
123).

55. Citing the evidence in Douglass's speeches and in firsthand accounts of his ef-
fectiveness, Franchot argues that "Douglass typically deflected audience attention from
the 'feminine' exposure of his body (taking off his shirt to reveal his scars) to the
'masculine' display of his face." In so doing, he presented "his features on the podium as
evidence against the racist pseudoscience of the new ethnology" (Franchot 1990, 145).

56. See Scarry (1985, 181–277).

57. See Byerman (1982).

58. Others might take a more skeptical view of these passages, as Foster argues that the slave narrators faced the knotty narrative problem of how to critique the master class even as they relied on this class for their readership. "It became almost axiomatic," therefore, "that for every two or three bad experiences related, one good experience must be recounted" (Foster 1994, 14).

59. Dickson Preston has argued similarly in his biography that Douglass's early experiences as a favored child left him open to the sufferings of others as well as inspired him with the rage to end them (Preston 1980, 66). See also Franchot (1990, 147).

60. In *Being and Time* (1927a), Heidegger argues that "[b]ecause Being-in-the-world is essentially care, Being-alongside the ready-to-hand could be taken in our previous analyses as *concern*, and Being with the Dasein-with of Others as we encounter it within-the-world could be taken as *solicitude*. Being-alongside something is concern, because it is defined as a way of Being-in by its basic structure—care" (193). He continues: "That very potentiality-for-Being for the sake of which Dasein is, has Being-in-the-world as its kind of Being. Thus it implies ontologically a relation to entities within-the-world. Care is always concern and solicitude, even if only privately" (194).

61. In *History of Mary Prince*, for example, the narrator recalls how mean her master was to his wife, "a kind-hearted good woman, [who] treated all her slaves well" and how much, as a consequence, the slaves not only loved but "pitied" her (Prince 1831, 1). See more on this in the next chapter. Compassion is also a key element in Mrs. A. E. Johnson's post-Reconstruction polemical narrative, *Clarence and Corinne; or, God's Way* (1890).

62. Compare my argument with that of Andrews, who, borrowing from Ricoeur, argues that the slave narrators needed a style "of autobiographical discourse that subtly reoriented a reader's response to [their texts] away from a distanced perspective and toward one that authorized appropriation" (Andrews 1986, 65). Of Douglass himself, Andrews argues that he sought an authentic "discursive relationship of equals in the slave narrative," one independent of "preconceived roles, instituted agendas, and programmed responses" (1986, 137).

63. The illustration Douglass refers to is the Head of Rameses. For commentary on his choice, see Franchot (1990, 159). In a speech delivered in 1854, Douglass invokes various authoritative accounts to argue that even though, strictly speaking, the Egyptians were not Negroes, nonetheless it is correct to assert that the race enjoys "a strong affinity and a direct relationship" with that greatest of ancient civilizations (Blassingame 1982, 517). He also uses the unity of these two peoples to argue for the unity of all human beings.

64. Or he was writing too much under the watchful eye of the abolitionists who wanted him to stress how slavery destroyed the nuclear family.

65. Stuckey reads Douglass's narratives as providing evidence that his grandmother "represented, unbroken from Africa, certain traditions of work that were shared by significant numbers of slaves" (Stuckey 1990, 39). For a full accounting of his grandmother and the rest of the Bailey clan, see Preston (1980).

66. As Anderson puts it, contemporary society "could learn much from the moral performances of slave families. The slaves successfully fought off the apathy, the blunting of emotions, and the feeling that one could not care any more, all of which often characterize the psychological reactions of the oppressed" (Anderson 1978, 131).

67. In offering a Freudian reading of the experiences of infants in general and en-

slaved infants in particular, Genovese darkly asserts that our entry into the world is
marked by "terror." "The newborn child lives, has sensations, and experiences the world.
What else, then, can that first projection of a sensate but as yet unreasoning being into
the unknown be except traumatic? All the love and affection provided by the wisest and
most loving parents cannot . . . wholly draw the fear and terror from the child's being"
(Genovese 1978, 32–33).

68. Stephanie Smith argues convincingly that "Douglass's sentimental revisions [of
his *Narrative*] seek to rescript a politics of community so that the ties that bind the flesh
do not mean enslavement" (Smith 1994, 123). Andrews makes a similar claim by tracing
Douglass's growing desire for a supportive community of black people. At first Douglass
thought he had found a satisfactory community among the abolitionists. But it is not long
before he recognizes the need to leave them behind, since they would have him conform
to their vision of what kind of black spokesman the anti-slavery movement required. "To
create community for himself required," on Andrews's view, "that he recreate himself
into a communal entity," which he attempts to do in the second autobiography, "for by
1855 he was not trying just to prove who he had been in the past . . . but who he wished
to become in the future—a man with a community-affirming mission for the truly free
black men and women among whom he could feel . . . at home" (Andrews 1986, 239).
Of the earlier *Narrative* and Douglass's speeches on the lecture circuit, Gray claims that
through them Douglass "places himself in the tradition of American self-reliant individualism. He is, by his own strength, making himself a part of the culture that has failed
him and is demonstrating that he possesses to an extraordinary degree one of its most
admired characteristics" (Gray 1990, 40). For a full discussion of the competing narrative
drives that faced the slave narrators as they struggled to reconcile their own claims to an
individual identity with the abolitionist-driven need to represent oneself as a typical
slave, see Foster (1994, especially 5–6, 68–70).

69. For a summary of some of these arguments, see Awkward (1990; 1995).

70. Lunsford Lane asserts similarly (and disingenuously) that he has not "in this
publication attempted or desired to argue anything. It is only a simple narration of such
facts connected with my own case, as I thought would be most interesting and instructive
to readers generally" (Lane 1842, iii). Yet he confesses midway through his narrative that
while still in the South, like all blacks there, he never revealed how smart he was (31).
Olney argues that "in one sense the narrative lives of the ex-slaves were as much pos-
sessed and used by the abolitionists as their actual lives had been by slaveholders"
(Olney 1985, 154). It is my argument that the slave narrators escaped this possession by
listening to their bodies' recollection of *being*. The slaves and ex-slaves had no need to
hear from the abolitionists that they were equal to whites; their own embodiment had already revealed this truth to them.

71. Commenting on the plantation's isolation and self-sufficiency, Douglass had remarked that "[c]ivilization is shut out, but nature cannot be" (Douglass 1855, 160).

72. For the slaves, of course, motility also symbolized freedom—the opportunity to
escape enslavement by, quite literally, running away. Thus it was that the escape itself
provided the thematic focus of many slave narratives. See, for example, Pennington
(1849) and Brown (1847). For a discussion of this theme, see MacKethan (1982). James
L. Smith reports in his narrative how his motility was reduced by a childhood accident
that left him lame. Years later, when he and some fellow slaves set out for the North,
they are forced to leave him behind to fend for himself because he cannot keep up with
them. But of his crippling accident, he recalls in addition to the more gruesome details

the fact that he "would have died if it had not been for Miss Ayers, who was house-keeper in the 'great house.' She came into the kitchen every day to dress my knee, till I could get around" (Smith 1881, 148).

73. For a slightly different take on this subject, see Blassingame (1979, 280), in which he argues that "because the planters recognized that slaves voluntarily limited their work . . . many of them set the standard of labor so low that every slave could meet it." Even so, Blassingame also argues that plantation owners felt that if they could get slaves to behave morally, if their slaves "rested during the hottest part of the day, spent all of their time on the plantation, marched to the fields, ate, and went to bed at the sound of bugles or bells, and were kept under proper subjection, they would be healthy and in-dustrious" (239). Hedin reads these limitations on the slaves' motility as "one of the cruelest and most pervasive aspects of slavery; to expose it accurately was one of the nar-rator's purposes. The narratives are therefore filled with loose ends, with incidents whose outcomes remain unknown, especially with characters who drop out of the narrator's ken and whose fate we never learn" (Hedin 1982b, 29). For a more extensive discussion of the production and management of docile and useful bodies, see Foucault (1975).

74. On the "ritual of deference," see also Blassingame (1979, 256).

75. Even as he walks the seven miles from Master Thomas Auld's to Mr. Covey's place, Douglass reports that all he could do along the route was *think* (Douglass 1855, 258).

76. Elizabeth Keckley describes herself as having come "upon the earth free in God-like thought, but fettered in action" (Keckley 1868, 17). Although at four years old she has the full responsibility of caring for an infant, she is later able to see that this lesson in responsibility "was not a bitter one, for I was too young to indulge in philosophy, and the precepts that I then treasured and practised I believe developed those principles of char-acter which have enabled me to triumph over so many difficulties" (19). Blassingame re-ports that while not all slaves enjoyed "idyllic childhoods," many in fact did enjoy the unstructured pleasures of youth to such an extent that they were unable at first to see the fact of their own enslavement (Blassingame 1979, 185). See also Foster (1994, 93–96).

77. For a comprehensive study of how early modern Western cultures became civi-lized by modifying people's public behavior—by teaching them such things as table manners—see Elias (1939).

78. Signifying on Douglass's own words, McDowell argues that "black women's backs become the parchment on which Douglass narrates his linear progression from bondage to freedom" (McDowell 1991, 201).

79. Compare my claim with that voiced by a southern woman of abolitionist leanings in William Wells Brown's *Clotel*. After listening to the slaves sing, Georgiana Peck re-marks that whites can do any number of things to a slave, including placing "him under any process which, without destroying his value as a slave, will debase and crush him as a rational being; you may do this, and *the idea that he was born to be free will survive it all*. It is allied to this hope of immortality; it is the ethereal part of his nature, which op-pression cannot reach; it is a torch lit up in his soul by the hand of Deity" (Brown 1853, 120). For a discussion of how Henry Bibb's narrative includes "echoes of the official human rights philosophies of the United States," see Foster (1994, 117). As Bibb himself recalls, his new situation "gave me a longing desire to be free. It kindled a fire of liberty within my breast which has never yet been quenched. This seemed to be a part of my nature; it was first revealed to me by the inevitable laws of nature's God. I could see that the All-wise Creator, had made man a free, moral, intelligent and accountable being; ca-

pable of knowing good and evil" (Bibb 1850, 17).

80. The Reverend John Sella Martin (1832–76), a poet, editor, and orator, who also enjoyed a relatively idyllic childhood, when reflecting back on the exact moment he realized that he must be "a slave for life," is able to find his own saving grace in the event, explaining in his brief autobiography that while it was true that he "lost by the blow the ministrations of an affectionate mother," this grievous loss was nonetheless "partially compensated . . . in the production of sympathy for my suffering fellow-bondsmen, and hatred of the system that oppressed us" (Blassingame 1977, 708).

81. Compare this with what Josiah Henson reports of the man who first taught him about religion. John McKenney was a baker "and his character was that of an upright, benevolent Christian. He was noted especially for his detestation of slavery, and his resolute avoidance of the employment of slave-labour in his business. He would not even hire a slave, the price of whose toil must be paid to his master, but contented himself with the work of his own hands, and with such free labour as he could procure" (Henson 1881, 23). More negatively, however, Douglass describes Covey as "one of the few slaveholders who could and did work with his hands. He was a hard-working man" (Douglass 1845, 56). This suggests that a willingness to work with one's hands, in the absence of other redeeming characteristics, is not sufficient to remind a person of our mutual relatedness-to-*being*.

82. For a comprehensive history of the development of Western literacy, see Graff (1987). For a discussion of the symbolic and practical role of reading in our own era—an era in which the highly prized and hard-won literacy of our ancestors is experiencing a precipitous decline in value—see Birkerts (1994). For an account of exactly how difficult it was for slaves to learn to write, because of the absence of pen and paper, see Cornelius (1991, 72). Learning to read was hard enough, but learning to write involved, for the slaves (as well as for other poor people), the manufacture of tools with which to write and the production of smooth surfaces on which to write.

83. Cornelius reminds us that for the slaves, "literacy . . . was a communal *act*, a political demonstration of resistance to oppression and of self-determination for the black community. Through literacy the slave could obtain skills valuable in the white world, thereby defeating those whites who withheld the skills, and could use those skills for special privileges or to gain freedom" (Cornelius 1991, 3).

84. Cornelius reports that "[e]ven though laws banning the teaching of slaves were seldom enforced, and were only in effect in four states for the entire period from 1830 to 1865, slaves recognized their symbolic power. Former slaves accurately recalled the existence of such laws in Virginia, North and South Carolina, and Georgia"—but, strictly speaking, no such laws existed in Maryland (Cornelius 1991, 64).

85. Years later, when he has returned from Mr. Freeland's to Baltimore to work as a carpenter in Mr. Gardiner's shipyard, Miss Sophia again reacts compassionately when Douglass is injured during a fight. So comforted is he by her ministrations he finds the beating almost worth it because it allows him to see once again her "originally characteristic kindness" (Douglass 1855, 334). Strikingly, when Hugh Auld tries to get the magistrate to arrest the men who have beaten Douglass, his word is insufficient to get him to act, as are the wounds on Douglass's body. Auld tries to use Douglass's body as a text in this scene—"'look at his head and face . . . ; *they* show *what* had been done'"—but the magistrate will accept only the testimony of a white witness, the word of one who has seen (Douglass 1855, 335). Once Douglass has escaped and found refuge and work among the abolitionists, however, they are only too willing to use his body as their text,

introducing him as one who has a *"diploma written on my back"* (365). On this, see Sánchez-Eppler (1993, 30).

86. For a discussion of the complex motives that led antebellum whites to teach slaves to read, see Cornelius (1991).

87. Ziolkowski argues that the *Narrative* provides readers with a species of "textual self-reflection, one concerned with the relations of words to social power as well as with the ways in which the very acquisition of the hegemonic means of expression situates the text in a kind of mediatory limbo" (Ziolkowski 1991, 149).

88. For a discussion of what is left unspoken in the 1845 account of Douglass's exchange with Covey, see Van Leer (1990).

89. This is an interpretation that Olney completely overlooks when he claims that "we have literacy, identity, and freedom, the omnipresent thematic trio of the most important slave narratives, all conveyed in a single startling image" (Olney 1985, 158). It is a measure of how beholden Olney is to Western metaphysics that he cannot see that the body lies at the heart of the image. It would appear to me that Douglass knows far more than his reader how to avoid undue influence. Not only did Douglass evade editorial pressures, as Olney argues, but he also managed to evade the crucial metaphysical construction that elevates the mind at the expense of the debased body. As I have suggested previously, that it is impossible to evade metaphysics entirely goes without saying. That Douglass was, furthermore, unable to evade all liberal humanistic thinking is also to be expected. Nonetheless, he does offer a pointed critique of many humanistic principles. More aligned with my approach, Stephanie Smith asks of other humanistically bound readings, "Might this image also be read as a metaphoric refusal of an identity bound to a logic requiring that bodily wounds be forgotten?" (Smith 1994, 117).

90. The Reverend Sella Martin reports that he learned to read by first acquiring great skill in playing marbles—and trading his vast hoard of marbles for literacy when a less-skilled player, with a passion for gaming, invites him to become his "partner," an arrangement the young slave boy is only too happy to accommodate (Blassingame 1977, 710). Not only does his "partner" teach him how to write the alphabet, but Martin has used the labor of his own hands, his great skill in marbles, to earn the right to learn to write. In a complex layering of submissions, Martin must first make his "partner" think that he (the other boy) has initiated the idea of a partnership so that Martin can seem to submit to the boy's suggestion that they team up. But even though Martin entices the other boy into making him an offer he has no intention of refusing, if he is to learn to write, he must, after all, submit to the boy's teaching. But the lessons pay off handsomely. Not long after he has mastered that to which he has submitted himself, he is asked by some fellow African Americans to read a newspaper for them. Thinking he will fool them into believing he is a competent reader, he discovers to his surprise that he can, after all, make sense of the article, thus beginning his career of secretly reading aloud to other slaves. Strikingly, when Martin first discovers the act of reading, he describes it as having the ability to "make paper and the little black marks on it talk" (709).

91. For a completely different take on this question, see Andrews (1986) and Gates (1989). For a related argument, see Sánchez-Eppler (1988; 1993), who argues, for example that "[t]he problem, for the antislavery writer," such as Stowe, "lies in depicting a black body that can be instantly recognized not only as a loyal or a rebellious servant, but also as a hero or a heroine" (Sánchez-Eppler 1993, 28).

92. In her *Story*, Mattie J. Jackson is disarmingly candid about her purpose, admitting that her objective is to obtain "sympathy from the earnest friends" of persons who

had been enslaved against their will (Jackson 1866, 3). She needs people to buy her book, furthermore, so she might secure the education necessary to help her "emancipated brothers and sisters" (3). Writing fifteen years later, James L. Smith is equally candid in telling his readers that by "purchasing this narrative you will be assisting one who has been held in the chattels of slavery: who is now broken down by the infirmities of age, and asks your help to aid him in this, his means of support in his declining years" (Smith 1881, 144).

93. Ironically, this is exactly what Gates does in his introduction to Harriet Wilson's *Our Nig*, when he authenticates this 1859 autobiographical novel as having indeed been written by a black woman and not, as originally thought, by a white one.

94. Scarry describes a similar narrative dilemma faced by letter writers for Amnesty International, who attempt to engage readers in helping to end the physical suffering of the person whose torture is being described in the letter (see Scarry 1985, especially the Introduction).

95. Baker, while arguing that the very language in which Douglass gains instruction restricted him, also asserts that "the slave can arrive at a sense of being only through language. But it is also true that, in Douglass's case, a conception of the preeminent form of being is conditioned by white, Christian standards" (Baker 1980, 36). While I would not disagree that our subjectivity is formed by language, I argue throughout this study that the language of our metaphysical system works to deny our inborn, preconceptual knowledge of our relatedness-to-*being*. The more we become a being—an individualized, Westernized, Christianized being; that is to say, a subject—the harder it is for us to recollect *being*. Douglass, on my view, never lost this capacity because of the intensively embodied experience of slavery. Never permitted to forget his body, he never forgot what his body knew.

96. For a different but equally positive take on the significance of wandering in the slave narratives, see Hedin (1982a; 1982b). On a related issue, see Piccinato (1994). For a reading of Douglass in the context provided by Thoreau and other major figures of the American Renaissance, see Reising (1986, 256–72).

97. With this rhetorical question I am, of course, challenging most previous interpretations of Douglass's work. Barrett, for example, in a recent essay continues to argue that Douglass achieves in his *Narrative* a "repudiation of the body" (Barrett 1995, 432). On my view, readings such as Barrett's fall prey to the same metaphysical thinking that Douglass was able to challenge. See also Gates, who claims that "surely this must be the literary critic's final judgment of Frederick Douglass: that he was Representative Man because he was Rhetorical Man, black master of the verbal arts. Douglass is our clearest example of the will to power as the will to write" (1989, 108).

98. Again, my goal here is to demonstrate that Douglass did rise above what Valerie Smith has called "the very premises that contributed to his enslavement" (Smith 1987, 28). See also Baker (1980, 38–44). For a summary of some of the more conservative readings of his autobiographies, see Gates (1989, 112–24). Gates takes issue with their arguments but fails to take his argument as far as I have taken mine.

3

Disappearing Acts

I have broken my discussion of African American antebellum narratives into two chapters because of the different cultural expectations facing male and female authors in the nineteenth century.[1] I have argued that Frederick Douglass turned to rhetorical advantage (in print and in person) the fact of his manly embodiment. In stark contrast, nineteenth-century women, whether white or black, could gain little by being associated with their bodies—except, of course, to the extent that Euro-American women enjoyed the power and prestige attendant upon their "whiteness."[2] While it is true that woman's character also was thought to be readable in physical signs, being considered physical at all was a distinct disadvantage to a woman.[3] Middle-class white women, shaped by the restrictive if glorified habitus of domesticity, lived in the paradoxical condition of being disembodied as far as literature, polite discourse, and social convention went—and yet being so thoroughly identified with their bodies that they were known collectively as "the sex." Their indisputably second-class standing, relative to their middle-class male counterparts (in the persons of their fathers, husbands, brothers, and even their sons), was also, of course, a direct consequence of their own biological differences—differences that were exaggerated not only in the political arena but also in medical textbooks, as even purportedly objective artistic renditions of women's skeletons exaggerated the width of their hips and the smallness of their cranial capacity.[4] Readers trying to find convincing evidence of women's embodiment in the literature of this time, however, must content themselves with these flawed descriptions—or, if they are readers of novels, with elaborate metaphoric displacements.[5] As Helena Michie reminds us, even though it was commonplace for "Victorian novels [to] center on a physically beautiful heroine and trace the disposition of her body in either marriage or death, the body itself appears only as a series of tropes or rhetorical codes that distance [sic] it from the reader in the very act of its depiction"

(Michie 1987, 5). Moreover, Michie asserts that "[a]lthough Victorian language—even and perhaps especially women's language—is rich with metaphoric allusions to the body, discussions of the body itself are always immediately supplemented with metaphors from other fields of discourse" (5). For this was an era of polite conversation, in which women's "legs" became the more socially acceptable "limbs," an era when women's skirts brushed the floor, when even tables and pianos wore fringed shawls to hide evidence of their legs, and when doctors gained reputations by developing skill in examining the modest sex with their own eyes closed or averted so as not to embarrass their patients. Although well-to-do women, to all appearances, no longer had legs in the nineteenth century, they certainly had buttocks and wore voluminous bustles and tight-laced corsets to enhance them, to the serious detriment of their health and energy. Much as American feminists felt the need of immediate dress reform, the public was so hostile to such change that even the redoubtable Elizabeth Cady Stanton was prevailed upon by her fellow Suffragists to give up the idea since her scandalous practice of wearing loose-fitting clothes and the newly introduced "bloomers" was keeping would-be sympathizers out of the Suffrage movement.[6] Although middle-class white women were said to have no sexual desires, a few miserable creatures nonetheless had their clitorises excised to keep them from masturbating—and were operated on by J. Marion Sims, the so-called "father of American gynecology," who perfected many of his gynecological procedures on the unwilling bodies of black women.

If white women enjoyed the questionable class privilege of becoming socially disembodied, black women had the even worse fate of becoming mythically overly embodied.[7] In virtual opposition to their white counterparts, African American women were identified with their bodies and commonly "known" among whites to be highly sexed.[8] Harriet Jacobs describes the problem succinctly when she reports that what "commands admiration in the white woman only hastens the degradation of the female slave" (Jacobs 1861, 28). As even the male slave narrators themselves acknowledged, being a slave brought African American women additional psychological, emotional, and physical burdens. Writing in 1881, James L. Smith recalls, for example, that "[t]he wretched condition of the male slave is bad enough; but that of the woman, driven to unremitting, unrequited toil, suffering, sick, and bearing the peculiar burdens of her own sex, unpitied, not assisted, as well as the toils which belong to another, must arouse the sympathy in every heart not dead to all feeling" (Smith 1881, 166–67).[9] So unwomanly was the embodied experience of hard-working African American women thought to be, in comparison to the protected, ethereal status of the white ladies of the leisure class,[10] that in 1851 Sojourner Truth took it upon herself to lecture the audience at a women's rights convention on this very subject, attempting in the process to insert herself into the category "woman" and thus, in the process, transform it, asserting, for example, "I have as much muscle as any man, and can do as much work as any man. I have plowed and reaped and husked and chopped and mowed, and can any man do more than that?" (Washington 1993, 118).[11]

Not all African American women would be equally willing to risk alienating their audience or readers in going head to head with the repressive ideology of nineteenth-century society. But the tradition of African American women's fiction begins, remarkably enough, with a writer who was willing to do just that. While *Our Nig*, as other critics have argued, is indeed an indictment of Northern racism and the repressive socioeconomic practices of nineteenth-century America,[12] it is also a brilliant reconfiguration of what it means to be a woman as well as an exposé of the strained relations between black and white women.[13] As such, it is also an exposé of the myth of domesticity, calling particular attention to the cruelty mothers can wreak on their children, the tyranny wives can wield over their husbands, and the dependence of middle-class women on the household labors of working-class women.[14] Although neither Truth nor Harriet E. Wilson refers to herself as a "lady"—the idealized model of nineteenth-century womanhood—this former slave and her free-born sister in suffering nonetheless contribute to the reconstruction of nineteenth-century womanhood, and they do so by calling attention to their bodies. Very much like Douglass himself, Wilson, in her long-neglected autobiographical novel, which for decades was thought to have been written by a white woman, dares to describe the quotidian experiences of the African American body-self.[15] I find Wilson's book to be an extraordinarily compelling and critically undervalued account of the centrality of embodiment to the human experience and thus another founding text of proto-Bohemianism. Equally stunning is Wilson's ability to convert into a perdurable commodity the nearly unremitting physical suffering she endured throughout her life, a life tragically marked by the demands that were placed on her by the white family she lived with as a so-called free black woman. The commodity that Wilson produced is, of course, the novel itself—a commodity that continues today to have economic value. Those of us who buy her book, even now, discharge a longstanding debt born of her mistreatment at the hands of the Bellmonts.[16] Although Wilson's novel is less complex than Douglass's narratives, speaking proportionally, the body-self takes up much more space as the subject[17] of her account than does Douglass's body-self. While Douglass's body-self informs his story, Frado's body-self constitutes her story.

Two years after *Our Nig* appeared, however, Harriet Jacobs, writing under the protective pen-name Linda Brent, published *Incidents in the Life of a Slave Girl* and in so doing hastened the movement underground of the African American body-self. As Douglass's *Narrative* stands as the most conspicuous founding text of proto-Bohemianism, Jacobs's *Incidents* stands as the most conspicuous founding text of proto-Gentility. While Jacobs could not have freed herself from slavery without the extraordinary discipline of her self-imprisoned body, her body is virtually absent from her text—becoming in its absence a portent of things to come.[18] That is to say, the traces of Frado's body-self and the manual labor she performed for the Bellmonts can be found in the "work" of racial uplift that provides the focus and purpose of much of the post-Reconstruction fiction written by African Americans. This work, while "real," is, nonetheless, a displaced metaphor of the physical labor performed by the slaves and free blacks. It will be my argument, therefore, that these turn-of-the-century novels continue the tradition of what one might call *narrative couvade* that is begun in Jacobs's *Incidents in the Life of a Slave Girl* and other African American narratives written by women, such as Nancy Prince's 1853 *Narrative* and even the transcription of Louisa Picquet's 1861 interview, *The Octoroon: or Inside Views of Southern Domestic Life*. That is, in the Epilogue, I will argue that a dominant concern of African American writers, during the post-Reconstruction era, was not only to uplift the race but also to protect the racialized body from the white reader's gaze—whether this gaze was considered to be disciplinary, scopophilic, or voyeuristic in nature. It is my belief that postbellum writers and their successors (especially those who were associated with the Genteel School of writing) hid the black body from view because they no longer felt they could trust their (white) readers.[19] As I conceive of it, this narrative distrust had its literary origins in Jacobs's antebellum autobiography and various other, less well-known female narratives.[20] Before discussing these earlier narratives, however, I want, like others before me have done, to contextualize them in the tradition of the American sentimental novel.

Because of the clear overlapping of these two literary forms, it has not been uncommon for critics to read African American women's slave narratives in connection with this other hugely popular nineteenth-century literary genre[21]—which until recently has been critically reviled largely because of its widespread popularity among women readers. Perhaps in part because of its association with the more politically respectable genre of slave narratives, this previously vilified body of literature has recently undergone substantial critical rehabilitation in the capable hands of Nina Baym, Robyn Warhol, and Karen Sánchez-Eppler.[22] What makes this reconsideration of sentimental fiction particularly useful to me is the renewed attention these studies have given to the bodies of readers. For, as Baym, Warhol, and Sánchez-Eppler remind us, readers have not always been as disembodied as they appear in contemporary literary theory, even in most forms of reader response criticism. In her 1984 study, *Novels, Readers, and Reviewers*, for example, Baym lays the groundwork for much of the current work being done on this subject. Reminding us that for the nineteenth century a novel was mostly likely to be evaluated on the basis of the "interest" it was able to stimulate in readers, Baym notes that not all interest was thought to be beneficial, especially if it was of a particularly excitable sort (Baym 1984, 54–56). She then describes the unresolvable dilemma of nineteenth-century reviewers who wished somehow to be able to distinguish between a novel's ability to engender in readers either a "natural [or an] unnatural excitement." "Only the *Ladies' Repository* with its view that *all* excitement is unnatural—or more precisely that all excitement, though natural, is a mark of original sin—could escape the issue," on Baym's view, "and it did so, inevitably, by condemning the novel genre as a reprobate form" (1984, 56). Those who gazed disapprovingly on the many pleasures novels stimulated in their devoted readers were wont to describe reading in terms of "metaphors drawn from bodily appetites implying physical stimulation, intoxication, and addiction" (56). At the same time, "those arguing for 'wholesome' fiction did so with the same metaphors" (58). In the selections that Baym quotes from, good novels are said to have a salutary effect on the reader, while bad ones are said to have a deleterious effect. But whether individual novels were seen as beneficial or harmful, reviewers tended to conceive "of the novel as a *substance taken into the body*, there to work an effect beyond the reader's control" (Baym 1984, 58; emphasis added).[23] Warhol picks up this theme in "As You Stand, So You Feel and Are," where she responds to Herbert F. Smith's attack on sentimental fiction (in his 1980 study, *The Popular American Novel: 1865–1920*). As Warhol describes it, on Smith's view "sentimentality is the disease infecting the body of the text, whereas in the nineteenth-century model, textual pathos was the medicine for the body of the reader" (Warhol 1992, 106). Challenging the positions of other twentieth-century critics of sentimentality, Warhol utilizes the work of Joseph Roach to argue that the form "is pointedly *not* cathartic, but that it rather encourages readers to rehearse and reinforce the emotions it evokes" (112). Drawing on the work of the nineteenth-century French philosopher François Delsarte as he is used in Martha Banta's study of American women's cultural history, Warhol argues further that, in acting, "the gesture not only expresses the emotion and the state of mind, it *brings them into being*" (114). Arguing finally that "the Victorian idea that we feel sad *because* we weep puts a radically different spin on weeping's ultimate effect," she is able to conclude that the act of crying over a sentimental novel "did not drain a reservoir of stored feelings, nor did it debilitate readers from taking action in the extra-textual world. Instead, crying created and promoted the feelings, which then might presumably serve as goads to action" (114).[24] Warhol then aligns herself with those "who argue that criticism can no longer afford to overlook the physically present body of the reader who brings the text into being through the act of reading" (116). In both her 1988 essay and her 1993 book Sánchez-Eppler makes a similar claim about the importance of bodies in the nineteenth-century reading experience. Like Warhol, Sánchez-Eppler also believes in the ability of these texts literally to move their readers, arguing that "[t]he tears of the reader are pledged in these sentimental stories as a means of rescuing the bodies of slaves" (1988, 36; 1993, 26). On her view, then, it was fitting that abolitionist texts took the form of sentimental fiction, not just because it was so widely read, "but also because sentimental fiction constitutes an intensely bodily genre" (Sánchez-Eppler 1988, 35; 1993, 26).[25]

Writing about class differences in Victorian England, Michie notes that three competing schools of thought approached the woman question from a single "rhetorical source"—that being the idiom of women's bodies (Michie 1987, 34): "While conservatives focussed on sexual fall, protectionists focussed on disease, and the protofeminists, paradoxically enough, on the healthy effects of work and the moral and physical corruption that attended idleness" (33). Sánchez-Eppler argues similarly of nineteenth-century feminist-abolitionist American fiction that it relied on the idiom of the slave's body: "For women and slaves the ability to speak was predicated upon the reinterpretation of their flesh. Feminists and abolitionists share a strategy: to invert patriarchal readings and so reclaim the body" (Sánchez-Eppler 1988, 30). In the slave narratives themselves, of course, the ex-slaves were reinterpreting their own embodied experience—not merely to enter liberal humanism as equal to whites, but, as I have been arguing throughout, to reconfigure it. To my mind, it is unnecessary to argue that the slaves consciously knew this was their project. Although, indeed, they hoped to destroy the "peculiar institution" by exposing its cruelties, perversions, and degradations, in doing so they must, by necessity, write about what they had experienced. And what they had experienced thematized, as few other documented events in the history of the West, the importance of embodiment to human be-ing. That much of this experience was designed to degrade the body, and often succeeded in doing so, does not in any way nullify what the body-self of the slaves knew. Neither did all the slaves necessarily interpret their embodiment as shameful. While I think it is reasonable to assume that many female slave narrators remained silent about their sexual misuse out of a deep-seated sense of privacy or even a sense of shame,[26] many did not hesitate to describe the work they were required to do. This willingness to describe their work contrasts with the pattern Michie detected in the canonical texts of nineteenth-century British literature, which remained silent on the subject of both work and eating because both were seen "as closely involving women's bodies" (Michie 1987, 30). Given this silence, it is possible to read the detailed accounts of women's work in the slave narratives not just as representing or speaking for women's bodies, but as displaced metaphors of the sexual mistreatment they received at the hands of their white masters.

Before turning to *Our Nig*, therefore, I want to examine the 1831 narrative of Mary Prince, the first female slave narrative, as William Andrews notes (1988, xxix), to have come out of the Americas, and a narrative that does not at all shy away from depicting the work of a woman's body.

Mary Prince

The History of Mary Prince, A West Indian Slave. Related by Herself (1831)

The History of Mary Prince, A West Indian Slave was edited by Thomas Pringle after Prince sought him out and, with his permission, told her story to one of his house guests. While we cannot be entirely sure how much in this history is Prince's recollection of conditions and how much the product of her editor's imagination, I find this relatively neglected text notable for many reasons. One I have just alluded to—that being the detailed account of the work Prince is required to do and the pain and torture to which her body is subjected by her masters. Another is the fact that, like Douglass, Mary Prince, in anticipation of his narratives, also includes an account of the compassion she experienced as a young slave. Not only does Prince recall feeling compassion toward Mrs. Williams (her first mistress) and Mrs. Williams's daughter Betsey (to whom she technically belongs), but she recalls the love the white woman and her daughter had for her. Of her attachment to Mrs. Williams, Prince recalls that, excepting her own mother, she loved this woman more than anyone else in the world (Prince 1831, 1). When Mrs. Williams can no longer afford to keep her and hires her out to Mrs. Pruden, Prince becomes similarly attached to the two young children she supervises, one of whom teaches her the alphabet and to read a few words—thus linking the gestural expression of compassion with the acquisition of literacy, a linkage that is also thematized in Douglass's narratives. Looking back on those days before Mrs. Williams's untimely death (the fate of all too many kind mistresses), Prince recalls fatalistically from her vantage point of an adult that they had been "too pleasant to last." Yet thinking of them never fails to "soften" her "heart" (2). As she tries to describe what it felt like to learn she was about to be sold away from the Williams family and her own beloved mother, she admits that she can hardly bear to think of the day, confessing that she wishes she were able to "find words" to express what she "felt and suffered" (3). Once she has left the relatively tolerable conditions of being slave to Mrs. Williams, Prince learns the brutal reality of her servitude—a servitude that would, quite literally and legally, treat her as chattel personal. The men bidding for her at auction, for example, she describes as having "examined and handled" her just like "a butcher would a calf or a lamb" that is for sale. So habituated are these men to treating slaves in this fashion, they discussed her "shape and size in like words—as if I could no more understand their meaning than the dumb beasts" (4).[27] But the suffering she experiences at losing her home, her mother, and her kind mistress is nothing to the suffering that awaits her with her new master, whose behavior is quite literally so unspeakably vile he is known here only as Captain I—— in deference to any living relatives who might be innocent of the sins of the father. Although Prince is received kindly enough by Hetty, her fellow slave, Hetty dies soon after Prince arrives at Captain I——'s household. Hetty's early death is brought about by a severe beating she receives while pregnant, the details and fatal consequences of which Prince recounts as part of her efforts to inform the people in England about the true horrors of West Indian slavery.

In recalling her instructions at the hands of her new mistress, Prince (perhaps with the assistance of her amanuensis or editor, who admits to polishing her account, or perhaps on her own, as hers is an unusual intelligence) describes not just the household tasks she is taught to perform but, in a brilliant play on words, the other kinds of bodily knowledge she also learns at the hands of her mistress. In addition to teaching her all the conventional household chores from washing clothes to washing floors, from doing the cooking to picking the cotton, this woman "caused me to *know the exact difference between the smart of the rope, the cart-whip, and the cow-skin*, when applied to my naked body by her own cruel hand" (1831, 6; emphasis added). In this brief passage, Prince summarizes the essence of slavery as a dreadful combination of unceasing labor and physical pain. The lessons in human compassion she received in her first mistress's household are here supplemented by the more negative lessons in human brutality, but both kinds of lessons are physical in origin and remembered forever in her body, as she well knows when she exclaims, "how can I ever forget it!" (6). As she narrates the physical suffering of her fellow slaves, therefore, it is not altogether surprising that she describes the communion she feels with those who share her bondage. In exchanging Captain I—— for a different master, Mr. D——, she tells us that she has simply gone from "one butcher to another" (10). Mr. D——, for example, has a crippled slave, "old Daniel," whom he beats until his skin is raw and then throws buckets of salt water over the wounds until "the man writhed on the ground like a worm" and shrieked in agonizing pain (11). But it is with this pitiful "worm" that Prince herself identifies. Recalling that his open sores were more than once crawling with "maggots," she says that all the slaves pitied him, "and in his wretched case we saw . . . our own lot," if they were to live as long as he (11). In recollecting the torment of yet another elderly slave, Prince admits that the act of recounting her own pain and "sorrows" has inevitably brought back memories of how others suffered (12).

But like all the slaves, whether she was "sick or well," Prince had her "work to do" (1831, 18). She works so hard, under such harrowing conditions, that she concludes her narrative with a peroration on work as the essence of slavery. First she assures her British readers that slaves would not mind working so hard if they were treated well, paid a living wage, and allowed to observe the Sabbath. But, in contrast to the English aristocracy, American slave holders refuse to treat their workers in this humane and decent fashion. Instead, they require "work—work—work, night and day, sick or well," until they are quite used up, a disciplinary regime that the slaves are not allowed to contest, no matter how much they are ill-treated. "And then when we are quite done up, who cares for us, more than for a lame horse? This is slavery" (23). Since work is done by enslaved bodies, Prince's claim is not very different from James Pennington's claim that slavery would be nothing without the chattel principle. In his narrative, Lunsford Lane also understands how work differentiates slave from master. While he was still a child, he reports that he "knew no difference between [himself] and the white children" (Lane 1842, 6). But once he begins "to work," he says that he "discovered the difference," for then his former playmates "began to order [him] about" (7). Henry Bibb reports similarly that once he was hired out to pay for the education of his own playmate, his "sorrows and sufferings commenced" (Bibb 1850, 15). Once Prince has escaped John Wood, her last master, however, she willingly works for those who will pay for her labors, but she is incapable of doing very much since she has been ill-treated for so many years. This willingness to work for herself once freedom is obtained is a common theme in slave narratives, with many former slaves bragging about the extent of their work and sometimes even the wealth that accrues to them as a result of it. In Lucy Delaney's case, for example, once she secures the freedom that is legally hers,[28] she finds, as she puts it, "a great difference between slave and free labor, for while the first was compulsory, and, therefore, at the best, perfunctory, the latter must be superior in order to create a demand, and realizing this fully, mother and I expended the utmost care in our respective callings, and were well rewarded for our efforts" (Delaney c. 1891, 52–53). In William Wells Brown's novel, *Clotel*, once the Carltons tell their slaves that they can earn their right to freedom, a similar change occurs: "The bricklayers had been to work but a short time, before their increased industry was noticed by many. They were no longer apparently the same people. A sedateness, a care, an economy, an industry, took possession of them" (Brown 1853, 128). Given the proper incentive and permission, slaves did not wait for freedom to demonstrate a willingness to work. Lane, who bought his own freedom for $1,000, brags, for example, about the work he does while still a slave to support his wife and children who are owned by another man, recalling that virtually "every article of clothing worn either by my wife or children, especially every article of much value, I had to purchase" (Lane 1842, 12).[29]

On one hand, of course, such accounts of industry and responsibility are to be read as evidence of the slaves' suitability for freedom and for their acceptance into the human family as equal brothers and sisters. On the other, such accounts, especially when they assume such central importance as they do in Prince's narratives, exceed what Jehlen has called the "merely thematic" and begin to function formally (Jehlen 1981, 595). That is, in contrast to many of the best-known African American novels that were written after the Civil War, Prince's autobiography is structured around or shaped by her body and its exertions. It is throughout constituted by her body, its pain and suffering and labors. For Prince, the body-self *is* her narrative self. Unlike her immediate, postbellum successors and her middle-class English contemporaries, Prince and her amanuensis have the narrative freedom to write the body. The body is not absent here but present in its pain. Although she may indeed rely on work to carry the additional metaphoric burden of representing sex, the fact that this woman's work is represented at all in this nineteenth-century text is significant in and of itself. One might be tempted to read this as a scandalous commentary on the slave woman's experience, scandalous in that to write about her life she, shamefully, must write about her work and thus, if only metaphorically, write about her body. Given the desire to conceal women's bodies that dominated nineteenth-century genteel discourse, the need to talk about a slave woman's work in an abolitionist text might have in and of itself been shocking enough to inspire outrage among the middle class. But at the same time, titillated as some genteel readers might have been by her account of working, Prince was writing the body into narrative and at the same time revising, if only minimally, the prevailing myths of what it was to be a woman. She was, moreover, on my view also critiquing the disembodied notion of subjectivity itself. For how could Mary Prince deny the body? How could she not see herself as a body-self?

Mary Prince not only transforms her body-self into a new kind of autobiography, she also, as I will argue of Harriet Wilson, transmutes her bodily suffering and labors into the body of her text by which she reaches out to us and invites our reciprocal compassionate response. In the editor's supplement to her narrative, Thomas Pringle attests to Prince's good character (partially to counter her last master's libelous claims that she is depraved and licentious), observing that she has "strong attachments" to others and responds deeply to acts of kindness. She is also decent, well-behaved, and, most especially, known for her *"delicacy"* in all matters, large and small (1831, 35). Her faults he lists as "a somewhat violent and hasty temper, and a considerable share of natural pride and self-importance," which he admits to having seldom seen and by which he claims to be largely unbothered (35). Having only the narrative by which to judge her, I would attribute Prince's good character to the early compassion she experienced in her first home, slave though she was. I find it significant to my argument that, even after the terrible experiences she had at the hands of her masters, she still retains the capacity to form attachments to others and enjoys what, to my eyes, is a healthy amour propre—both of which are evident in the fact that she, on Pringle's account, had the idea herself of writing her history so "good people in England" could learn of the horrors and suffering of slavery from one who had herself been enslaved (Prince 1831, iii). Not only is she testifying in this *History* on behalf of all those still enslaved, she is reaching out to decent people in England, seeking their compassion. Although the bulk of her previous experiences might have convinced her of the natural depravity of whites, especially those in the West Indies, those few years she spent with Mrs. Williams and then Mrs. Pruden seem to have had the same kind of salutary effect on her as Douglass's early years with his grandmother had on him. In both instances, I would argue, the slave's body was allowed to remember our preconceptual and inherent relatedness-to-*being*. Like Olaudah Equiano before her, Mary Prince composes a narrative designed to help sympathetic British subjects recollect their own relatedness-to-*being*, a recollection that both former slaves trust will have the effect of moving the British Parliament to action.

The tension in this, the first of the American women's slave narratives, between pain and abuse on one hand and a seemingly ineffectual compassion on the other, is one that also informs the first novel to be written by an African American woman, Harriet Wilson's long-neglected 1859 novel, *Our Nig*.

Harriet E. Wilson

Our Nig; or, Sketches from the Life of a Free Black, In a Two-Story White House, North. Showing that Slavery's Shadows Fall Even There (1859)

In this first novel written by a black person to be published in the United States,[30] we can clearly see the role of the body in African American narrative already being negotiated. Like Frederick Douglass before her, Harriet Wilson meditates on the meaning of human embodiment—but in her case as it relates to the experience of *free* African Americans. Like Mary Prince before her, she also meditates on the meaning of human embodiment as it pertains to African American women and the work they must do. It is a meditation marked by the extraordinary tension between what is spoken and what is left unspoken, that is to say, between what is spoken and what Pierre Macherey would call its gaps and silences[31]; for in this novel Wilson is working against the grain of nineteenth-century genteel discourse in explicitly describing the travails and fate of Frado's working body. In his introduction to *Our Nig*, Gates addresses what he sees as the "tensions between autobiography and fiction" that are evident throughout this novel (xxxvi), tensions that help explain many of these silences, as Wilson clearly does not feel able to tell everything about either herself or the family she works for.[32] Gates then profitably "compare[s] the plot structure" of Wilson's novel to the "'overplot' of nineteenth-century women's fiction" as it has been described by Baym (1984), finding in the process instances of both correspondence and difference (xli). He also argues that Wilson's novel pivots on the issue of the "economic bond" that defines the unequal relationship between white mistress and black servant (xliv), suggesting further that Wilson wrote her novel to show "the suffering of a black, wearied, wornout daughter of toil" (xlv).[33] But having established his intellectual understanding of the physical economies of *Our Nig*, Gates goes on to assert that "[t]he great evil in this book is not love-betrayed . . . or the evils of the flesh; rather, it is poverty, both the desperation it inflicts as well as the evils it implicitly sanctions" (xlvi). By implicitly relegating the "evils of the flesh" to carnal relations or sexual abuse, Gates fails to remark that the body is all too implicated in the evils of poverty.[34] While impoverished peoples surely suffer grave spiritual, emotional, mental, and psychological despair, this despair is felt (as it needs must be) in their bodies, which are already weakened and afflicted by exhaustion, hunger, illness, and excessive temperatures.

This deeply felt and unremittingly physical experience of poverty, it seems to me, is what Wilson's novel is about. Although her eponymous heroine ("Our Nig"), whose given name is Frado (and not, as one of Wilson's character witnesses seems to think, Alfrado), is portrayed as brave, intelligent, witty, and spiritual, the overriding characteristic that appears without surcease is one of Frado's utter, debased embodiment—yet hers, like that of the Southern slaves, is an embodiment that accomplishes something. Although she is not rewarded for doing it, and is often punished for doing it incorrectly, Frado, unlike any of the Bellmonts living at home, does work. At the same time, by portraying the utter uselessness of the entire Bellmont clan, the novel itself works to imbue Frado's own unceasing labors with dignity. As such, it is a novel that also critiques the capitalist system, which is built on the labors of the working poor.[35] Although, to one degree or another, all the privileged Bellmonts function as foils to the hard-working Frado, it is primarily Mrs. Bellmont who seems to think she owns Frado's labors. Thus, what she intends to be a disciplinary regimen that will humble her unpaid, virtually enslaved servant girl and, simultaneously, improve her own social standing, instead has, in the realm of interpretive economics, the unanticipated reverse effect of increasing Frado's value even as it diminishes her own. There are many things that differentiate the humorless, ambitious, and pitiless Mrs. Bellmont from her high-spirited, sensitive charge. At the heart of them are Frado's capacity for and willingness to work—characteristics that readers can only admire. Work also brings Frado's body to narrative presence. As Michie has argued, in novels as in life, "[w]ork marks the body, making it representable, marked, remarkable" (Michie 1987, 35). But unlike the canonical nineteenth-century British novelists who, associating women's work with their unmentionable middle-class bodies, remained largely silent on the subject, Wilson does not avert her own or the reader's gaze from the fact of her heroine's embodiment. She rather insists we gaze upon it. One might even say *our work* as readers is to gaze unceasingly upon the spectacle of Frado's working body. Although we are not overburdened with specific descriptions of Frado's appearance,[36] we are burdened by the painful reality we are forced to witness page after terrible page.[37] Frado's body-self works and is therefore seen. It is punished and is therefore seen. It suffers and is therefore seen. In its highly conspicuous presence—both in Frado's own daily experience and in the pages of Wilson's autobiographical novel—this body-self announces itself as re-markable. For it is common neither in real life nor in fiction to see a body *qua* body be so thoroughly and vividly thematized.

It goes without saying that all of us are embodied—and that is precisely my point. It goes without saying. As I have discussed in previous chapters, it is the nature of human embodiment to go largely unremarked. Because our engagement with the world is a perceptual engagement, we find ourselves the majority of the time attending to the world and away from our bodies. It is when something goes amiss that we withdraw our attention from the world and use our perceptual capabilities to attend to ourselves, our bodies. The body in pain gets our attention. The hungry body gets our attention. The tired body gets our attention. And, as Frantz Fanon discovers, the racialized body gets our attention[38]—as, of course, does the sexualized body. Conversely, the well-cared-for, well-rested, healthy body—especially if it is a white male body—provides the unremarked means by which we engage the world. At the same time, of course, this world, which is, after all, *our* world, can, in its beauty and complexities, offer our body-self extraordinary pleasures. Who among us has not felt the swelling of emotions that seems to make the heart grow large with joy when a loved one comes into view, a favorite flower is smelled, or a melody is heard? But except for those intermittent moments of pain and pleasure, most of the time our bodies remain ciphers to us.[39] They are, to repeat, how we know and have the world and are therefore necessary to human be-ing, but they can be *consciously* ignored even as, by their very presence—their unremarked and unremarkable presence—they engage us in the world. This is not to say that we ought to ignore the body, only that, physiologically speaking, we can and, philosophically speaking, we are trained to.

But what of Frado, whose body, in the terms of indenture that bound her out to the Bellmonts,[40] was not her own to work as she might—but, in the terms I am using, is still her very own body-self? The tension here is reflected in the title, *Our Nig; or, Sketches from the Life of a Free Black*. What do we make of the fact that "Our Nig" is a "Free Black"?[41] On one hand, the notion of freedom as it pertains to nineteenth-century black persons is seriously challenged by this despairing novel. As I have argued earlier, the daily experience of nineteenth-century African Americans could not help but undermine the transcendental claims made on behalf of the universal principles of freedom, equality, independence, and reason—those noble concepts that lie at the heart of liberal humanism. If Frado's experience is *freedom*, what, then, is slavery?[42] Except for the moments of charitable intervention by kindly but mostly ineffectual relatives, Frado's body is virtually never free of repression, correction, exhaustion, or pain. It is thus almost always the subject of her attention, seldom capable of mercifully receding into the background. Contrary to the ordinary experience of others, she does not experience the world through her absent body; she experiences her all-too-present body through the vices and devices of the world, in the form of beatings and the threat of beatings, an inadequate diet, insufficient clothing, a demand that she work almost continuously, and a chronic lack of sleep. Because her body is treated so harshly by others, she herself must constantly be attentive to it. Thus, except for those stolen moments when she confides in her beloved dog Fido or tricks a wily sheep, those moments Aunt Abby and the sons James and Jack comfort her, and those moments she attends church, her narrative recounts the suffering presence of her racialized black body. Except for the occasional brief moments of respite when we get a glimpse of what an unfettered Frado could become, we observe this young servant girl working for Mrs. Bellmont and her demanding daughter Mary, or being beaten by her mistress for not working hard or obediently enough. But, on the other hand, as I asked less rhetorically of Mary Prince's body-self, does this abused body not think? The answer here, as my earlier answer in Chapter 1, is most assuredly it—that is, *she*—does. Frado's body is beaten and otherwise debased, but the labor she performs, though she herself does not gain material advantage from it, provides her with a human *presence* and a dignity far surpassing those of her brutal mistress. And, as others have also observed, in the end Frado is able to convert her bodily suffering into a commodity that she (as Harriet Wilson) offers up for sale to what she hopes will be a sympathetic and receptive audience. Indentured to Mrs. Bellmont and having worked most of her life quite literally for nothing—no pay, no appreciation, no respect, no love—she now attempts in one final, and tragically futile, gesture, to exchange her life-story into sustenance for her ailing son. Where the two mothers she has known, Mag Smith and Mrs. Bellmont, exchanged the labor of their child (Frado) to improve their own lives, she, a more "natural" mother, will exchange her labor to help her child—which is where the labors of her readers come into play.

Although her book failed to save the life of her ailing child, it can, given the proper reception by her readers, exchange her view of intertwined, embodied human be-ing for the prevailing Western view that isolates, debases, and discounts the body. For Frado, as her text makes quite clear, without a body would be no-body—nothing at all. Take away what happens to her body and nothing of the text is left. Like all the rest of us, who are so keen to deny it, Frado is a body-self. Without question she would have preferred to know life differently and not to have suffered for her racialized embodiment. For who among us would choose to work ourselves to death, or suffer beatings, deprivations, and illness as she did? But that she did experience these physical hardships revealed to her truths about human be-ing to which we more privileged readers are blind. Like her contemporaries, the fugitive slave narrators, Harriet Wilson was no professional philosopher. Her prose is not infused with abstract arguments or buttressed by learned reasoning. She does not prove Hegel wrong with an elo-quent display of irrefutable logic. She simply wrote what she knew. And what she knew, as did so many other nineteenth-century African Americans, was the body. On my view, therefore, we do not give this novel the reading it deserves unless we understand it as a book about the body-self. But to say that *Our Nig* is about the body-self is also to claim that it, like Douglass's narratives, is a cri-tique of liberal humanism. In the weak sense it is a critique simply in its attack on the so-called Christian household of the comfortably middle-class Bellmonts and on the economic system that makes it nearly impossible, even in the so-called free states, for poor people to enter the middle class. In the strong sense it is a critique in its insistence on the centrality of embodiment to the human condition and its revelation that the wealth of the bourgeoisie depends upon and is produced by the bodily effort of the working poor.[43]

It is no accident that this novel begins with a conventionally sentimental de-scription of Frado's mother, Mag Smith, who is portrayed as a young girl "walk[ing] with downcast eyes and heavy heart" (5). Behind this passage, we can almost see the allegorical painting this verbal description is meant to evoke—silently but urgently admonishing its girlish viewers to protect their chastity or risk destruction. Foolishly, what this orphaned and impoverished girl has dared to imagine on the cusp of womanhood is a life of "ease and plenty" (Wilson 1859, 5). Hoping for release from poverty and drudgery, she has fatally given herself to a well-to-do (presumably white)[44] man without securing his le-gal protection. When she has a child out of wedlock (who dies shortly after birth), she is further driven to the margins of society. There she lives in a hovel, struggling with recent immigrants for the few scraps of wages their untrained labor could garner them from an unfeeling petit-bourgeoisie. During this time, a hard-working African man notices her plight and befriends her. As her fortunes continue to languish, he finally convinces her to marry him. The text is quite clear on what he is able to provide his new wife—that is, "a more comfortable dwelling, diet, and apparel" (14). In short, his (black) body-self has relieved her (white) body of the pains of poverty; she now has a place to live, food to eat, and clothes to wear. Neither does the text remain silent about Mag's motives. Once Jim becomes ill with consumption, Mag dutifully nurses him but does so merely "to subserve her own comfort" (15). It is not losing her husband that she fears; it is reverting to a state of hopeless poverty. After his death, she returns to her hovel with their two children and her husband's former partner, Seth Shipley, who has taken a proprietary interest in her. When work disappears again, they slip back into indigence, for even though Mag "toiled and suffered," she cannot earn enough to support her family (16). Finally, out of desperation, Seth and Mag conclude that they must give her two children away though Mag thinks no one will want the "black devils" (16). In this estimation she is proved wrong, as Mrs. Bellmont, after initially resisting Frado's presence in her household, determines to put her to good use. Although Mag has called Mrs. Bellmont a "she-devil" (22), this is the person with whom she and Seth resolve to leave Frado. There they deposit her without explanation, never to return. What thus begins as an account of the mother's bodily suffering becomes an account of the daughter's bodily torment—literally at the hands of yet another (but this time a surrogate) mother.

In this bizarre exchange, where Frado is given away by her biological mother so that she and her new husband can leave town in search of economic security for themselves, Wilson seems to turn the plot of slave narratives on its head.[45] What slave mother would have, even if she could have, given her child away to whites in an informal but apparently binding indenture that is designed not to help the child but to improve her own fortunes?[46] In leaving her daughter with Mrs. Bellmont, this fallen white woman, who has twice been rescued by a black man, behaves more like the master than the mother. But Mag does not sell her offspring into servitude as a white master likely would have; she gives her up in the hope that having one fewer mouth to feed will allow her and her husband to escape wrenching poverty. In so doing, the natural mother (a white person) is shown to be "unnatural."[47] Thus the only party to enjoy positive economic gain from this transaction is the aptly named she-devil (yet another "unnatural" white mother).[48] The question must then be raised as to why Mrs. Bellmont so despises this young girl who will enrich her household and purchase with her own labors unlimited free time for her mistress. What is it that inspires Mrs. Bellmont to such hatred? Although it is never mentioned, it must be a form of sexual jealousy, for Frado, as will become typical of many nineteenth- and early twentieth-century African American heroines, is "a beautiful mulatto, with long, curly black hair" and "handsome, roguish eyes" that sparkle in a sign of her virtually unstoppable high spirits (17). It is, moreover, significant to my argument that Mrs. Bellmont cuts off Frado's curls (70) and forbids her from protecting herself from the harsh sunlight, no matter how hot the day (39). In so doing she is intent upon distinguishing this light-skinned mulatto from her own daughter. (Something similar happens to Louisa Picquet, who has her hair cut short by her master because he thought it was prettier than his daughter's hair [Picquet 1861, 17].)[49] It is also significant that three of the Bellmont men—the father, James, and Jack—pay Frado particular attention and do the best they can in a repressive matriarchal regime to offer her some gestures of compassion. Finally, it is significant that the two Bellmont women who offer Frado kindness—the maiden Aunt Abby and the invalid daughter Jane—would hardly be threatened by Frado's sexuality. Aunt Abby seems to be beyond sex and Jane, while she insists on marrying a man against her mother's wishes, seems to be too frail to worry about sexual competition. It is only the spiteful virago, Mrs. Bellmont, and her equally vile daughter Mary who seem to take untoward, sadistic pleasure in brutalizing this young servant girl. Why, then, since she so improves their lives at the cost of her own, would they beat her if not from some sort of misplaced (and/or displaced) sexual envy?[50] While Wilson could bring herself to fictionalize her white mother's sexual degradation—which itself was apparently born of a misdirected and naive ambition to remove herself from poverty—she seems not to have been able to describe her own, whether it was a case of actual sexual misuse or simply being punished for being an attractive and thus threatening sexual presence in the Bellmont household.[51] We should not expect her to describe what happened. She as much tells us that she cannot when she says in her Preface that she has intentionally left out those details that would be likely to "provoke shame in our good anti-slavery friends at home" (n. p.). Although she has omitted specific reference to sexual relations or sexual tensions, she has, I believe, used the metaphor of work as a stand-in for sex. On my argument, then, work functions here to reinstate the importance of the body-self and as a fairly conventional nineteenth-century substitute for the sexualized woman's body. It is Jack, after all, who first takes Frado to her bedroom and thus introduces her to her first degradation—the sleeping quarters in the attic that are so restricted that Jack remarks to his family that "the child would soon outgrow" them (27). He notices, in other words, that she will soon enough become a pubescent girl. And it is Jack who intervenes on her behalf when Mary tells lies about her (35–37). It is not necessary to my argument that Frado be sexually abused; it is enough that she be *seen* as a potential sexual threat by the white women in the novel. Because of their love of material goods, Mrs. Bellmont and her daughter do not wish Frado to leave, for her presence will increase their worth. But if she is to stay, her disruptive black female body must be made both harmless and useful.

Thus, the body that will bring the family relief from an extraordinary range of labors is early instructed in its inferior status as Frado is introduced to her cell-like sleeping quarters. In contrast to the "nicely furnished rooms" that the Bellmonts use, her room is "an unfinished chamber over the kitchen" (27). Although she entertains rebellious thoughts as she lies in bed waiting for her chamber to cool down enough so she can sleep, the next day the disciplining of her body begins in earnest.[52] She is instructed in exactly how to feed the hens and warned that if she does not follow instructions she will be whipped. She is taught how to herd the cows. Only then is she permitted to eat her meager breakfast of skimmed milk and bread crusts, which, humiliatingly, she must consume while standing up—even as the family sits down to breakfast in the dining room.[53] Although she is only six years old, she is also to be responsible for washing all the dishes. With few exceptions this "discipline" defines her life, as it is intended to do (29). In Foucauldian terms, Mrs. Bellmont is converting Frado's body-self into a docile, useful body, whose unpaid labors will enrich the Bellmont household. Neither can Frado protest her condition. Whenever Mrs. Bellmont catches the little girl crying, for example, she beats her with a strip of rawhide since she considers weeping to be a "symptom of discontent," which must be disciplined out of her new servant girl (30; see also 101).[54] The work Frado does brings no praise but instead is often accompanied by harsh words and "blows on her head" (30). Like other repressive regimes, that in the Bellmont household is designed to normalize the virtual enslavement of the least powerful inhabitant. In Althusserian terms, Frado is being trained to respond to the abject interpellation "Our Nig," someone whose body—by virtue of her color *and* her parent's poverty—effectively if not literally belongs to others.[55] This is not just a novel about racial divisions and prejudice; it is equally a novel about class differences. Mag Smith ends where she does because she is white and poor, and Frado ends where she does because she is black and poor.

Although Mrs. Bellmont does not believe that blacks can benefit from a formal education, her husband insists that Frado be allowed to attend school. In this instance he succeeds in challenging Mrs. Bellmont's formidable will and in doing so once again thematizes the connection in African American narrative between the gesture of compassion and the gestural acquisition of literacy.[56] At school Frado enjoys some relief from the harsh domestic world after the teacher admonishes the other children to be kind to the "poor and friendless" (32). Although Mary Bellmont continues to mistreat Frado, the other children at school find "Nig" quite lively and entertaining, and at home Jack consistently intervenes on her behalf with his mother. But the feelings of joy and comfort that Frado gains from being away from "home" (32)[57] or talking to the farm workers are constantly being undone by the disciplinary cruelties she receives at the hands of Mrs. Bellmont. Once Frado has learned to read and write, Mrs. Bellmont brings her schooling to an abrupt halt, feeling that this nine-year-old servant girl's "time and person" are her property and hers alone (41). And even though Jack, James, and even Aunt Abby try to intervene on Frado's behalf, the narrative makes it perfectly clear that in a very real sense, her "person" does indeed belong to Mrs. Bellmont, who beats and kicks her at will. As Frado matures, she is given additional tasks to perform for the family, until by the time she turns fourteen, she is doing virtually all the household tasks. And, if the truth be known, in the capitalist economy that marks the Bellmont household, each and every family member, however sympathetic to her plight, benefits from Frado's unceasing labors. The person who benefits the most, however, is the "angel" of the house, the she-devil Mrs. Bellmont. But, except for the visits she makes to her married children, what Mrs. Bellmont does with all the leisure time that Frado's work earns her remains unspoken. What happens to Frado's body, however, continues to mark the narrative, as she becomes more and more prone to illness—in part because of overwork and in part because she is not allowed even to wear shoes until after it has snowed (66). Excessive labor and beatings are not the only other abuse she is subjected to, for Mrs. Bellmont continues to berate, taunt, and threaten her almost unceasingly (66). Although the disciplinary regime is intensified as she matures, Frado's high spirits remain largely intact, as when she is discovered to be standing on the roof of the barn or tricking a particularly willful sheep into the stream. While Jack and James, Aunt

Abby and Jane, and even to a degree Mr. Bellmont offer some consolation to Frado, significantly, it is no human but her little dog Fido—a gift from Jack— who seems to listen to her most sympathetically and with the greatest under- standing (41–42).

I want to conclude this discussion, therefore, by claiming that in *Our Nig* Harriet Wilson models for us what Catherine Ross would call a new metaphor of reading (Ross 1987). On one hand, we can argue that by counterpoising ac- counts of the horrific physical suffering Frado endured at the Bellmonts— primarily at the hands of Mrs. Bellmont—with accounts of the compassionate sympathy she received from other members of the Bellmont household, Wilson instructs her readers how to respond to her pain-filled narrative. As Cynthia Davis has argued, Wilson might be said in this novel to be "speak[ing] of her own pain" in an authoritative (and authorizing) gesture by which "both pain and the black female body are redefined via powerful language as capable of both power and language" (Davis 1993, 399).[58] By including in her text many in- stances of human compassion, gestures that serve to reduce if not eliminate her pain, Wilson does seem to invite us to reach out to her in a similar fashion. But, as readers, we are silently admonished to do more than the Bellmonts have done. We must go beyond James's and Aunt Abby's Christian homilies.[59] We must act to end Frado's physical, and not just her spiritual, suffering. This in- junction is echoed in the Appendix, where one of Wilson's character witnesses, Margaretta Thorn, calls upon the friends of African Americans to "lend a *help- ing hand*, and assist our sister, not in giving, but in *buying a book*" (Wilson 1859, 140; emphasis added).[60] Wilson makes clear in her Preface that she has written "these crude narrations" in hopes of finding a way to support herself and her sick child; of her African American readers in particular, she asks "patron- age, hoping they will not condemn this attempt of their sister to be erudite" but support and defend her in her effort to improve her lot (n. p.). Clearly, it is com- passion she is after—an efficacious compassion that will manifest itself, as Thorn puts it, in the pragmatic act of "buying a book" and in understanding her travails. Although twentieth-century readers no longer have the opportunity to help her financially, we can still rally around her, in my new metaphor of read- ing, by giving her a hand—that is, by reaching out across time and understand- ing her novel in the fullest Gadamerian sense of internalizing it and applying its insights to our own lives. As I have indicated, for Gadamer, understanding, in- terpretation, and application are all of a piece.[61] The act of interpretation there- fore might be said to thematize, or to foreground, the act of understanding. But each involves the other, just as each involves application. Thus understanding *is* interpretation *is* application (see Gadamer 1989, 307–11). For Gadamer, then, the problem of application is the central problem of hermeneutics—the problem I wish now to address as it pertains to *Our Nig*.

It is my argument that Frado/Wilson asks us to go further than either James or Abby was able to go in helping her, as both were unable to see beyond their own horizon of understanding. That is to say, although their impulse to help Frado was a positive one, their Christian prejudices blinded them to Frado's different understanding of life and its meaning. I take the concepts of horizon and prejudices also from Gadamer. Without belaboring too much the details of his complex argument on the nature of philosophical hermeneutics, let me simply summarize his ideas as they pertain to my discussion of this novel. In describing the phenomenon of understanding, Gadamer uses the metaphoric image of a horizon, by which he means to suggest the limitations on our understanding and the possibility of moving beyond these limitations (Gadamer 1989, 302). For Gadamer, as for Heidegger, we are able to understand a text at all because we bring to the interpretive experience a pre-understanding of its meaning, what Gadamer calls our "prejudices," a term he attempts here to rehabilitate from the disgrace it has known since the Enlightenment (Gadamer 1989, 270–85). Although some of these prejudices are indeed to be rejected as disenabling because they interfere with understanding, others are to be embraced and utilized as enabling or productive as they make possible the act of understanding itself (298–99).[62] Gadamer describes as a horizon the historical differences between contemporary reader and traditionary text that limit the understanding in any interpretive event. Thus both readers and texts can be said to have a horizon. And so, when readers attempt to understand a text that falls outside their immediate historical purview, they will understand some of it but fail to understand other aspects—as, of course, occurs in my own reading of these nineteenth-century narratives. When a relatively full understanding occurs, a "fusion of horizons" is said to take place (306–307). This is not to say that the historical differences have been overcome. Since all readers are in a Heideggerian sense "thrown pro-jects," overcoming history is an impossible task. But these differences can be used by well-intentioned readers to see their own prejudices in a new light. Much more respectful of traditionary texts than I, as a rule, could ever wish to be, Gadamer believes that the burden mostly falls to the reader to submit freely to the text's superior, time-proven, and well-deserved authority—which is exactly the burden I have accepted in this project (279–81).[63] The reader should, therefore, attempt to understand the traditionary text as much as possible on its own terms, even if doing so means temporarily suspending one's own fore-knowledge—suspending, that is, what Gadamer would consider one's disenabling prejudices—again, much as I have been trying to do.

While I do not here wish to critique Gadamer for being overly respectful of tradition, as I have done elsewhere,[64] I cannot proceed without at least mentioning the dangers to the disenfranchised of submitting themselves to the traditionary texts they are asked to read and respect unquestioningly. On my view, in these interpretive situations, what Gadamer would consider disenabling prejudices, we might consider enabling; that is, they are enabling in the sense that they help us to understand what it is we should resist in these texts.

But in this study I want to suggest how Gadamer can help us with Frado and her would-be mediators. If we treat Frado and her embodied experience as a kind of cultural text, we can see that both James and Aunt Abby make no effort to suspend their own disenabling Christian prejudices when they try to help her. The interpretive problem they unknowingly face is therefore not born of histori-

cal differences but of class and religious differences. Both James and Aunt
Abby are convinced of the righteousness and rightness of their Christian faith, a
faith that elevates the soul above the body, a faith that willingly accepts the need
for physical suffering if such suffering leads to spiritual healing and transcendence. They can literally afford to take this view because they do not have to
rely on the labors of their own bodies to provide themselves with shelter and
sustenance. To a large degree, in fact, they rely on Frado's labor. How, then,
could these two otherwise well-intentioned, devout, and economically privileged persons possibly hope to understand what Frado's body-self knows? Attending to this dilemma helps to answer one of the probing questions Barbara
White asks of the novel. "Why . . . is there so much emphasis on Frado's near
conversion to Christianity . . . when the [subject is] never resolved?" (White
1993, 22). If we treat Frado's near-conversion not in terms of *her* failure to become a Christian but instead as symbolic of the failure of well-to-do Christians
to understand her, I think we can resolve the issue. When the "pious" Mrs.
Bellmont makes it clear that she will not take Frado to church,[65] Aunt Abby
steps in and willingly takes this servant girl to the evening service. "Many of
less piety would scorn to present so doleful a figure," the narrative informs us,
since her beautiful hair has been shorn and she has been outfitted by the miserly
Mrs. Bellmont in only a "coarse gown and ancient bonnet. . . . But Aunt Abby
looked within. She saw a soul to save, and immortality of happiness to secure"
(Wilson 1859, 68–69). On the face of it, the narrative seems to be endorsing
Aunt Abby's more truly Christian proclivity to ignore Frado's appearance and
attend to her soul. But, unexpectedly, the narrative continues in a different vein
by asserting that Nig looks forward to these outings because they were "*such a
pleasant release from labor*" (69; emphasis added). Aunt Abby may think she is
saving Frado's soul; but Frado apparently sees her as saving her body from otherwise unremitting work.

For his part, James endorses his aunt's behavior, thinking that Frado bears
certain characteristics "which, *transformed and purified by the gospel*, would
make her worthy the esteem and friendship of the world" (69; emphasis added).
But James is doomed to an early, painful, and prolonged death—a drawn-out af-
fair during which he seems to play Eva to Frado's Topsy. "With all his bodily
suffering," the privileged but Christ-like white man remembers Frado and protects her as best he can from his mother's abuse (76). But as he is fixated on the
state of Frado's soul, he cannot see that his own selfish need for Frado's ministrations is wearing her out and ruining her health. Constantly called upon to
move him by James himself, Frado readily agrees to help her friend, with the result that not only does she work all day but she is frequently "deprived of her
rest at night" (76–77). Inevitably, as James's health deteriorates, so does
Frado's, until she is finally "reduced as to be unable to stand erect for any length
of time" (81–82). This is an extraordinary passage that should not be overlooked. Even this caring and compassionate man has the power—and apparently
the will—while he is on his deathbed to work Frado until she no longer has the
strength to stand. Although on my view he has not served his friend well in his

final days, from a Christian perspective he seems not to have served her particularly well either. For, once he dies, Frado is only interested in going to heaven if it means seeing James there; that she also would see Christ seems not to interest her (103). And, most assuredly, she has no interest in going if it means she will spend eternity with Mrs. Bellmont (104). James might have prayed for Frado, but apparently he has not saved her. Neither has he read her right. He reads her correctly in that she does desire and require compassionate attention, which he provides as best his prejudices permit him. But he fails to understand the cost to her own body that his bodily demands have made upon this girl who, though ill herself, wishes, in her turn, to provide him with the compassionate attention he requires. Frado may act like a Christian by intervening to reduce James's suffering, but it appears that this humble servant girl is more Christ than Christian, more Christ-like than James himself. Although it is true that James dies, he does not die in order to save her—and she seems not to have been saved. She, in contrast, dies trying to save him, though the full extent of her sacrifice is delayed for years. It is not his soul she strives to save, however, but his body-self. So even she is no Christ, and her actions must be understood in more secular terms. To put it in the terms of my argument, therefore, it is in and through the ongoing suffering of her own body-self that she understands our relatedness-to-others and to *being* itself—an understanding she applies by reaching out to her more privileged "master," though doing so hastens her own death.

Let me return to the claim made by Sánchez-Eppler that "[t]he tears of the reader are pledged in these sentimental stories as a means of rescuing the bodies of slaves" (1988, 36; 1993, 26). It is significant that the only person in Wilson's novel who responds to Frado's suffering by weeping is Frado herself (though Mr. Bellmont at one point does detect a tear welling up in Jack's eye [Wilson 1859, 36]), and without exception, when she is seen to cry she is punished for it—as when she first arrives at the Bellmonts and weeps "over her sad fate" (30) or when, upon learning that James is fatally ill, she is discovered to be weeping uncontrollably by Mrs. Bellmont (77). After James has died, Frado weeps once more as she secretly listens to the words of prayer and consolation offered the family by their clergyman. Returning to her work, she is sought out by the tireless Mrs. Bellmont and instructed to work yet more diligently. Bone-tired, ill, and deeply offended by this unwarranted reprimand, she lets the tears flow freely. To the she-devil this is nothing more than another "act of disobedience" that must be punished by applying the rawhide yet again to her young servant girl, who craves nothing more than "healing mercies" (101). Thus, no tears are shed for Frado among the Bellmonts, and I am not sure that tears are what Wilson wants from her readers. Sánchez-Eppler may be correct in arguing that the reader's tears are pledged to help the enslaved, but, then again, it seems to me that, rather than an emotional exchange, Wilson is after something more in the lines of an economic exchange. As I have suggested previously, just as she shows that the North is no different from the South in constructing its myth of domesticity on the backs of laboring black women, Harriet Wilson, with the publication of this autobiographical novel, quite literally asks her readers to pay for the suffering she has known. But in what coin are we asked to cancel this debt? As I have argued elsewhere of *Native Son*, *Our Nig* is, in Elaine Scarry's terms, an artifact. Working out of pain, working to end her pain, Harriet Wilson crafted this artifact as a public and durable expression of her bodily suffering.[66] Like the slave narratives, it is a dispatch sent from her body-self to our body-selves, a dispatch that reminds us of the reversibility of the flesh and calls to us to reciprocate in kind.

Clearly, then, it is time for someone else's body to do the work. And the work required of us as readers is threefold. First, it is the kind of work that earns us enough money to buy Wilson's book. Second, it is the interpretive work involved in understanding the centrality of embodiment to the human experience. For, on my view, Wilson's novel does not only call upon her readers to behave as the Christians they might claim to be. More radically, she calls upon us to recall the fact of our own human embodiment and thus recollect, by the example of Frado's body-self, our common relatedness-to-*being*.[67] Once we have done so, her novel implies, we must, finally and most important, work to end the suffering of Frado and those like her. Frado does not need our tears—though they may, indeed, be the body's first response to her suffering. Like Frederick Douglass and the other slave narrators, she too needs justice in the flesh, and she needs our action to achieve it. Having been betrayed and deserted by the scoundrel she marries, on a purely practical level she needs to be paid a living wage so she might support herself and her child. On a more philosophical level, she needs the kind of understanding that Gadamer describes, one that entails application, one that she herself has modeled for us. What does it mean for me to claim that understanding *Our Nig* entails application? In a practical sense it means what I have just laid out: It means Wilson's readers can truly be said to understand her text only if they act to end her misery. In a philosophical sense it means her readers can truly be said to understand her text only if they internalize her insights regarding the body's recollection of *being*. Thus does the philosophical understanding put in motion the practical understanding. Once we *understand* (in the Gadamerian sense) our interrelatedness with other body-selves, we cannot do anything else but move to end their suffering.[68]

In writing her pseudonymous slave narrative, Harriet Jacobs hopes to inspire a similar kind of active response in her female readers. Yet she has not written her narrative for monetary gain but, instead, "to arouse the women of the North" to a full understanding of the suffering caused by the enslavement of black women (Jacobs 1861, 1). In appealing to the implied bodies of her readers, however, Jacobs, in an antebellum gesture of *narrative couvade*, might be said to veil her body behind the discursive scrim of sentimentality. While she hopes to inspire revulsion of the institution of slavery by describing her master's unwelcome sexual advances and her own loss of chastity, she knows she risks inspiring revulsion of herself in doing so. Therefore, even though the problem of embodiment is as central to her narrative as it is to Wilson's novel, in the economics of the interpretive exchange that Jacobs seeks with her readers, she obviously feels she cannot afford to thematize the spectacle of her enslaved body. What she offers us, therefore, is the paradox of her body's absent presence—that is, her (body-)self.[69] In offering this paradox, she produces perhaps the founding text of proto-Gentility, a narrative tradition that relies on the body's tacit or unspoken recollection of *being*.

Harriet Jacobs ("Linda Brent")

Incidents in the Life of a Slave Girl, Written by Herself (1861)

If one were to come to Harriet Jacobs's autobiography straight from a reading of Prince's narrative and Wilson's novel, one would be struck immediately by the relative absence of the body in this 1861 account of female enslavement. Moving to *Incidents* from other female narratives would not be quite so striking a transition, however, as most of the other well-known female narrators did not speak the body or assert their own embodiment.[70] In *Louisa Picquet, The Octoroon*, for example, the ex-slave clearly would prefer to leave details of embodiment out of her text, but they are urged upon her and her readers by the prying insistence of her male interviewer, who plagues her for details of the beatings she received and the adulterous relations she has witnessed. Where she is content to relate that a Mr. Cook whipped her so she would not "forget another time" to go to his room at night, her abolitionist interviewer, the Methodist minister Hiram Mattison, insists on more graphic details—whether out of legitimate political necessity or his own prurient interest is not clear. Thus he inquires of her (and records their exchange almost as a Foucauldian examination or Althusserian interpellation),[71] "Well, how did he whip you?" To which she replies laconically, "With the cowhide." That this is not what he had in mind is clear from his next question, "Around your shoulders, or how?" Again Picquet replies laconically, "That day he did." Not hearing what he wants to hear, Mattison finally shows his hand in the next two questions he asks of this former slave, virtually forcing her to describe her physical humiliation. "How were you dressed—with thin clothes, or how? . . . Did he whip you hard, so as to raise marks?" (Picquet 1861, 12). Submitting to his interrogation, Picquet finally seems willing enough to give him the details he desires. Yes, she tells him, he always left marks—but then she proceeds to bombard him with details Mattison would, no doubt, consider beside the point. For example, she tells him about how Mr. Cook got drunk, how he gave her a lot of money, how she spent it on material for a new dress ("white, with a little pink leaf all over it"), how he wanted her to sew a button on his shirt, and, then, how he beat her. Although Mattison includes these *feminine* details, he will not be distracted by them in his *masculine* search for truth and asks of this beating if Mr. Cook had broken the skin. "Oh yes," she replies, "in a good many places. I don't believe he would whip me much worse, if I struck his wife or children" (15). But again taking refuge in silence, his "subject" refuses to elaborate.[72]

This refusal to elaborate also characterizes Harriet Jacobs's narrative, a refusal that suggests it was not only dangerous to be enslaved but dangerous to discuss the experience in any great physical detail if one were a woman.[73] I have already suggested the possibility that descriptions of work stand in for descriptions of sexual abuse in Wilson's autobiographical novel. Whether I am correct in this interpretation, detailed descriptions of the work they must do, as I also have mentioned, bring both Frado's and Mary Prince's body-self to narrative presence. But Jacobs does not even dare to describe in any great detail the work she does for Dr. Flint—and what she admits to is safely confined to the kind of domestic chores with which her intended readers could identify.[74] Although she acquires freedom through the extraordinary self-discipline she imposes on her body for nearly seven years, she is unwilling to allot it much narrative space. Valerie Smith offers a possible explanation for this narrative omission when she argues that "Jacobs's class affiliation, and the fact that she was subjected to relatively minor forms of abuse as a slave, enable her to locate a point of identification both with her readers and with the protagonists of sentimental fiction" (Smith 1987, 36).[75] In a very real sense, Jacobs attempts the impossible task of taking the body out of her text—of leaving her body-self out of the narrative account of her *Life*, an account specifically designed by its reluctant author to show women of the North how their Southern sisters in bondage were prevented from protecting their own virtue.

Mine is an argument that other critics would no doubt contest. Jean Fagan Yellin, for example, while noting that Sojourner Truth completely omits reference to her sexuality, argues that this "tabooed subject is central" to *Incidents in the Life of a Slave Girl* (Yellin 1989, 87). Sidonie Smith argues similarly that "Jacobs recognizes that only by speaking the unspeakable can she hope to bring the history of the slave woman's body before the body politic" (Smith 1993, 43). It is my argument that Jacobs, contrary to the introductory apology offered by Lydia Maria Child, did not withdraw the veil that concealed the "monstrous features" of slavery that afflicted the black woman's body-self (Jacobs 1861, 4). I intend to argue, against Smith's and Child's position, that Jacobs did not speak the sexualized woman's body. She certainly intimates what could occur to her body-self were she not to remain vigilant against Flint's improper, importunate, and unwanted sexual overtures—but she never says directly what would happen. Neither does she say what he wants, other than to tell us that he whispered "foul words" in her ear, corrupting her "young mind with unclean images" (27), constantly reminding her that, as she "belonged to him," he would and could force her "to submit to him" (28).[76] Make no mistake about my motives here: I do not need these details; neither do I, in contrast to Louisa Picquet's interlocutor, particularly want them. I do see their absence, however, as one way the ex-slaves—especially the female ones—negotiated the problem of embodiment in their narratives, a response that would have far-reaching narrative implications for the next two generations of African American writers, male and female alike.

Apparently Jacobs's readers did not either need or want these details, as

Child herself, for example, seems to believe they have already been provided. What the text fails to include, the readers (or at least, in this case, the editor) supply—telling us as much about themselves as the text tells us about Jacobs, in that, given the proper hints, these women *knew* (as do we) what Jacobs left out of her text.[77] Returning to Macherey, then, we could argue that these gaps in the significantly named *Incidents in the Life of a Slave Girl* reveal the limits of the very ideology from which it would distance itself—the same ideology that has produced the text we read. Because, as Terry Eagleton puts it, a text might be described as "ideologically *forbidden* to say certain things," it falls to the reader (or critic) to make it speak (Eagleton 1976, 35; emphasis added). On one hand, we can argue, then, that Jacobs wittingly leaves out the prurient details in the full knowledge that her otherwise "careless" readers will supply them.[78] On the other, we can argue that even had she wanted to include these details (which she clearly did not, as her prefatory matter makes clear), the ideologies that have shaped both herself and her text forbid her to name them. The dominant or hegemonic discourse from which Jacobs's text emerges is the capitalist, liberal humanist, Christian, and bourgeois ideology of mid-nineteenth-century America. The counter-hegemonic discourses that give it shape—persuasive and domineering in their own right within their own circles of influence—are the discourses of the abolitionist movement and the myth of domesticity (this last so influential one might call it hegemonic).[79] Both discourses had their own literary form (the slave narrative and the sentimental novel, respectively); both discourses mark the production of Jacobs's text; and both discourses (as several critics have argued before me)[80] are modified by the work each is expected to do in the presence of the other in this text. Thus Jacobs, utilizing the conventions of abolitionist discourse, can describe the disruptive influence of slavery on her family and end her modified version of a sentimental novel with the assertion that it does not end in the conventional way, with marriage, but with freedom— that is, with the (male) slave narrative's ending (201). Conversely, utilizing the conventions of sentimentality and domesticity, Jacobs can structure her slave narrative less around herself and her heroic escape (which would be conventional in a male slave narrative) and more around her family and her attempts to rescue her children.[81] For Jacobs, escaping slavery, paradoxically enough, primarily involves staying at home, sequestered in the arms of domesticity—that is, hidden in her grandmother's garret.

And the discourse of sentimentality seems to carry the day when it comes to questions of Jacobs's describing the sexual abuse to which she was subjected. Where the male slave narrators describe in detail what happens to slave women, Jacobs, like others of her sex, does not. The strict conventions of sentimentality—and the contract she has made with her intended female readers—prevent her from talking about her female body as anything other than the unwilling recipient of her master's own vile *discourse*. Thus, on her accounting, the master's unwelcome sexual advances become *whispers* and secret *notes*, while sexual relations between blacks and whites are transmuted into discursive phrases that are virtually limited to the fact of parentage. Of the kind mistress who, while still single, tried unsuccessfully to manumit her slaves, Jacobs reports, for example, that, after this woman's marriage, one of her young slave girls becomes a *"mother*; and, when the slaveholder's wife looked at the babe, she wept bitterly"—knowing that her husband had impregnated the girl (Jacobs 1861, 51; emphasis added). Of the white woman who has unsanctioned sex with her father's slave, Jacobs reports that this "daughter had selected one of the meanest slaves on his plantation to be the *father of his first grandchild*"—a grandchild who, like others born in similar circumstances, would have been immediately put to death in order to protect the family's name and reputation (52; emphasis added). Of her own decision to establish a sexual relationship with Mr. Sands, Jacobs says she "shuddered to think of being the *mother* of children that should be owned by my old tyrant" (55; emphasis added). Legally, of course, any children she might have would belong to Flint and his daughter, but at least she would have the comfort of knowing that, if past patterns held, he would be less likely to sell her babies if they had been fathered by someone else. Feeling she simply has no choice in the matter, she finally takes a "headlong plunge" but does not say into what she plunged except that it is an "abyss" (55, 53). Apparently made pregnant by Sands, although the text does not report the event that would have occasioned her pregnancy, she confesses to us that she had wished in those agonizing months to "confess" to her grandmother that she "was no longer worthy of her love; but I could not utter the dreaded words"—neither, of course, has she uttered them to us (56). Finally, when Flint informs her that the cottage he has been building for her is nearly ready, she replies, "I will never go there. In a few months I shall be a *mother*" (56; emphasis added). Thus she announces her fallen state to him and to her readers by announcing her impending motherhood—and confirms it by documenting the birth of her two children.

Her children thus become not only her socially sanctioned motive for escaping slavery and, paradoxically, for delaying her escape (so that she might effect their freedom, too) but also the displaced sign and symbol of her own sexuality. The spectacle of a pregnant woman's body and that of her live offspring have long stood in the West as signs and symbols of an unmarried woman's sinful fall from both heavenly and social grace, so Jacobs's nineteenth-century readers would have had no trouble understanding what she left unspoken.[82] But just so there is no mistake about what the births of her children are intended to represent, she surrounds these events with supplementary explanations that "[t]he slave girl is raised in an atmosphere of licentiousness and fear. The lash and the foul talk of her master and his sons are her teachers" (Jacobs 1861, 51). She freely admits that Flint had done his best to corrupt her imagination with "foul images" so that she, like others, had become "prematurely knowing, concerning the evil ways of the world" (54). She admits that what she has done in seeking out Sands, she did quite intentionally (54). She invokes the rhetoric of sentimental fiction to gain pity for a "poor desolate slave girl" whose future has been blighted by "the powerful grasp of the demon Slavery" (54). She asks her privileged, protected, and "virtuous" readers to pity and pardon her, but warns them that they have not had the kinds of experiences that would allow them to under-

stand why she did what she did (55). She knows she has done wrong: "No one
can feel it more sensibly than I do. The painful and humiliating memory will
haunt me to my dying day. Still, in looking back, calmly, on the events of my
life, I feel that the slave woman ought not to be judged by the same standards as
others" (55–56). Thus she has called on her readers' common fears of being
sexually victimized, even as she distinguishes her own experience from theirs.
John Ernest has argued that, given the differences that divide her from her readers, Jacobs "cannot hope to have any readers actively value her 'standpoint'";
she must therefore "work towards a fundamental breakthrough in the ways in
which knowledge about this field is grounded and constructed" (Ernest 1995,
98). She achieves this, Ernest continues, through indirection: "By saying indirectly that which she cannot communicate directly, Jacobs deflects the reader's
attempt to acquire knowledge from her text; she disrupts the subject/object dy-
namic of the gaze, and locks eyes, if only momentarily, in a quiet glance of
mutual understanding" (Ernest 1995, 98). "In the silent reciprocity of locked
eyes, Jacobs could speak through the stories she tells and, yet more powerfully,
through those untold and untellable stories she implicitly draws from her readers" (99). Ernest calls Jacobs's narrative strategy a form of "*deferred* discourse,"
whereby she postpones, through indirection, what her readers are not at first capable of comprehending (98). Once they have learned to see themselves and
their world differently, she and they, in Ernest's metaphor, can lock eyes "to
begin the mutual task of re-forming knowledge, discourse, and community"
(107).

I want to pursue this line of thinking in a different direction, supplementing
rather than challenging Ernest's interpretation. I suggest that while Jacobs's discourse is indeed deferred, her body symbolizes the paradox at the heart of this
and other slave narratives—that is, how to maintain what Harry Berger has
called the "order of the body" within the "order of texts" (Berger 1987, 147). In
"Bodies and Texts," Berger distinguishes between what he identifies as "two
hypothetical orders of communication and semiosis—one centered on speaker
and hearer, the other on reader and writer" (147). The first, the order of the
body, transmits all its communications through "the body and its extensions,
while in the second, all messages are abstracted from the body and reconstructed
in graphic media so they can pass through written channels" (147). Speech belongs to the order of the body; print belongs to the order of texts. Writing falls
somewhere in between. Moving from speech, through writing, to print (and beyond, in hyperspace) can be viewed as extending the body into the world, even
as the communication itself becomes "progressively *abstracted* from it" (149).
Each mode of communication has its advantages and disadvantages. For my
purposes I want to examine, very briefly, what the fugitive slaves (thought they)
had to gain or lose by using speech or print to make their abolitionist points.
Public speaking, as Frederick Douglass soon discovered, carried the built-in (but
ultimately specious) authority of what Derrida has called the "metaphysics of
presence" (Derrida 1967, 23), which, as Jonathan Culler succinctly explains it,
"locates truth in what is immediately present to consciousness with as little me-

diation as possible" (Culler 1975, 132).[83] To this way of thinking, language, when spoken, is transparent—a window to pure consciousness and thus to truth itself. Speech therefore carries more authority than writing because the person speaking is thought to be present in the words. To put it differently, the speaker is thought to be invested, by his or her very presence, with the power to control the meaning of the words. It follows from this reasoning that no interpretation would be required of the listeners, as all meaning would be made immediately clear by the speaker. Writing, in this system, is regarded as a debased form of speech since its meaning is less certain, more open to interpretation in the absence of the author (speaker).[84] That Douglass's physique and physiognomy worked effectively to reinforce the authority of what he said in the minds of his listeners, I have already suggested. But because public speaking in the nineteenth century was strictly a local phenomenon, it would have taken enormous effort to reach large numbers of people (an effort Douglass apparently thought worthwhile, as he was a regular on the abolitionist traveling lecture circuit). Print, on the other hand, would and did ensure a larger audience for the fugitive slaves,[85] but it would have to be a *reading* audience and readers are notorious for finding their own meaning in texts, no matter how authoritatively they are written. Thus what the fugitive slave gained in numbers, he or she—to all appearances—lost in control. In what Derrida would regard as a futile (and entirely misguided) attempt to maintain interpretive control by retaining the authority vested in the speaking body,[86] the fugitive slaves and their interfering editors consistently invoked the narrator's body in the forematter that preceded the texts and the testimonials that were appended to them. Thus, all the slave narrators, to one degree or another, rely on the speaking body to give their words weight and authority. As I have discussed, many of the narratives are accompanied by affidavits that testify to the real (that is to say, embodied) existence of the author-narrator, whose existence precedes the text and authorizes it.[87] Many are printed with the slave's likeness and signature. If a real person, an ex-slave, has written (or narrated) the events contained within the text, the affidavits and signatures imply, the narrative can be believed. Many narratives are also quick to claim that they are providing the reader with the plain, unadorned truth—promising, in effect, to engage in no fictionalizing or philosophizing that might cast doubt on the authenticity and accuracy of the document in question. In so doing, these narratives attempt to pass themselves off as transparent, unmediated—and therefore utterly truthful—accounts of slavery. In short, they are invoking the metaphysics of presence with a thoroughness seldom seen in literature, which ordinarily—if only tacitly—accepts the inevitability of its own purportedly debased status. To return to Berger, the slave narrators and their editors employ a carefully chosen combination of rhetorical, pictorial, and autographic strategies to ensure that the order of the body will extend into the order of the text. In a gesture we might describe as inversely Derridean, they try to give the illusion of presence to textuality.

Jacobs's narrative certainly seems to fit this profile. The author opens her text with the assertion, "Reader, be assured this narrative is no fiction" (Jacobs

1861, 1). With this statement Jacobs claims not only truthfulness for her account but also immediacy, as she gives the appearance of being able to address the reader directly, in person. The narrative is nestled between the authorizing testimonials of the well-known abolitionists Lydia Maria Child and Amy Post, both of whom claim to know the author personally. Although it carries no likeness of the author, the title page of the first edition carries the additional authorizing claim that it has been "Written by Herself." Yet Jacobs wrote her narrative under the pseudonym Linda Brent. And even though the burden of her argument against slavery relies on readers' sharing her horror that young girls like herself were doomed to sexual abuse, Jacobs's own body is hardly to be seen. In short, in *Incidents in the Life of a Slave Girl*, the body is the absent signifier, the meaning of which, in true Derridean fashion, is endlessly deferred. Echoing Derrida yet again, we might say that like all signifiers, the body in *Incidents* is but a *trace*—the term Derrida uses to suggest the fact that language knows only difference and deferral, what he calls *différance*. There is no originating moment or location in language; there are only traces.[88] This, it seems to me, is exactly analogous to what *Incidents* tells us of the slave woman's body—as signifier and as signified. Linguistically speaking, Jacobs's body, like language itself, knows only difference and deferral—*différance*. It is and it means only in that it is not—not a white woman's privileged female body, not a white man's privileged male body, not a black man's male body. This is the burden of Jacobs's argument, to show what can happen to a black woman's body (as signified) because of what it is not (as signifier). Unmoored as a material body from what could ground it, provide it with origins, safety, and certainty—that is, the myth of true womanhood—her body carries within itself the *trace* of what might have been but never was.

To put it differently, Jacobs's material body functions simultaneously as signified and as signifier. In its materiality it is what the signifier points to, represents, and stands in for—it is the signified. But at the same time, by virtue of this same materiality, it also conveys meaning itself. That is to say, it also functions as a signifier. To see a slave woman like Harriet Jacobs is to know her. She is "known" by her color to be a slave, a correct enough deduction. But she is also "known" by her appearance to be deserving of enslavement and naturally licentious, an incorrect deduction. Because Jacobs is known in these ways by her visible body, if she is to evade the construction (or interpellation) of herself as slave and licentious woman, she must make her material body invisible, to owner and reader alike. In her efforts to make her material body (as the signified) invisible to her owner (the man who would name her his whore), she hides in her grandmother's garret for seven years and sends out misleading missives that seem to place her body safely in the North. She would thus make her body doubly (or even triply) absent. In her efforts to remove the material body (still as the signified) from the narrative that she is writing for Northern white female readers, Jacobs would convert her own body into text, until, as Foreman intimates (1990), all that is left of it is discourse—paradoxically, a signifier without a signified. In a move that would have impressed twentieth-century poststructuralists, this ex-slave, who says of her efforts that "it would have been more pleasant to me to have been silent about my own history" (1), attempts to make true what will become Barthes's as yet unspoken assertion: "the *I* that writes the text is never, itself, anything more than a paper *I*" (Barthes 1971, 79). Or, as he put it in an earlier essay, "Linguistically, the author is never more than the instance writing, just as *I* is nothing other than the instance saying *I*: language knows a 'subject,' not a 'person,' and this subject, empty outside of the very enunciation which defines it, suffices to make language 'hold together,' suffices, that is to say, to exhaust it" (Barthes 1968, 145). Thus, in order to claim subjectivity for herself, Jacobs would relinquish her person. No body, of course, can appear in a text as the signified; its materiality can only be represented by other signifiers. But, in stark contrast to *The History of Mary Prince* and *Our Nig*, *Incidents in the Life of a Slave Girl*, as I have argued, does not thematize the body as body. In a narrative that purports to be about the body, the body is remarkably absent. To return to my Derridean claim, Jacobs would convert her material body-self wholly into a linguistic *trace*.[89] But—to shift from Derrida through Heidegger back to Merleau-Ponty—the body will not be erased. Perhaps it can be written *sous rature* (that is, under erasure), but, as a transcendental signifier, it can not be erased. Neither can what the body knows be lost to us forever. As Equiano recognized, what the body knows cannot be rubbed out. And the subject, though constructed in language, is nevertheless, contrary to metaphysical and poststructuralist principles, always already embodied. This is my metaphysical claim—and, on my argument, the claim of the slave narratives, even the ones that seem (or try) to deny it. Thus the problem of embodiment is the problem of the slave narratives, and this problem is nowhere more evident as a problem than in Jacobs's narrative.

Harriet Jacobs, writing under the tutelage of her friend and sponsor Lydia Maria Child and wresting her story from Harriet Beecher Stowe, a woman she has come to distrust, is faced with the paradoxical situation of having to make her own anti-slavery argument by talking about her sexualized body, the very subject she does not want to discuss. The more her argument requires the body, the more it recedes from view—in the text and in the story. Once her body is hidden from the appropriative, scopophilic gaze of Dr. Flint, however, it apparently loses its representative potential as a sexualized body and can therefore be safely portrayed as a suffering body—that is, a body in pain. Although, as I have already shown, Jacobs has been careful to represent all sexual activity that occurred between whites and slaves only obliquely by reference to parentage and offspring, she has been much more straightforward in her accounts of the pain and suffering experienced by other slaves, most particularly in the chapter called "Sketches of Neighboring Slaveholders" (46–52).[90] She has described her Uncle Benjamin's failed bid for freedom and the subsequent physical punishment that he suffered. She has also admitted that some slave men "have been so brutalized by the lash" that they will permit "their masters free access to their wives and daughters" (as though they might have the opportunity to prevent such abuse) (44). She also has not been entirely silent on the subject of her own punishments. She documents, for example, how Flint struck her for the first time when he learned from her that she loved another slave (39). After the birth of her son, she admits that she was quite ill for nearly a year, a time during which "there was scarcely a day when I was free from chills and fever" (61). And she reports that Flint, upon learning she is expecting a second child, cuts off all her beautiful hair and a few months previously, in another fit of anger, had thrown her down the stairs (77). On the surface it would appear that she feels she can safely relate these forms of physical punishment because they are not forms of sexual abuse. But, of course, it is also possible to read them all as a doubly perverted form of "spousal" abuse, arguing that Flint strikes her out of sexual jealousy when faced with the fact that she loves a black man and has had sex with another white man. Her body is also the agent of her rebellion, although she cannot speak its primary role in this insurrection. Recounting how it is that she came to have a sexual liaison with Mr. Sands, she tells her readers forthrightly, "I knew what I did, and I did it with deliberate calculation" (54). What she does not—and apparently cannot—say in so many words is that she had sexual intercourse with Sands. She is prevented from speaking by the formal choice she has made to participate in the discourse of sentimental fiction. She is prevented by the modesty that, by all nineteenth-century hegemonic accounts, marks the female sex. She is also prevented, perhaps, by a desire to silence what has already been spoken in too many nineteenth-century "anthropologies," pro-slavery tracts, and male slave narratives.

She does, however, tell us in some detail what it was like for her body to spend nearly seven years in her grandmother's garret, her "Loophole of Retreat" (114). I argue that, in a modified version of what Mary Prince and Harriet Wilson did before her, Jacobs finally gives a full accounting of the work she did— not the obligatory work she did for her tormentor but the freely chosen and ennobling work she did to save herself and her children. Hiding her body in the garret gives her permission, as it were, to bring her body to narrative presence. Once she is actively engaged in securing her own and her children's freedom, no longer need she be ashamed on anybody's terms to talk about her body-self.[91] Thus she tells us of her hiding place, "The air was stifling; the darkness total" (114). While she could rest "quite comfortably on one side," the slope to the room "was so sudden that I could not turn on the other without hitting the roof" (114). She says that she longed to see the faces of her children "but there was no hole, no crack," through which she could gaze (114). She found the dark "oppressive" and reports that it "seemed horrible to sit or lie in a cramped position day after day, without one gleam of light." Even so, she assures us, "I would have chosen this, rather than my lot as a slave, though white people considered it an easy one; and it was so compared with the fate of others" (114). She then, astonishingly, enumerates in graphic detail what she never had experienced in slavery: "I was never cruelly over-worked; I was never lacerated with the whip from head to foot; I was never so beaten and bruised that I could not turn from one side to the other; I never had my heel-strings cut to prevent my running away; I was never chained to a log and forced to drag it about, while I toiled in the fields from morning till night; I was never branded with hot iron, or torn by bloodhounds" (114–15). On one hand, this litany of horrors is inclusive enough that it invokes by its very absence the real reason she fled: She was about to be sexually abused. On the other, one cannot assert a negative without invoking a positive: "I was never lacerated" paradoxically makes us see her being whipped—just as the body she tried to leave out of her text inevitably finds its way back in (if, in places, only through the efforts of her readers). Once she finds a gimlet and bores some breathing holes for herself, her physical conditions improve somewhat. But after that, for weeks she was "tormented by hundred of little red insects, fine as a needle's point, that pierced through my skin, and produced an intolerable burning" (115). In summer the heat is intolerable, as are the cold and damp in winter. The second winter of her confinement she becomes deathly ill, and she vacillates between trying to "be thankful for my little cell" and despairing that there is "no justice or mercy in the divine government" (123). Weakened from her months of imprisonment after she sneaks outside to communicate to Mr. Sands who, she has learned, is on his way to Washington, she is too weak to climb back into the garret. Her friends worry that she will be crippled for life as a result of her hiding and she confesses that, had it not been for her children, she would have been happy to die, "but, for their sakes, I was willing to bear on" (127). Looking back on the years she spent in the garret, she admits that "my body still suffers from the effects of that long imprisonment, to say nothing of my soul" (148). She also recounts that having been sequestered for nearly seven years, she became restless, confessing that she "had lived too long in bodily pain and anguish of spirit" (150). But her work— that of outwitting Flint—is very nearly over and shortly thereafter she escapes North on a ship. Before she leaves, however, she visits the garret one last time, only to discover that, on the cusp of liberty, "[i]ts desolate appearance" no longer had the power to "chill" her (155).

As miserable as she has been while entombed in the garret, she confesses to feeling terribly sad to leave "that old homestead, where I had been sheltered so long by dear old grandmother; where I had dreamed my first young dream of love; and where, after that had faded away, my children came to twine themselves so closely round my desolate heart" (155). She invokes here an image of human connectedness, by which we affirm our relatedness-to-*being*. Although she has found it difficult to speak the body, she finds it easy to speak what the body knows. Thus, we need not seek graphic evidence of what her body suffered if we are to learn what her body has to say. Others have noted the fact that while the male narrators decried the sexualized abuse to which the female slaves were subjected, they themselves were not above describing it in sometimes explicit detail. They have also noted the fact that such graphic accounts of abuse account for many of the gaps and silences in the narratives written by women. For the most part these critics explain the difference by arguing that the male narrators tried to elevate themselves to manhood on the lacerated backs of the women, whose victimization they described so graphically. No doubt there is considerable merit to such an explanation—even though, as I have myself been at pains to argue in this book, I do think the male narrators question both the liberal humanist and metaphysical grounds of "manhood" or (male) subjectivity. But, just as important, the male body-self is brought to narrative presence in many different ways, as I have suggested in my discussion of Douglass's first two autobiographies. But even in those cases where the body-self is most present, most obvious, there is a tension in the narratives born, I think, of certain Christian refusals to value the body as much as the soul, of the liberal humanistic refusal to value the body as much as the subject, of the metaphysical refusal to value the body as much as reason—of the West's refusal to value the black as much as the white. All four of these modalities of denying the body are learned, as they were, to a degree, by the fugitive slave narrators. But we all begin and end life as bodies. And even though virtually all our discursive systems deny it, we journey through life as bodies, which bear a primordial knowledge of human connectedness. This is the great gift of the slaves to ourselves. What the fugitive slaves and the freed slaves carried into the North and their narratives was the body's (*their* bodies') recollection of *being*. Sometimes, as with Equiano, Douglass, Prince, and Wilson, this recollection is thematized to such an extent that it is visible to the naked eye, if only we will believe what the texts themselves ask us to see. Sometimes, as with Jacobs, it is hidden and must be unconcealed by the most painstaking of efforts. But it is always already there.

NOTES

1. For discussion of some of the different expectations facing male and female slave narrators, see Foster (1985). On a related subject, see Tate (1992). For a comprehensive history of African American women, see Giddings (1984).

2. On the other hand, the physical characteristics of a strong and either presumably or demonstrably fertile black woman were an economic advantage to her white owners, who stood to profit by her (re)productivity. On this, see Carby (1987).

3. For a white woman, being perceived as having a body was tantamount to being seen as a whore. Michie reports, for example, that in England women who worked "inevitably made their bodies, as well as their work, public. The angel who left her house was, on some metaphysical level, seen by the more conservative elements of Victorian culture as a streetwalker" (Michie 1987, 31). On a related issue, see Gilman (1985–86; 1990).

4. Londa Schiebinger has written extensively on this subject, arguing that it was no coincidence that "anatomists focused attention on those parts of the body that were to become politically significant. When the French anatomist Marie-Geneviève-Charlotte Thiroux d'Arconville published drawings of the female skeleton in 1759, she portrayed the female skull as smaller than the male skull, and the female pelvis as larger than the male pelvis." But, on Schiebinger's view, this was not because anatomical renditions had become more realistic. Instead, "[t]he depiction of a smaller female skull was used to prove that women's intellectual capabilities were inferior to men's"—thus giving biological support to the widely held belief that women were not fit to participate in the world outside the home. Similarly, the depiction of a woman's outsized pelvis was intended "to prove that women were naturally destined for motherhood" and thus best

suited to remain in the domestic sphere (Schiebinger 1987, 42–43). This was a pattern of political-biological representation that proved irresistible to subsequent generations of anatomical illustrators. By the nineteenth century, "[a]natomists attempted to rank the sexes and races in a single, hierarchical chain of being according to the cranium and pelvis size. . . . In respect to skull size, the European male represented the fully developed human type, outranking the African male, the European female, and the African female" (Schiebinger 1989, 211). Thus, the same kind of politically influenced exaggerated disfigurations occurred in scientific and medical portraits of African Americans, American Indians, and other non-European groups; on this also see Gould (1981). "Scientific definitions of human 'nature' were thus used to justify the channeling of men and women (as well as whites and blacks) into vastly different social roles" (Schiebinger 1987, 72). Thomas Laqueur's findings support those of Schiebinger, as he writes that "no one was very interested in looking at the anatomical and concrete physiological differences between the sexes until such differences became politically important. It was not, for example, until 1797 that anyone bothered to reproduce a detailed female skeleton in an anatomy book so as to illustrate the difference from the male. Up to this time there had been one basic structure for the human body, the type of the male" (Laqueur 1987, 3–4). On the role of metaphor in science, see Stepan (1990), in which she reminds us that during "the nineteenth century . . . gender was found to be remarkably analogous to race, such that the scientist could use racial difference to explain gender difference, and vice versa" (Stepan 1990, 39). "Woman was in evolutionary terms, the 'conservative element' to the man's 'progressive,' preserving the more 'primitive' traits found in lower races, while the males of higher races led the way in new biological and cultural directions" (40). Given these intersections, Stepan is able to conclude that "[w]ithout the metaphor linking women and race . . . many of the data of women's bodies (length of limbs, width of pelvis, shape of skull, weight or structure of brain) would have lost their significance as signs of inferiority and would not have been gathered, recorded, and interpreted in the way they were" (48). For a more comprehensive study of the relationship between race and science, see Stepan (1982), in which she discusses, among other texts, Prichard's 1813 *Researches into the Physical History of Man* and Lawrence's 1819 *Lectures on Physiology, Zoology, and the Natural History of Man Delivered at the Royal College of Surgeons*.

5. For a comprehensive survey of the ways in which the "surrender of woman's reason to embodiment . . . contaminates her relationship to the word," see Sidonie Smith (1993, 15).

6. As part of her campaign to improve the condition of American women, in 1841 Catherine Beecher urged women to give up the practice of tight-lacing, warning them that as "long as it is the fashion to admire, as models of elegance, the wasp-like figures which are presented at the rooms of mantuamakers and milliners, there will be hundreds of foolish women, who will risk their lives and health to secure some resemblance to these deformities of the human frame" (Beecher 1841, 96). Fourteen years later, she published a survey in which she again warned the country that women's health was being imperiled by foolish behavior (Fishburn 1982, 12–13, 171–75).

7. For an account of how this "exposure" of the African American woman's body affected the writing of politically active antebellum Northern black women, see Peterson (1993, especially 192–200).

8. See Carby (1987, 25–27). For a graphic discussion of how the supposedly archetypal female African body (most particularly, the body of Saartjie Baartman or Sarah

Bartmann, the so-called Hottentot Venus) became virtually indistinguishable from that of the unclean, dangerous, and diseased prostitute in Victorian England, see Gilman (1985–86). See also Sidonie Smith, who argues that the "black female body served the slave system as both the ground upon which the patriarch satisfied his desire and the metaphorical ground upon which the slave owner asserted his cultural authority over the black male" (Smith 1993, 40). Given what I have said about the corset and bustle enhancing the size and angle of middle-class white women's buttocks, it is worth noting that what especially fascinated the Europeans and thus made Sarah Bartmann worthy of exhibition was her steatopygia, her exceptionally large buttocks, which were regarded as the visible physical sign not just of her pathological femaleness, but also of her primitiveness and racial inferiority. That African women were subjected to the normative gaze of white men and women is clear from this example. It also helps explain the disappearance of black bodies from much post-Reconstruction fiction. On the subject of how the working class commodified black bodies, see Lott (1993). On the subject of how the grotesque performed a representational purpose among the emergent bourgeoisie, see Stallybrass and White (1986). On the subject of the female grotesques as they appear in theory and literature, see Russo (1986). On the subject of black male sexuality in the nineteenth century and the myths surrounding it, see, for example, Jordan (1968). On all these subjects, see Hernton (1965; 1987). On the subject of how African American women have had their literature and their experiences co-opted and commodified by African American men and white feminists, see duCille (1994).

9. Foster goes so far as to argue that the popular image of the African slave woman as "sexual victim" was in part a consequence of the male slave narrators' rendition of them, claiming that, because of the prevailing literary and social attitudes of the nineteenth century, "most slave narratives stereotyped slave women as sexually exploited beings" (Foster 1994, xxx; see also 127–41).

10. Lott reminds us that if at this time "women were responsible for household order and spiritual hygiene, all that was dirty, disruptive, and disorderly was projected onto working-class women" (Lott 1993, 122). And Michie reports that in England, "[b]y the middle of the nineteenth century, physicians had constructed two entirely different bodies for working-class and leisure-class women" (Michie 1987, 30).

11. I have elected here to quote from the version of this speech that has been authenticated by Margaret Washington (1993) in her new edition of Sojourner Truth's 1850 *Narrative*. Readers can find Frances Gage's more familiar version ("Look at my arm! I have ploughed, and planted, and gathered into barns, and no man could head me! And a'n't I a woman?") in Guy-Sheftall (1995, 36). See also Yellin (1987, xxxi; 1989, 87).

12. See, for example, Carby (1987), Gates (1983), and Ernest (1995).

13. For a discussion of the symbiotic relationship between the mythic configurations of black and white women in the nineteenth century, see Christian (1980), Fishburn (1982), Gwin (1985a), and Carby (1987). For a comprehensive history of black and white women's multi-faceted relationship, see Fox-Genovese (1988). For a history of the role of black and white women in the anti-slavery moment, see Yellin (1989).

14. On the subject of domesticity, see Welter (1976).

15. Whether *Our Nig* should be treated as fiction or autobiography is a question raised by Barbara White in a recent genealogical essay that documents the real-life identity of the Bellmonts; see White (1993, especially 40–45). In his introductory essay to *Our Nig*, Gates treats it as a transitional work that bridges the gap in the nineteenth century between the established genre of African American autobiography and a newly

emergent tradition of African American fiction (Gates 1983, lii). Priscilla Wald calls it "a *narrative about* autobiography" (Wald 1995, 169). For a reading of it as satire, see Breau (1993).

16. Or, as Ernest puts it, "when we purchase this book, we fulfill, belatedly, the terms of its existence" (Ernest 1995, 55). On this, see also Baker, who has argued more generally that "[t]he nineteenth-century slave, in effect *publicly* sells his voice in order to secure *private* ownership of his voice-person" (Baker 1984, 50).

17. By this, I do not mean to suggest that Wilson is endorsing the metaphysical definition of self as subject. Instead, I would argue that Wilson, by devoting so much attention in her narrative to the body, is redefining the liberal humanist concept of the subject as a *body-self*.

18. For a contrary view of Jacobs, see Sidonie Smith (1993).

19. This was clearly not a concern of the Bohemian school of writers, as is clear, for example, from Claude McKay's sensual novels *Home to Harlem* (1928) and *Banjo* (1929), or Zora Neale Hurston's short stories, such as "Sweat" (1926) and "The Gilded Six-Bits" (1933).

20. According to Andrews, for many years the "slave narrators had worried publicly over their readers' distrust of them, but Jacobs was the first to acknowledge her distrust of the white reader as a brake on her candor" (Andrews 1986, 240–41). For a discussion of the competition between readers and writers that would lead to distrust on the part of writers, see Foster's 1993 essay, in which she takes Fox-Genovese (1988) to task for not believing (that is, trusting) Jacobs's descriptions of her own life.

21. Braxton argues, for example, that Jacobs's novel "combines the narrative pattern of the slave narrative genre with the conventional literary forms and stylistic devices of the 19th century domestic novel in an attempt to transform the so-called 'cult of true womanhood' and to persuade the women of the north to take a public stand against slavery, the most political issue of the day" (Braxton 1986, 384). Nudelman argues of *Incidents* that, "[w]hile sentimentality aspires to the unmediated exchange of felt experience, it relies structurally on the translation of marginal experience by a privileged and unimplicated author. Jacobs, telling her own story, must find ways to mediate its transmission. Emphasizing the distance between her experience and that of her readers, she critiques a sentimental model of communication that aspires to the expression of universal feeling" (Nudelman 1992, 961). See also Gates (1983), Valerie Smith (1987), Foreman (1990), Doriani (1991), Sánchez-Eppler (1993), and Wald (1995). While agreeing that *Our Nig* bears resemblance to sentimental fiction, Carby treats it as "an allegory of a slave narrative" (Carby 1987, 43).

22. For yet another recuperation of sentimental fiction, see Tompkins (1985). For an approach that combines historical, rhetorical, and ideological issues as they pertain to a process analysis of sentimental fiction, see Harris (1993), in which she includes a list of eight questions we might use to evaluate this literature. For a spirited—and influential—attack on the doleful consequences of sentimentalism on the American character, see Douglas (1977, 13), in which she asserts that "[i]n America, for economic and social reasons, Calvinism was largely defeated by an anti-intellectual sentimentalism purveyed by men and women whose victory did not achieve their finest goals; America lost its male-dominated theological tradition without gaining a comprehensive feminism or an adequately modernized religious sensibility."

23. See also Ross's study of this phenomenon, in which she detects two complementary patterns of metaphors: "reading is eating" and "reading is a ladder." Quoting from an

1877 description of fiction readers, Ross finds that

> [t]he up and down directions of the ladder are what bring into alignment such pairs of opposites as good/bad, progress/retrogression, virtue/depravity, healthy development/debility. If reading matter is food, then nourishing food such as the "spare diet of statistics" and "the simple beverage of plain narrative" are up on the ladder of up/down; sugar and "confectionery" are down, as are "poisoned stimulants." A reader with an "incessant craving" for fiction reading is under a spell. (Ross 1987, 149)

Ross also notes that "READING IS EATING has the advantage of being compatible with the orientational metaphor of the ladder, so that the two metaphoric systems are congruent and can be used together, as they are in the term 'elevated (or debased) reading taste'" (155). Examining the consequences of relying on these metaphors of reading, Ross concludes that "[w]ithin the conceptual frame provided by the metaphors of ladders and eating, it is easier to tell a story of active texts and passive readers. In this story, the text . . . is a thing to be swallowed. Because meaning is fixed in the text itself, all the reader can do is to swallow it whole and incorporate its content in altered form" (158). See also Johnson (1987) and Barrett (1995).

24. For a general discussion of why we cry under various circumstances, see Neu (1987).

25. For a critique of these ideas, see Barrett (1995).

26. In the account of slavery that Louisa Picquet narrated to the Reverend Hiram Mattison, she is much more reluctant than he to describe her personal experiences in detail. At various parts of her story, Mattison questions Picquet on details of her beatings and transcribes their exchange as an interview he is conducting—apparently resorting to this devise to disguise (perhaps even to himself) the prurient interest he takes in these sadomasochistic rituals. At one point the details are seemingly too much not only for Picquet but also for Mattison himself, however, as he is content to insert parenthetically into the text the information that here Mrs. Picquet "declines explaining further how he whipped her, though she had told our hostess where this was written; but it is too horrible and indelicate to be read in a civilized country" (Picquet 1861, 15). No such narrative modesty afflicts Mattison when Picquet's story is published, however, as he ends her story with a chapter titled "Slave-Burning, or the 'Barbarism of Slavery,'" which is a series of detailed eye-witness accounts of lynchings, none of which have anything directly to do with Picquet's own experiences. One can only imagine how Picquet herself might have felt to see these extraordinarily detailed accounts of physical mutilation and torture appended to her own more reserved account of the horrors of enslavement. To compare the difference between what a white male editor is willing to describe and what a black female author will report, one need only compare this seven and a half-page chapter written by Picquet's male interviewer with the bare statement made by Susie King Taylor on the subject. After the Civil War, while visiting the South, she writes, without further detail: "At Clarksdale, I saw a man hanged. It was a terrible sight, and I felt alarmed for my own safety down there. When I reached Memphis I found conditions of travel much better" (Taylor 1902, 74). For more discussion of Picquet's reluctance to detail the atrocities to which she was subjected, see below in this chapter. In an oft-cited description of the fugitive slave narratives, Robin Winks has called them "the pious pornography of their day, replete with horrific tales of whippings, sexual assaults, and explicit brutality, presumably dehumanized and fit for Nice Nellies to read precisely because they dealt with black, not white, men" (Winks 1969, vi).

27. Compare this with Elizabeth Keckley's account of the sale of a little slave boy who was literally "placed in the scales, and was sold, like the hogs, at so much per pound" (Keckley 1868, 28).

28. Delaney is legally free because in slavery the child followed the condition of the mother, and her mother was free.

29. For other accounts of a hard-working ex-slave, see the narratives of William Grimes (1855) and Venture Smith (1897).

30. William Wells Brown's *Clotel, or The President's Daughter* was published in London in 1853. For another candidate for the first novel to be published in the United States by a black person, see Gates's discussion of the fraudulent (i.e., fictionalized) *Narrative* of James Williams, which was published in 1838, after being dictated to John Greenleaf Whittier (Gates 1990, 57–59).

31. For Macherey, texts are by necessity both open and incomplete in that they are prevented from saying certain things by their relationship to ideology. On his view, "We always eventually find, at the edge of the text, the language of ideology, momentarily hidden, but eloquent by its very absence" (Macherey 1966, 60). Because a writer gives form to ideology in the fixed and determinate structure of the novel, readers, by detecting what is unspoken or absent in the novel, can see its ideological limits: "Thus the work cannot speak of the more or less complex opposition which structures it; though it is its expression and embodiment. In its every particle, the work *manifests*, uncovers, what it cannot say. This silence gives it life" (84).

32. On this subject, see also Barbara White (1993) and Wald (1995, 156–71). On a related issue, see Yarborough (1989).

33. Karla Holloway argues that, in contrast to the more open and dialogic *Iola Leroy*, "Wilson's largely monologic work subordinates the textual structure, the characters' voices, and the narrative to its economic intent, effectively making the economies of narrative spaces a primary metaphor in the novel" (Holloway 1993, 127). On this subject, see also Barbara White (1993, 33–34).

34. Ernest also takes Gates to task, claiming that "'the great evil in this book' is . . . the will to dominate, which feeds upon cultural and personal vulnerability in whatever form it takes"—a domineering will most clearly seen in Mrs. Bellmont (Ernest 1995, 71).

35. Dyer has argued that

[t]he rhetoric of capitalism insists that it is capital that makes things happen; capital has the magic property of growing, stimulating. What this conceals is the fact that it is human labour and, in the last instance, the labour of the body, that makes things happen. The body is a 'problem' because to recognise it fully would be to recognise it as the foundation of economic life; how we use and organise the capacities of our bodies *is* how we produce and reproduce life itself. (Dyer 1986, 138)

Furthermore, he continues, as a result of both "slavery and imperialism, black people have been the social group most clearly identified by and exploited for their bodily labour. Blacks thus became the most vivid reminders of the human body as labour in a society busily denying it. Representations of blacks then function as the site of *remembering and denying* the inescapability of the body in the economy" (138–39). See also Gordon (1995).

36. In his study of description, Michel Beaujour finds "a consistent affinity between description, allegory and the dream or vision (as literary genres). It follows from this that *description* may have a peculiar and even paradoxical relationship to the 'real' world of waking; conversely, there may not exist any compelling artistic reasons to describe (in

literature) the familiar and instrumental objects of daily life" (Beaujour 1981, 35–36). In fact, when an ordinary object is described "in some detail," it has the perverse effect of becoming "*defamiliarized*, and as it ceases to be taken for granted, it assumes the enigmatic aura of things in dreams and fantasy" (36).

37. Davis has also remarked on this phenomenon, observing that "[w]hat we are forced to witness throughout Wilson's tale (even more, perhaps, than we might wish) is a body whose primary and delineating experience is not sexuality, but pain" (Davis 1993, 396).

38. See my previous footnote on Fanon, in the Introduction (Note 48).

39. For a cultural study of pain, see Morris (1991).

40. On this subject, see Barbara White (1993, 46–47, Note 9).

41. On the transformation of Frado into "our nig," see Wald (1995, 159–63).

42. This is a question also raised by Susie King Taylor, when, after narrating her own experiences among a "Colored" regiment during the Civil War, she asks rhetorically, "Was the war in vain? Has it brought freedom, in the full sense of the word, or has it not made our condition more hopeless?" (Taylor 1902, 61). She then questions whether it is possible to claim the country is truly united under a single flag "when one race is allowed to burn, hang, and inflict the most horrible torture weekly, monthly, on another" (61–62; on this see also Barthelemy 1988). On the slaves' inability to find freedom, see Sidonie Smith (1974, 24).

43. Stallybrass and White remind us that "one of the most powerful ruses of the dominant [is] to pretend that critique can only exist in the language of 'reason', 'pure knowledge' and 'seriousness'. Against this ruse Bakhtin [1965] rightly emphasized the logic of the *grotesque*, of excess, of the lower bodily stratum, of the fair" (Stallybrass and White 1986, 43). While I do not for a minute think that *Our Nig* qualifies as an example of the grotesque or lacks seriousness, I do think in its unrelenting emphasis on the body it stands out from most forms of "serious" literature.

44. We must presume he is white because he is racially unmarked.

45. As duCille notes, this novel also "uses both material considerations and racial ideology to turn the marriage ideal in on itself" (duCille 1993, 5).

46. One could almost pick a female slave narrative at random to counter Mag's heartless attitudes toward her child. In an apostrophe to her genteel white female readers, Bethany Veney, for example, reminds her audience that, secure as they are in the love of their own family, they will never be able to

understand the slave mother's emotions as she clasps her new-born child, and knows that a master's word can at any moment take it from her embrace; and when, as was mine, that child is a girl, and from her own experience she sees its almost certain doom is to minister to the unbridled lust of the slave-owner, and feels that the law holds over her no protecting arm, it is not strange that, rude and uncultured as I was, I felt all this, and would have been glad if we could have died together there and then. (Veney 1889, 26)

See also Foster (1994, 133–37).

47. For a nuanced and historicized defense of Mag's treatment of her daughter, see Tate (1992, 33–36). For a different slant on her unnaturalness, see Wald (1995, 160).

48. That both the surrogate and the natural mother behave "unnaturally" in this text suggests that motherhood itself is a construction—as the novel makes quite clear. In a racist economy, even motherhood is corrupted by the marketplace of greed, prejudice, and poverty.

49. When Dr. Flint learns that "Linda Brent" is pregnant with her second child, he, too, cuts her hair (Jacobs 1861, 77).

50. On this subject, see Gwin (1985a; 1985b).

51. For another approach to this question, see Tate (1992, 48). See also Davis (1993) and Breau (1993).

52. See Foucault (1975).

53. Here, as elsewhere, the female slave narratives were working against two competing conventions. It was common in the male narratives to describe the meager portions slaves had to eat and thus how hungry they were, but, as Michie reminds us, to the Victorians a woman's "hunger cannot be acted out in public" (Michie 1987, 23).

54. Much has been written in an attempt to explain the phenomenon of human tears, with Darwin providing a physiological explanation and William James arguing that feelings of sorrow do not precede tears but actually follow them. In his discussion of this history, Jerome Neu offers his own explanation by claiming that as we develop in infancy we learn from others what our physically induced and as yet psychologically unmotivated tears mean to them (Neu 1987). Using Neu's argument that crying is one of the (learned) activities that makes us uniquely human, we might argue that Mrs. Bellmont is so enraged by Frado's crying because it reminds her that in brutalizing this young black girl she is brutalizing a fellow human being.

55. Gates argues that Frado reverses the objective status, which has been thrust upon her, "by *renaming herself* not Our Nig but 'Our Nig,' thereby transforming herself into a *subject*" (Gates 1983, li). To this I would add that Wilson also contests and transforms the notion of subjectivity itself.

56. According to Barbara White, under the terms of Frado's "binding out," as a girl, she would have been indentured until she was eighteen and during this time permitted a minimal education (White 1993, 46–47, Note 9).

57. Surely this use of "home" is an act of signifying on Wilson's part.

58. Davis, however, argues that "the project of *Our Nig* is essentially a humanist one, designed to clear a space in which 'our nig' can assert her essential humanity" (Davis 1993, 400). On my view, Wilson's project interrogates liberal humanism because this political philosophy debases the body.

59. Ernest argues that Wilson's novel "presents a vision of Christianity in which *redemptive* faith requires that one *redeem* one's resources in an economic management of selfhood" (Ernest 1995, 77). See also Tate (1992, 45–47).

60. Although their efforts to help Frado are largely ineffectual, both Jack Bellmont and the schoolteacher are nonetheless described as taking Frado "by the hand" when they show her compassion (27, 32).

61. See Chapter 1, Note 48. I do not always agree that application is necessary to understanding. For an explanation of my demurral, see Fishburn (1995, 14, Note 11).

62. In short, both Gadamer and Heidegger endorse the concept of the hermeneutic circle. See Gadamer (1989, 265–67, 292–94) and Heidegger (1927a, 153).

63. As he puts it, "the miracle of understanding consists in the fact that no like-mindedness is necessary to recognize what is really significant and fundamentally meaningful in tradition. We have the ability to open ourselves to the superior claim the text makes and to respond to what it has to tell us" (Gadamer 1989, 311).

64. See Fishburn (1995).

65. It is a common theme in the slave narratives, as many have noted, to have the most religious of the whites act the worst. Of the pious and religiously devoted Benjamin

B. Smith, Lunsford Lane, for example, writes that "grace (of course) had not wrought in the same *manner* upon the heart of Mr. Smith, as nature had done upon that of Mr. Boylan, who made no religious profession" (Lane 1842, 11).

66. As Davis says, "rather than allowing pain to silence her, it is precisely her pain which compels Wilson/Frado to speak" (Davis 1993, 393).

67. In a personal correspondence, John Ernest reminds me of the complex role Christianity takes in the slave narratives. For comprehensive studies of the relationship between African Americans and Christianity, see Paris (1985; 1995).

68. Ernest argues similarly that Wilson's object is to help create "a reconfigured community of understanding" (Ernest 1995, 59). She hoped to achieve this, on Ernest's view, by working through "conflicts" and their kernel of "mutual dependence" (exemplified by Mag Smith and Jim) to arrive at "a genuine and morally secure community of interests" (79).

69. Andrews has argued that Jacobs "wrote on a precarious margin," revealing just enough autobiographical details to inspire compassion in her female readers without deeply offending them (Andrews 1986, 240). See also Lewis Gordon's work on absence and presence in antiblack racism (1995, 97–103), which I briefly discuss in a footnote in the Introduction (Note 42).

70. See Davis (1993, 396).

71. See Foucault (1975, especially 170–94). In Althusserian terms, the questions Mattison asks Picquet invite—if not encourage—her to respond affirmatively to his construction of her as a sexually violated woman.

72. In contrast to Picquet, the ex-slave Sylvia Dubois, during her postbellum interview with Cornelius W. Larison, is quite forthcoming with details about her physical exploits, frankly discussing her dancing ability, her drinking, and her extraordinary strength. See Larison (1883).

73. Andrews notes the irony in Jacobs's self-appointed task, claiming that there is an inverse relationship between the magnitude of the wrongs done to a person and the willingness of an audience to learn "from the victim herself" (Andrews 1986, 249). See also Baker (1991), in which he asks rhetorically, "What tale can the daughters tell without incurring *contempt*?" (20).

74. One of the few times we learn about her responsibilities occurs after her daughter and second child is born, when she is outwardly obedient but inwardly planning some way to rescue her children from enslavement. Flint's daughter is getting married and Jacobs's "task was to fit up the house for the reception of the bride. In the midst of sheets, tablecloths, towels, drapery, and carpeting, my head was as busy planning, as were my fingers with the needle" (Jacobs 1861, 86). Although Flint had entrusted the "entire management of the work" to her, the focus in the chapter is on her children, how much she loves them, and how she might save them (88). And most of the details she includes, it will be noted, have to do not with her work per se but with the Flint's material possessions, which have been given over to her for attention.

75. This notion of class differences is one to which I shall return at the end of the chapter. The passage I have quoted here is reprinted in Valerie Smith (1990, 219).

76. According to Foreman, "[a]s Jacobs translates her life to the level of discourse in writing her narrative, she transcribes the *events* of her life to that level. Dr. Flint's sexual abuse of Linda takes place almost completely in the terrain of language" (Foreman 1990, 317–18). Foreman finds it "telling," for example, that "the passion in her language does not seem to have a direct correlation with what she claims Flint 'says.' Jacobs transfers

Linda's (unacknowledged) violated body to the body of the word. By serving for and providing the trope for physical abuse, words act both to describe her violation and to absorb it" (318).

77. This issue is perhaps more complex than my remarks suggest. On one hand, though other twentieth-century readers may feel differently about the absence of these details, I feel, somehow, that I want to respect her modesty. On the other hand, because Jacobs provides so few details, much of what we supply in filling these gaps or making the text speak is necessarily pure supposition—born of fanciful imagination or, one would hope, informed scholarship. In any event, under such conditions as Jacobs experienced, there is a danger both in speaking and in remaining silent.

78. I take this characterization from the title page of the first edition, on which appear a statement by "A Woman of North Carolina" and a verse from Isaiah: "Rise up, ye women that are at ease! Hear my voice, ye careless daughters! Give ear unto my speech." For a discussion of the relationship between Jacobs and her intended readers, see Foster (1993).

79. On this, see Ziolkowski (1991, 163).

80. For a sampling of the extensive literature on this text, see, for example, Andrews (1986), in which he argues that Jacobs wrote *Incidents* "as much to assert the power and potential of women's community in the South and the North as to denounce the state of commonage under which all resided under the patriarchy of slavery" (254); Carby (1987), in which she argues that "*Incidents* . . . is the most sophisticated, sustained narrative dissection of the conventions of true womanhood by a black author before emancipation" (47); Yellin (1989), in which she argues that "*Incidents* embodies the conflict between patriarchal definitions of true womanhood and the definition advanced by the antislavery feminists" (92); Valerie Smith (1990), in which she argues that "[r]estricted by the conventions and rhetoric of the slave narrative . . . Jacobs [also] borrows heavily from the rhetoric of the sentimental novel," a form with its own restrictions—but in combining the two, she "seized authority over her literary restraints" (213); Tate (1992), in which she argues that the "disparity between the representations of freedom in *Incidents* and male slave narratives . . . illustrates how the goal of freedom becomes problematic in a female text" (27). See also Yellin (1985), Braxton (1986), Gray (1990), Foreman (1990), Nudelman (1992), Foster (1993), and Ernest (1995). The collection of essays edited by Garfield and Zafar (1996) appeared too late to be included in my discussion.

81. This generalization is not entirely accurate, as Henry Bibb (1850), for example, expends considerable energy and narrative space in documenting his numerous attempts to rescue his wife and daughter from slavery—attempts that ultimately all failed.

82. As Yellin remarks, "Pregnancy outside wedlock presented a serious problem in nineteenth-century American life and fiction. . . . Popularly, the cult of motherhood enshrined the relationship of a mother and child only if the mother was first a wife; in popular fiction, pregnant girls found their way to the riverbank and drowned themselves and their unborn babies" (Yellin 1989, 88). In Jacobs's text the two illegitimate children nonetheless help her resist Flint's unwelcome sexual advances; and, although she first despairs when her son is born, ultimately she describes him as a "tie to life" (Jacobs 1861, 58). In so doing, on Yellin's view, Jacobs "implicitly criticizes the notion that extramarital sex and illegitimacy involve sin and death" (Yellin 1989, 88).

83. Culler continues: "Thus, the Cartesian *cogito*, in which the self is immediately present to itself, is taken as the basic proof of existence, and things directly perceived are

apodictically privileged. Notions of truth and reality are based on a longing for an unfallen world in which there would be no mediating systems of language and perception but everything would be itself, with no gap between form and meaning" (Culler 1975, 132). As Jameson puts it, "The very problem of a relationship between thoughts and words betrays a metaphysics of 'presence,' and implies an illusion that univocal substances exist, that a pure present exists, in which we come face to face once and for all with objects; that meanings exist, such that it ought to be possible to 'decide' whether they are initially verbal or not; that there is such a thing as knowledge which one can acquire in some tangible or permanent way" (Jameson 1972, 173). Or, as Hartman puts it, "Writing, Derrida believes, undoes the illusion of the simple location of meaning or self-presence: an illusion fostered by what is nearest ourselves, our body (as Bergson had remarked) but particularly our voice, or the affective voice of others when it haunts us with their likeness" (Hartman 1981, xx).

84. In Aristotle, for example, according to Derrida, "[t]he feelings of the mind, expressing things naturally, constitute a sort of universal language which can then efface itself. . . . In every case, the voice is closest to the signified, whether it is determined strictly as sense (thought or lived) or more loosely as thing" (Derrida 1967, 11). Or, as Culler explains it, "Plato condemned writing because the written word was cut loose and liberated from the communicative presence which alone could be the source of meaning and truth" (Culler 1975, 132).

85. Firsthand accounts as well as verbatim transcripts of Douglass's speeches were widely circulated in newspapers of the time.

86. In Derrida's system, contrary to Plato and Aristotle, writing is not a form of speaking but just the opposite: Speaking is a kind of writing. Culler is critical of Derrida on this point, arguing that "within Western culture there are crucial differences between the conventions of oral communication and those of literature which deserve study whatever their ideological basis" (Culler 1975, 133). Barthes argues that writing "is not an open route through which there passes only the intention to speak. A whole disorder flows through speech and gives it this self-devouring momentum which keeps it in a perpetually suspended state. Conversely, writing is a hardened language, which is self-contained and is in no way meant to deliver to its own duration a mobile series of approximations. It is on the contrary meant to impose, thanks to the shadow cast by its system of signs, the image of a speech which had a structure even before it came into existence" (Barthes 1953, 19).

87. As Barthes puts it, "The Author, when believed in, is always conceived of as the past of his own book: book and author stand automatically on a single line divided into a *before* and an *after*. The Author is thought to *nourish* the book, which is to say that he exists before it, thinks, suffers, lives for it, is in the same relation of antecedence to his work as a father to his child" (Barthes 1968, 145).

88. Derrida writes:

The trace is not only the disappearance of origin—within the discourse that we sustain and according to the path that we follow it means that the origin did not even disappear, that it was never constituted except reciprocally by a nonorigin, the trace, which thus becomes the origin of the origin. From then on, to wrench the concept of the trace from the classical scheme, which would derive it from a presence or from an originary nontrace and which would make of it an empirical mark, one must indeed speak of an originary trace or arche-trace. Yet we know that the concept destroys its name and that, if all begins with the trace, there is above all no originary trace. (Derrida 1967, 61)

Or, as Jameson explains it, "to attempt to go back behind the sentence or the word that already exists, behind the thought that has already taken verbal form, is to submit to the prestige of a 'myth of origins,' and to attempt to re-place ourselves artificially in a past in which that living unity had not yet taken place, in which there still was such a thing as pure sound on the one hand, and pure meaning or idea on the other" (Jameson 1972, 174–75). Providing a mini-history of the legitimating and empowering function of writing in all Western social, political, religious, scientific, and philosophical institutions, Derrida reveals that the "common root, which is not a root but the concealment of the origin and which is not common because it does not amount to the same thing except with the unmonotonous insistence of difference, this unnamable movement of *difference-itself*, that I have strategically nicknamed *trace*, *reserve*, or *différance*, could be called writing only within the *historical* closure, that is to say within the limits of science and philosophy" (Derrida 1967, 93).

89. Compare my reading of *Incidents* with a passage near the beginning of Douglass's *The Heroic Slave*, in which the narrator remarks on how little is known or left of Madison Washington, the heroic slave: "Curiously, earnestly, anxiously we peer into the dark, and wish even for the blinding flash, or the light of northern skies to reveal him. But alas! he is still enveloped in darkness, and we return from the pursuit like a wearied and disheartened mother, (after a tedious and unsuccessful search for a lost child,) who returns weighed down with disappointment and sorrow. Speaking of marks, traces, possibilities, and probabilities, we come before our readers" (Douglass 1853, 38). On the rhetorical strategy implicit in this passage, see Andrews (1990, 29).

90. Yellin reports that Child has moved these incidents into this chapter from other locations in Jacobs's original manuscript. Furthermore, she reports that "[p]erhaps in consequence of this editing, perhaps because Jacobs was a townswoman generally unacquainted with the countryside, perhaps because it was and is inherently difficult to document atrocities against slaves, this chapter, unlike the rest of the book, does not appear correct in its details" (Yellin 1987, 267, Note 1 to Chap. 9).

91. Lindon Barrett has argued that "it is at the moments when the body of the narrator is most enduringly menaced and figures most prominently in the narrative that the narrator attains her greatest measure of authority" (Barrett 1995, 434).

Epilogue: Justice in the Flesh

Having established the slave bodies' recollection of *being* in the previous two chapters, here I will suggest very briefly how the postbellum novels of racial uplift and passing continue this African American meditation on the meaning of human embodiment.[1] They are forced to do so, however, in an even more displaced fashion than that occurring in the slave narratives, given the truly venomous hostility that was directed not just toward black persons but, more basically, toward black *bodies* after Reconstruction. Though, to be sure, most of this egregious animosity was displayed in the South, the North was not without its own racial animus, as was evident in the patterns of segregated housing and the difficulties African Americans faced everywhere in learning trades or finding skilled work. What seemed to be occurring at this time, North and South, was a racially motivated program of disciplining the bodies of African Americans, an effort that was to be federally codified in *Plessy vs. Ferguson*, the 1896 Supreme Court decision that affirmed the legal fiction of so-called separate but equal facilities for blacks and whites, thus giving both encouragement and sanction to the emerging nationwide pattern of segregated housing, schools, transportation, entertainment, and restaurants. Much of the postbellum work of transforming free black persons into useful, docile bodies had already been codified in the late nineteenth-century Southern statutes that were known collectively as the Black Codes, local ordinances that were holdovers from slavery designed to control the association, mobility, and labor practices of African Americans. Many of these codes, according to John Hope Franklin, specifically set out "to limit the areas in which Negroes could purchase or rent property. Vagrancy laws imposed heavy penalties that were designed to force all Negroes to work whether they wanted to or not" (Franklin 1967, 303). Moreover, African Americans were assessed fines for "seditious speeches, insulting gestures or acts, absence from work, violating curfew, and the possession of firearms"

(303). In short, these laws were designed to regulate the activities of black *bodies*. As Herbert G. Gutman describes it, during the post-Reconstruction era it was widely believed that "essential 'restraining' influences on unchanging 'Africans' had ended with the emancipation, causing a moral and social 'retrogression' among the ex-slaves" (Gutman 1976, 531). This conviction was congruent with "southern Bourbon rhetoric that promised to redeem the South and save the nation from political corruption, economic extravagance, and racial and sexual 'irregularities' by reimposing dominance over a race and a class" that was said to have conclusively demonstrated "an incapacity to 'restrain' itself and thereby adapt decently to its changed status" (531–32). In the appendix to his book from which these passages have been taken, Gutman quotes from dozens of post-Reconstruction speeches, pamphlets, newspaper articles, and books—the depressing and influential arguments of which are the retrogression of "negroes" since Emancipation and the consequent need, for the well-being of the Republic, to bring them back under ameliorative white control. Of particular influence was Philip A. Bruce's favorably reviewed 1889 study *The Plantation Negro as Freedman*, which argues repeatedly, according to Gutman (1976, 535), that "blacks could not manage for themselves, and emancipation had caused a severe and increasingly menacing deterioration in their social and moral condition." Especially worrisome was the reputed inability of the so-called "Africans" to restrain their lasciviousness and honor their marriage vows (536). On this argument, it thus fell to whites, as it had before Emancipation, either to deport these dangerous barbarians, who were driven to sexual excess and criminal behavior by unchecked animal instinct, or to find new ways, in the absence of slavery, to train and civilize them. At the very least, the experts warned, blacks must not be enfranchised. As Gutman concludes, "[r]etrogressionist ideology" accomplished more than occasioning "the disfranchisement of American blacks" and driving them out of "the mainstream of national culture. It supplied a way of reinterpreting the entire Afro-American experience so that enslavement became essential to 'civilization' and emancipation became evidence of the essential social and moral incapacities of the Afro-American descendants of African slaves" (542–43).[2]

In his study of how whites perceived and portrayed black people, George M. Fredrickson has argued that in the late nineteenth century, "[l]ynching represented an ultimate sociological method of racial control and repression, a way of using fear and terror to check 'dangerous' tendencies in a black community considered to be ineffectively regimented or supervised" (Fredrickson 1971, 272). The need to justify such loathsome disciplinary measures, however, gave birth to neo-Hegelian arguments about the natural inferiority of Africans—the South's docile and childlike Negroes being said to have regressed to animalistic Africans with the abolition of slavery. On Fredrickson's view, in the post-Reconstruction era, "the only way to meet criticisms of the unspeakably revolting practice of lynching was to contend that many Negroes were literally wild beasts, with uncontrollable sexual passions and criminal natures stamped by heredity" (276).[3] As Claudia Tate summarizes it, "Academic scholarship, print media, plastic arts, manufactured goods, and colloquial speech of the post-Reconstruction era all reflected the ideology of retrogressionism and character-ized black people not merely as intellectually inferior but as lazy, ugly, intem-perate, slothful, lascivious, and violent, indeed bestial" (Tate 1992, 10).[4]

At the very least, as this brief, troubling summary is meant to suggest, being embodied as a black person after Reconstruction involved considerable incon-venience and a certain check to social and economic advancement. At the worst, it involved psychic distress, physical danger, and even death. It is no accident, therefore, that as well-paying jobs failed to materialize for blacks even in the North, as both de facto and de jure segregation received the imprimatur of the Supreme Court, as the Black Codes resurfaced with a vengeance, as the Ku Klux Klan spread its tyrannical tendrils into every corner of the South, and as lynching became the preferred mode of terrorizing and disciplining black indi-viduals and the black community at large, the physical bodies of identifiably black persons, so central to both the male and female slave narratives, seem al-most to disappear for nearly a generation of main characters in African Ameri-can fiction.[5] Little wonder, then, that most postbellum novelists took the path the similarly aggrieved and endangered Harriet Jacobs had taken in her antebel-lum narrative by relegating the disturbing fact of black embodiment to an absent signifier. This disappearance, as I have already suggested, was also partially driven by the conventions of nineteenth-century middle-class novels, the formal requirements of which seem not only, as Jehlen has argued, to necessitate a thematic focus on the interior development of an individual (Jehlen 1981), but also, as Michie implies, to necessitate the flight of mundane bodies into the ethereal realm of metaphor (Michie 1987). If, furthermore, as Stallybrass and White contend, the rising European middle or mercantile class had initially achieved a socially respectable identity by distinguishing itself from the working poor, it secured this hard-won distinction by carefully regulating the bodies of its own members and displacing onto the poor the shameful, all too visible bur-den of uncontrollable, undisciplined human embodiment (Stallybrass and White 1986). To be middle class, then, meant denying or at the very least disguising the fact of one's own embodiment, in real life as well as in fiction.

Thus it comes as no great surprise that that pre-eminently middle-class art form, the nineteenth-century novel of manners, would in its pages eschew or at least radically displace into more acceptable metaphors any graphic evidence of the human body. Even the fiction of the time that most relied on the emotional responses of its readers—the sentimental romance—had metaphoric strategies by which to contain the potentially unruly bodies of its characters.[6] Although heroes and heroines, as the fictional counterparts of human beings, by definition should have bodies, by the nineteenth century few novelists dared describe them in any detail. So it seems to have been with the middle-class African American novelists who wrote after the Civil War. Intent upon countering the hegemonic racist discourse that equated them with savages, if not animals, the post-Reconstructionist novelists could not afford to meditate openly on black bodies as either a physiological or a philosophical problem. That is to say, they were constrained in addressing both ontic and ontological issues as they pertained to the body-selves of dark-skinned African Americans. But they could—and did—meditate on definitions of race, on what makes one person legally (or even psychologically) white and another black, when there are no detectable differences in their features or color. Eager to uplift the race, moreover, and desperate to convince both black and white readers of the possibility of doing so, these novelists hardly dared explore in any detail the socioeconomic problems of working-class blacks, since to do so might have the unintended consequence of reinforcing the regressionist stereotypes they had set out to challenge.

But, limited as both the ante- and postbellum novelists were in terms of descriptive possibilities, what is notable is the ongoing commitment of both generations of writers to demonstrate how racial distinctions, in a racist environment, inevitably drive people apart even though they self-evidently share the same human characteristics—and frequently the same ancestors. If the overt argument in these sometimes overly didactic novels is that blacks are equal to whites because, under the skin, we are all human beings with similar ambitions and capacities,[7] the covert argument is that as embodied beings, we are necessarily and blessedly intertwined—inherently predisposed to engage the lives of other body-selves with our own body-self. Like the slave narratives before them, these post-Reconstruction novels remind us, in Levin's terms, that "what the body needs for its fulfillment is a social order governed by institutions of reciprocity" (Levin 1990, 43). In sum, they remind us that the same body-selves that make us human and constitute our very being always already carry with them both a capacity and a predilection for "justice in the flesh" (35–44). It was a desire to achieve this justice in their own lifetime that inspired the slaves to write. For how could any person—logically or legally—be kept enslaved if all persons were to recognize our common relatedness-to-*being*? Although the ex-slave narrators had done their work for two generations, although the Emancipation Proclamation had been enacted on 1 January 1863, and although the South had been defeated by 1865, as the advent of the next century loomed hard on the horizon, justice in the flesh remained but a dream, an unmet goal for African Americans, as workers were turned away from the factories, voters turned away at the polls, homeowners driven out of their neighborhoods, businesses burnt out, and reports of lynchings escalated. So, like their ancestors, the postbellum novelists shouldered the burden anew and worked, in their generation, to achieve justice in the flesh for themselves and their descendants—and, by necessary extension, for all the rest of us.

What I am arguing in this brief chapter can be seen quite clearly in Pauline E. Hopkins's 1900 novel, *Contending Forces: A Romance Illustrative of Negro Life North and South.* Although many late twentieth-century readers will no doubt find this romance and its tidy resolution far too sentimental for their tastes and straining credulity in its many coincidences, I think we can gain new ap-

preciation for it if we read it and others of its kind as a romance of the flesh.[8]
Hopkins contemplates in her novel the intertwining or interconnectedness of
human beings, one with another. But even as she makes her case for human interconnectedness—both cross-racially, white with black, and intra-racially, black
with black—she seems resigned to accepting at least some of her era's belief in
racial characteristics, if only to ensure a sympathetic white readership of her
sentimental romance. Very briefly, this is the story of two generations of Montforts. The first generation is composed of slave-holding landed gentry of English birth who eventually settle in Newbern, North Carolina. There the beautiful
and refined Grace Montfort, who is rumored to be of mixed blood, unwittingly
attracts the improper attentions of Anson Pollock, who has falsely befriended
Grace's husband, Charles. Jealous of Montfort's great wealth, enraged by Mrs.
Montfort's shocked and angry dismissal of him, and driven by the knowledge
that Montfort himself plans to free his slaves, Pollock incites other white ne'er-
do-wells to attack the plantation and murder the owner. During the attack, Pollock kidnaps Grace Montfort and her two sons (Hopkins 1900, 68). Shortly after
her abduction, however, Grace disappears, apparently preferring death by
drowning to becoming mistress to the man who has had her husband murdered.
Furious to have lost such a prize, the racist Anson Pollock comforts himself by
taking as his mistress Grace's maid-servant and foster sister, Lucy, herself a
black woman—while retaining the two Montfort children as his servants. At the
end of the first year, the older son, Charles, is bought by a stranger passing
through town, an English mineralogist who promises to recover the boy's right
of inheritance before he leaves the country. Although he hates leaving his
younger brother Jesse in bondage, Charles feels he has no choice but to accept
the Englishman's aid and, as soon as the deal is struck, departs with him. For his
part, Jesse bides his time until the aged Pollock trusts him to journey North on
his own. Once he reaches New York, he determines never to return South. Although his legal identity as a black man has only been established by those unfounded rumors about his mother's ancestry, these rumors nonetheless have
been sufficient to brand him a fugitive slave. Finding work first in Boston, he
soon must flee the city for Exeter, New Hampshire, having learned that Pollock
is coming after him. There he is sheltered by a black man and his family, whose
daughter he eventually marries.

The narrative then shifts to the story present and the lives of Jesse's daughter, the widowed but financially secure and well-respected Ma Smith, and her
two children, Dora Grace Smith and William Jesse Smith, who carry within
themselves and within their names their Montfort heritage. As we are introduced
to them, we learn that both generations live in harmony in the lodging-house
Mrs. Smith owns in Boston. Dora, who by now does most of the work running
the house, is engaged to an ambitious attorney and politico, John P. Langley,
while Will, a brilliant student, falls in love with the beautiful and mysterious
Sappho Clark, a woman of mixed race who has just moved into his mother's
boarding house. Langley proves as false a friend to Will as Pollock had to Montfort. Convinced (correctly) that Dora will someday come into great wealth be-

cause of her Montfort blood, Langley plans to marry her—but also lusts after the stranger, Sappho Clark, whom, in an astonishing act of betrayal to friend and fiancée alike, he hopes to set up as his mistress. After hearing a dreadful tale of kidnapping and forced prostitution from Lycurgus (Luke) Sawyer, a heroic and handsome black man who is a regular on the abolitionist lecture circuit, Langley deduces (again correctly) that the abducted victim was none other than the mysterious Sappho Clark herself, who has changed her real name to avoid public humiliation. Visiting a local fortune-teller, he accidentally discovers that the beautiful child this woman is raising is none other than Sappho's unacknowledged, illegitimate offspring whom she has borne to a rapist. In a brutal move to force her into concubinage, Langley confronts her with these truths about her past and inadvertently drives her out of town in self-proclaimed disgrace—to the inconsolable grief of Will Smith, who still longs to marry her even after learning about her painful past. Hearing what Langley has wrought, Dora angrily breaks her engagement with this man she has always intuited is not really the man to make her happy—and much later marries the worthy Dr. Arthur Lewis, who has founded an industrial school for blacks in Louisiana. In the meantime, Will graduates from Harvard, after which he travels to Europe to study science and philosophy. At the novel's dénouement, we learn that Langley is offspring of Pollock's grandnephew and one of Lucy's daughters, and we have confirmed the fact that the Smiths are the true inheritors of their grandfather Montfort's estate—an inheritance ensured by the timely intervention of their cousin, the honorable Charles Montfort-Withington, of Blankshire, England, who has been traveling in the United States. Returning himself from Europe and visiting his mother and sister in New Orleans, Will attends Easter Mass, where he is reunited with Sappho, whom he shortly marries, accepting her illegitimate son as his own. At novel's end the Smiths—mother, children, spouses, and offspring—are sailing for England to visit their relative.

While all of these coincidences and connections are dizzying in their abundance, I have reiterated them here in some detail because I think they should be understood not just as the literary devices of a sentimental romance of racial uplift but also as Hopkins's philosophical argument for the interrelatedness of human beings. For those of us weaned on twentieth-century realism, it may stretch the bounds of credulity that the lives of third-generation Montforts intersect by fateful coincidence the life of Pollock's descendant in a pattern that repeats the destructive relationship of the past—just as it seems beyond belief that long-lost relatives and long-lost lovers can be so conveniently reunited.[9] But what better way is there to illustrate the fact that we are, all of us, implicated in the lives of each other, for better or worse? By blurring racial distinctions, through the many inter-racial couples and characters in this novel, Hopkins reminds us still further that we are all flesh of the same flesh.[10] By this I mean to invoke the conventional meaning of "flesh" (that is, related by blood or by our common humanity) as well as Merleau-Ponty's usage of "flesh" as a manner of being. Although hers is purposefully and self-consciously a novel of racial uplift—as is evident in Hopkins's own preface,[11] in the many speeches delivered on this subject throughout the text, and in the many skills and accomplishments of the attractive, middle-class Montfort-Smith clan, as well as in the intelligence and good deeds of Dr. Lewis—even as it relies on conventional racial divisions, it also works, perhaps unexpectedly, to undo the concept of race altogether, since race is a concept that, by definition and design, would keep us separate, and *Contending Forces* is, above all, a tale of human connectedness overcoming oppression, opposition, and division.

It is also a tale that connects, by marriage, two men who seem to represent the lives and intellectual interests of those two eminent competitors, Booker T. Washington and W. E. B. Du Bois. It is no mere coincidence, as others have noted, that the esteemed Dr. Lewis argues that "industrial education and the exclusion of politics" should solve the nation's racial problems (Hopkins 1900, 124) or that, in a public oration, he argues that African Americans "should strive to obtain the education of the industrial school, seeking there our level, content to abide there, leaving to the white man the superiority of brain and intellect" (251). For his part, echoing the experiences of Du Bois, the intellectually gifted Will Smith has been sponsored by a well-to-do white man and given the opportunity to study at Heidelberg (168). Furthermore, the speech he gives at the American Colored League, in contrast to the more placatory one given by Lewis, stresses the importance of offering African Americans a comprehensive education and the urgent need for them to agitate for immediate social change (263–73).[12] Even though Sappho Clark is openly critical of Lewis's willingness to limit blacks to an industrial education (124), his unassuming tenacity is what finally wins the heart of Dora and thus ensures his acceptance into the Smith family. Thus, where the real-life Washington and Du Bois were bitter rivals, their fictional counterparts enjoy an exemplary filial harmony.

Although Will, moreover, states frankly in his speech that African Americans want no part of miscegenation, lawful or unlawful, as a solution to the race problem in the United States (Hopkins 1900, 264), he is himself, as are virtually all of the other major characters in this novel, the product of just such racial intermixing. The novel is unclear on whether such intermixing is necessarily good or bad,[13] yet it seems willing enough, as was common a century ago, to connect character and appearance—to read the one in the other. The admirable and successful Will Smith, for example, is described as "tall and finely formed, with features almost perfectly chiseled, and a complexion the color of an almond shell. His hair was black and curly, with just a tinge of crispness to denote the existence of Negro blood" (90). Although John Langley has Will's refinement and light complexion, with hair giving no hint of "Negro blood in its waves," nonetheless the manliness and probity found in Will are absent in John, whose ancestors, the narrative informs us, were "slaves and Southern 'crackers'" (90). For the narrator this is "a bad mixture—the combination of the worst features of a dominant race with an enslaved race" (91). The gentle and refined Sappho Clark, a model of decorous womanhood, nonetheless brings out in him (as she had brought out in her uncle) a defect in his personality, of which he had been heretofore unaware even though "[s]ensuality was prominent in the phrenologi-

144 The Problem of Embodiment

cal development of his head." Although he is apparently by nature predisposed to sensuality, none of his acquaintances had thought him "a libertine" (226). Luke Sawyer, however, is all nobility in his African appearance and demeanor. It is, moreover, given him to name the novel's theme and title in the address he delivers on the night Lewis and Smith speak. Following Lewis's speech, Sawyer rises to protest its accommodationist tenor and in doing so is described as "a tall, gaunt man of very black complexion" (254). Called to the podium to make his point, he makes his way through the crowd; as he does so, the audience observes "a man of majestic frame, rugged physique and immense muscular development. His face was kindly, but withal bore the marks of superior intelligence, shrewdness and great strength of character," calling to mind the appearance of Abraham Lincoln. So impressive are his looks that the narrator relates that those "of his physiological development—when white—mould humanity, and leave their own characteristics engraved upon the pages of the history of their times" (255). It is also given to him inadvertently to reveal Sappho's secret when he relates his part in rescuing the violated Mabelle Beaubean and lodging her in a "colored convent" in New Orleans where, in order to ensure her safety, he spreads the word that she had died upon the birth of her child (261). Seeing Sappho faint at the end of Luke's narrative is enough to convince Langley that she is the unfortunate Mabelle, who, throughout most of her own young life has had yet to experience herself her inborn right to justice in the flesh. The closest she has come is when she has been rescued from prostitution by Sawyer, who has used her tragic example to urge his shocked and silenced audience to action, ending with the peroration, "Under such conditions as I have described, contentment, amity—call it by what name you will—is impossible; justice alone remains to us" (262).

Through these abuses on the innocent and faultless Mabelle, Hopkins addresses one of the consuming issues of her time—the question of the African American woman's sexuality. Of her own estimable character there is no doubt, as her appearance makes clear in a novel that makes physiognomic distinctions, for she is "[t]all and fair, with hair of a golden cast, aquiline nose, rosebud mouth, soft brown eyes veiled by long, dark lashes which swept her cheek, just now covered with a delicate rose flush" (Hopkins 1990, 107). And hidden within these attractive features, her new-found friend Dora finds "a character of sterling worth—bold, strong and ennobling" (114). When Dora and she attend a talk given by the powerful Mrs. Willis, the widow of a prominent African American politician, Sappho, though we do not know it yet, has particular reason to paid heed to Mrs. Willis's thoughts on the role of a "virtuous woman" in uplifting and improving the race (148). Hearing Mrs. Willis claim that African women are naturally virtuous (as has been reported by travelers to the continent), Sappho asks, with a significance and a pathos we only come to appreciate later, whether Negro women will be held accountable for the charges of lasciviousness that daily bombard them or, more poignantly, does she think that the Almighty will find them at fault for the thousands of mixed race, illegitimate children to whom, against their own desires, they have given birth (149). To this naked plea for justice in the flesh, Mrs. Willis wisely responds by distinguishing between intentional and unintentional behavior, assuring her young interlocutor that African American women "are virtuous or non-virtuous only when we have a *choice* under temptation" (149). In the end, though she must suffer further humiliation and imagines the man she truly loves will scorn her for losing her virginity (if not her virtue) to a white man, she, like the other exemplary characters in Hopkins's complex novel, does eventually experience justice in the flesh, if not from the white world, at least among her own race, as Will seeks her out and persuades her to marry him. As we will see also occurs in the delayed marriage of Iola Leroy and Dr. Latimer, in this union of well-suited lovers, who have been "chastened by sorrow and self-sacrifice," we have a model of racial sacrifice, for their life's work will be that of bringing "joy to hearts crushed by despair" (401). Of this novel's plot and its dénouement in marriage, Tate has remarked that more than being a cry to end social injustice, *Contending Forces* (as well as *Iola Leroy*) is also an endorsement "of a racially validated and enlarged domesticity" (Tate 1992, 149).

Tate has written extensively on the artistic consequences that developed out of the differing conceptions of self and subjectivity that marked the transition from slavery to freedom, arguing that "the appropriation of bourgeois gender conventions in general [was] fundamental to the emancipatory discourse of nineteenth-century African Americans" (Tate 1992, 56). Just as Harriet Jacobs had displaced the dangerous subjects of rape and forced concubinage into the more acceptable—because more domestic(ated)—metaphors of motherhood and inter-racial offspring in order to achieve a kind of bourgeois respectability, her postwar successors displaced the newly inflammatory subjects of emancipated and threatening black bodies into conventional romantic plots that, as we have seen in Hopkins's archetypal example, pivot on questions of inheritance and disinheritance, family separations and reunions, racial loyalty and progress, and justice in the flesh—narratives that have as their main characters not dark- but light-skinned African American men and women, and, sometimes, even white persons (of varying character). Intent on portraying the suitability of African Americans for professional advancement, these writers created their own version of Du Bois's Talented Tenth, uncommonly successful heroes whose occupations include that of minister, teacher, doctor, and lawyer—highly respectable occupations that would be felt by their contemporaneous readers (as, indeed, by most contemporary readers) to require more mental ability than manual dexterity, work, in short, that would prove them intellectually and socially equal to whites. That these heroes (and their female counterparts) are predominantly light-skinned further served the programmatic goal of convincing white readers that those exemplary black achievers they read about were very like themselves.[14] In Merleau-Ponty's terms, these mixed-blood characters, who mirror both black and white readers back to themselves, vividly represent his principle of alterity in ontology as well as his theory of reversibility—that is, the imminent but always deferred reversibility of the seeing and the seen (in this case, white reader and light-skinned black character, mutually caught in the fold or the field of the visible).[15]

At the same time, in vivid contrast to their predecessors, such as William Grimes and Harriet Wilson, these post-Reconstruction sentimental novelists, with a kind of brutal pragmatism, mostly relegate the visibly black body to the margins of their text—whether it be the body-self of a professional or a manual laborer. Furthermore, the domestic spaces that provide the focus of the story lines in these novels are virtually without exception those of middle-class, light-skinned African Americans. There is also, in general, a strong correlation between those characters whose interior lives provide the burden of the plot and those whose households are described in detail. As we have just seen, for example, although Luke Sawyer is noble in appearance and behavior, he remains a minor character in Hopkins's novel. We may learn a little of his former history, but we see nothing of his current domestic environs. The Smiths' middle-class household, on the other hand, provides most of the novel's interior space and houses most of its main characters—certainly its most admirable ones. Similarly, in Frances E. W. Harper's 1892 novel, *Iola Leroy, or, Shadows Uplifted*, the focus is on the genteel Leroy household. It is true that the eponymous heroine rejects an offer of marriage from an aristocratic white man by reminding him, in response to his assertion that she is no longer suited to consort with black people, that it had been by virtue of their own unrewarded and unrecognized labors that she herself had been "educated, while they were compelled to live in ignorance" (Harper 1892, 235). But the novel itself does little to describe their lives or households. Yet common laborers abound as minor characters in the public arena of genteel late nineteenth-century fiction, and, almost without exception, they are the blackest of the black. Sometimes these working class blacks are good and decent people. Sometimes they are ignorant and shiftless. Or, sometimes, like Billy and Dave in Charles W. Chesnutt's 1900 novel, *The House Behind the Cedars*, they are merely careless and forgetful. While the main characters in this sentimental fiction, like their white counterparts, speak flawless standard English, the minor characters often speak a form of black dialect, as though to reinforce the difference in class between themselves and the novels' heroes and heroines.

Even with these class and color differences, however, the abiding fact of human embodiment as a material phenomenon (for black and white, rich and poor, male and female) seems, as a general rule, virtually to be ignored, if not denied outright, in most of this middle-class fiction. Aside from the adjectives detailing the creaminess or duskiness of a individual's complexion, those physical markers that do get into print would primarily be of interest to a phrenologist or physiognomist, as persons of both races (mixed and pure) have features and postures commensurate with their character. Those bodies that are most frequently acknowledged and thus described in some detail—even if their features are only minimally sketched out, which, as we have already seen, is typical of most novelistic description (Beaujour 1981)[16]—tend, for the most part, to be those of mixed-race persons, who are the middle-class heroes and heroines of the story. In many cases, these characters are white enough to cross the color line—and occasionally do so with disastrous consequences, as occurs, for example, in *The House Behind the Cedars*, thus giving birth to the literary phenomenon known as the tragic mulatto or mulatta.[17]

For the great majority of others who could pass, however, as occurs with several characters in *Iola Leroy*, it is a matter of pride to remain identified as and with what they would describe as the colored race. Stated briefly, Harper's novel—which also stands as an archetype of its kind—is about the unexpected enslavement, escape, separation, and eventual reunion of the mixed-race Leroy family, which is headed, until his untimely death by yellow fever, by a wealthy plantation owner and the former slave whom he has educated, manumitted, and made his wife. Although Eugene Leroy confides to his perfidious cousin, Alfred Lorraine, that he has married a woman with Negro blood, neither he nor his wife, Marie, tell their children the family secret. Many years later, while studying in the North, the son, Harry, receives a sobering letter from his sister, Iola, in which he learns not only of his father's unforeseen death, his cousin's treachery, and the family's disinheritance, but also, for the first time, of his mother's previous status as his father's slave—and the recently effected enslavement of his sister and re-enslavement of his mother. The news is so shattering to this privileged young man, who has lived all his life as a white aristocrat, that he falls seriously ill from the shock of it. Once he has recovered his health and after much soul-searching, Harry vows to return to the South, seek out his family, and fight in the war—in short, he will return home to pursue justice in the flesh. Before he comes to this noble resolution, which is the first real test of his young manhood, he must determine with whom his loyalty most rests. Because of his education and previous alienation from others of African descent, it is not an easy decision to make. To him, the white world represents "strength, courage, enterprise, power of achievement, and memories of a wonderful past," while the black world, of which he knows precious little, represents "weakness, ignorance, poverty, and . . . social scorn" (Harper 1892, 125). Being fair-skinned and having been raised in a position of privilege, Harry has known "colored people" only in their debased capacity as slaves, and, as a result, he initially recoils from the thought of regarding them as his equals (125–26). Love for his (legally) "colored" mother and sister prove stronger than his pride, however, and he ultimately concludes that "he must stand where he could strike the most effective blow for their freedom" and determines to do his part by enlisting in a colored regiment (126). In similar fashion, when the handsome light-skinned slave, Robert Johnson—who has "dark-brown eyes and [a] wealth of chestnut-colored hair" and is, in actuality, Marie Leroy's long-lost brother—deserts to the Union Army, he quickly rises "from the ranks [to become] lieutenant of a colored company" because of "his intelligence, courage, and prompt obedience" (201, 43). So effective a leader is he that one of the captains urges him to "take [his] place in the army just the same as a white man," but Robert declines, asserting his racial loyalty by declaring his place is with those who need him more (43).

The choice Iola must make is not in which regiment, colored or white, to enroll but whether to marry the white doctor beside whom she is working in a field hospital for wounded Northern soldiers—a man she has come to respect and admire, if not love. Although Dr. Gresham has been told confidentially of her mother's background, out of his own delicacy, he elects not to tell Iola he knows. Yet, having fallen in love with this beautiful blue-eyed woman who has been rescued from slavery by Tom Anderson—a man who is a friend of Johnson and a runaway slave himself—Gresham vows to marry her and take her North, where he will suppress the details "of her mournful past" so his own high-born relatives never learn her secrets (Harper 1892, 60). Twice he tries to persuade her to marry him, but twice she refuses, echoing her brother in confessing that it is her fate to "serve the race which needs [her] most" (235). Dr. Frank Latimer, close friend and colleague of Gresham, also elects to align himself with his "mother's people" even though, as the grandchild of a Southern white woman, "[t]he blood of a proud aristocratic ancestry was flowing through his veins, and generations of blood admixture had effaced all trace of his negro lineage" (238, 239). Learning that he has forgone his grandmother's offer to adopt him as her own if only he will forget his biracial heritage, Iola has nothing but admiration for this man who willingly offers his allegiance to the "weaker" race (239, 263). Hearing of her admiration, Latimer responds in kind, and a courtship is initiated, not just between two light-skinned African Americans who remain loyal to the race, but between two young people who long to serve their Southern brethren—to effect their own form of justice in the flesh, in the capacity of Sunday school teacher and medical doctor. In their passion to uplift other African Americans of lesser standing, "their hearts beat in loving unison. One grand and noble purpose was giving tone and color to their lives and strengthening the bonds of affection between them" (266). In short, having had the benefit of education, due primarily to the accident of their white parentage, they will translate their white-skinned advantage into labors of love for their dark-skinned people who are still living as field-workers and share-croppers in ignorance and poverty in the postbellum South. As this example suggests, the poverty, ill health, and general deprivation of the great majority of black people, which were important thematic concerns in the slave narratives, serve in the postbellum novels more as a kind of contrapuntal background, providing in this case, for example, the rationale for Iola Leroy and her husband to return South, as part of their self-appointed mission to uplift their race. But what is abundantly clear is that the characters we are to admire and emulate are those who, by aligning themselves with people of lesser means and opportunities, work to achieve justice in the flesh for all the race.

Sprinkled throughout this genteel postwar nineteenth-century fiction, perhaps as a sop to the authors' own conscience or as a way to include the ambitions and concerns of their darker-skinned readers into the narrative, however, are also examples of admirable men and women of achievement who are not what the time would have called amalgams or mixed-race persons. Tom Anderson, from *Iola Leroy*, is a case in point. Of his friend Tom, Robert remarks that "he is just as black as black can be. He has been bought and sold like a beast, and yet there is not a braver man in all the company" (44). It is Tom, after all, who effects Iola's release from enslavement by bringing her case to the attention of the Northern post commander, who has bivouacked his soldiers nearby. But this courageous and self-effacing man is an early casualty in the novel, having been fatally wounded helping a party of soldiers escape rebel fire. Conversely, the accomplished and highly respected Lucille Delany and Rev. Carmicle arrive late in the novel, the minister just in time for its dénouement. Unlike Iola, whose looks are described frequently, Lucille is described but twice, though her estimable qualities receive considerable narrative attention. We learn initially that "she is of medium height, somewhat slender, and well formed, with dark, expressive eyes, full of thought and feeling." Yet further details of what she looks like are left to our imagination, conveyed as they are in the negative: "Neither hair nor complexion show the least hint of blood admixture" (199). In response to this information, which has been provided by Harry, Iola replies that she is "glad" since each "person of unmixed blood who succeeds in any department of literature, art, or science is a living argument for the capability which is in the race"—an observation with which her brother concurs (199). After Harry has proposed marriage to this "ideal woman," whom Iola reveres as being "grand, brave, intellectual, and religious," we learn further about her own (unfounded) worries that Harry's mother might not wish to have her as a daughter-in-law because "complexional prejudices are not confined to white people" (278). This is all the physical description she merits—her accomplishments and potential for effecting good being of more importance than her looks. Just as Marie Leroy's story had been dependent upon the color of her skin, Lucille Delany's story, the narrative makes clear (though it fails to pursue it), will be dependent on her character and intelligence. Of the virtually disembodied Carmicle, we learn merely that "he [has] no white blood in his veins"—the fact of which is self-evident "from his looks" to the racist Dr. Latrobe (227). But as admirable as many of them are, and as hard as they work to achieve justice in the flesh for themselves and their race, dark-skinned African Americans such as these remain, virtually to a person, minor characters in whatever novels they appear.[18]

This ambivalence in describing main characters with African features can be traced back to two of the founding texts of African American fiction, William Wells Brown's 1853 novel, *Clotel, or The President's Daughter*, and Frederick Douglass's 1853 novella, *The Heroic Slave*.[19] For her part, Clotel, the eponymous heroine of Brown's novel, has, for example, "a complexion as white as most of those who were waiting with a wish to become her purchasers; her features as finely defined as any of her sex of pure Anglo-Saxon"; moreover, her entire appearance "[indicated] one superior to her position" (Brown 1853, 42). In vivid contrast to the cultured, raven-haired, and statuesque Clotel, Pompey, as befitting his role as servant to the ruthless slave speculator Dick Walker, "was of low stature, round face" and had extraordinarily beautiful white teeth; in addition, "his eyes [were] large, lips thick, and hair short and woolly" (46).[20] Unlike the refined Clotel, Pompey also speaks in dialect. But George Green—the courageous, rebellious, and eloquent slave of Horatio Green and eventual husband of Clotel's daughter, Mary—is virtually indistinguishable from whites, making it impossible to detect the fact that "any African blood coursed through his veins. His hair was straight, soft, fine, and light; his eyes blue, nose prominent, lips thin, his head well formed, forehead high and prominent"—features that would suggest, in the phrenological taxonomy of the era, both high intelligence and good breeding (181). At the same time, the other heroic black man in the novel is described in the first edition as "a tall, full-bodied negro, whose very countenance beamed with intelligence" (133). Remarking on these narrative ambiguities, Richard Yarborough argues that in the works of these antebellum novelists, "incongruities in their characterizations frequently reflect some degree of ambivalence on their part toward the social values and literary images they felt constrained to endorse in their fiction" (Yarborough 1990, 170). He finds it notable, therefore, that in the 1864 version of the novel, *Clotelle; A Tale of the Southern States*, Brown describes William as "a tall, full-blooded African" (Brown 1864, 46) and uses this change to contend that by the mid-1860s, Brown had forsworn "some of the racist ideological assumptions that supported popular white conceptions of blacks" (170).

Yarborough also invites us to compare the two versions of Douglass's description of Madison Washington. In "Slavery, The Slumbering Volcano: An Address Delivered in New York, New York, on 23 April 1849," Douglass recounts the story of the brave and manly slave, whom he describes as "a black man, with woolly head, high cheek bones, protruding lip, distended nostril, and retreating forehead" who, freeing himself from chains and taking control of slave ship, secures its passage to port in a free state (Blassingame 1982, 155). Yet four years later, he was to describe this same heroic slave of extraordinary oratorical powers as being "of manly form. Tall, symmetrical, round, and strong. In his movements he seemed to combine, with the strength of a lion, a lion's elasticity. His whole appearance betokened Herculean strength; yet there was nothing savage or forbidding in his aspect" (Douglass 1853, 40). Taken in conjunction with his 1854 claim that the ignorant and downtrodden Irish physically resembled blacks in their debased appearance (cited in Blassingame 1982, 521), Douglass, according to Yarborough, fails to challenge "one of the fundamental assertions of the racist, proslavery position: that the appearance of most blacks signified inferiority" (Yarborough 1990, 174).

In the post-Reconstruction era, these dark-skinned black men are not necessarily incidental to the plot. In fact, like the characters Luke Sawyer in *Contending Forces*, Frank Fowler in *The House Behind the Cedars*, or Josh Green in *The Marrow of Tradition*, they are often indispensable to it. Still, until the advent of the Harlem Renaissance, the visible proof of their black embodiment seems, if not to disqualify them as heroic, at least to disqualify them as heroes— especially in the pages of genteel novels of sentimental romance and racial uplift. Luke Sawyer and *Contending Forces* I have already discussed. Here let me quickly discuss the other two novels and the heroic black men I have just mentioned.

In Charles W. Chesnutt's 1900 novel of passing, *The House Behind the Cedars*, Frank Fowler—"a dark-brown young man, small in stature, but with a well-shaped head, an expressive forehead, and features indicative of kindness, intelligence, humor, and imagination"—is the loyal neighbor who has watched Miss Molly's (that is, Mary Walden's) beautiful light-skinned daughter, Rena Walden (Rowena Warwick), grow into womanhood and, as long as he can remember, has loved her from afar (Chesnutt 1900, 35). Yet, knowing that she thinks of him only as a friend or a brother and does not return his affection, he never speaks to her of his love. When she is still a child, he literally saves her life and, once she has grown, secretly looks out for her—recognizing, though she and her mother do not, the interconnectedness in the flesh of even those who are separated by class and degrees of color. Throughout the narrative, moreover, he serves as a foil to the two men who will make Rena desperately unhappy and eventually kill her. The unassuming Frank is both literate in the conventional sense and skilled in reading people's character in their demeanor—as Rena's mother is not, in either case. With the exception of the narrator, Frank alone can see in one of Rena's would-be suitors mere "affectation" and "hypocrisy," characteristics that make him quite unsuitable for this woman Frank adores (195). Of this Mr. Jefferson Wain, who is overbearing and insincere, the narrator has informed us that if he were to be scrutinized carefully in "a close or hostile inspection there would have been some features of his ostensibly good-natured face—the shifty eye, the full and slightly drooping lower lip—which might have given a student of physiognomy food for reflection" (189). Yet Rena's mother, Mary Walden, is not as careful a reader as Frank or the narrator and sees in Wain a man darker than she might have preferred but whose features, of the "broad mulatto type," were nonetheless, to her own prejudiced eye, "more than compensated . . . by very straight black hair, and, as soon appeared, a great facility of complimentary speech" (178–79). Because of her blindness, Mary Walden allows her daughter to leave Patesville with this unsavory fellow, while Frank watches her departure with deep misgiving (203). For his beloved Rena has already had her heart broken once by her aristocratic, white fiancé George Tryon, who has spurned her affection and broken their engagement upon discovering he had been about to marry a black woman who, like her brother John (his own friend), had been passing for white.

Overcoming her grief and her prejudice toward those darker than she, Rena has determined that she will do her part "for the advancement of those who had just set their feet upon the ladder of progress" and has secured employment as a country schoolteacher, to which job Wain is escorting her (Chesnutt 1900, 175). Seeing her leave with Wain inspires Frank—with justifiable cause—to worry again for her safety and happiness. Although it takes her a while to read him correctly, once she does she "soon fathomed his shallow, selfish soul, and detected, or at least divined, behind his mask of good-nature a lurking brutality" that frightens her (222). Shortly thereafter, caught between the unwelcome advances of her former fiancé, who seems to have become obsessed with her, and that of Jeff Wain, Rena, in a fateful moment, plunges deep into the woods seeking refuge from these unworthy suitors. Weakened by emotional trauma and fears for her virginity, she wanders around lost in a downpour and soon becomes delirious. It is there that Frank finds her, having driven to Sampson County to warn her that Wain had not only been married but had abused his wife. Mistaking her protector for both Wain and Tryon in her delirium, she nearly destroys him with grief, and in a moment of tenderness he finally confesses his love. But she is beyond love and help and dies shortly after he carries her back to her mother's. Before dying, however, she asks for Frank and sadly acknowledges that he, her "good friend" has loved her "best of all" (264). Thus it is that she finally affirms, in a moment of true reciprocity, her interconnectedness with this man who is darker than she. Moreover, in accepting his loving devotion she learns, perhaps for the very first time, that, had she only recognized it, she did have a chance to experience justice in the flesh—if not with the white people, whom she has been taught to admire and emulate, at least with her own race in the dark-skinned body-self of Frank Fowler. Thus, by the end, the novel has made it abundantly clear that in giving her heart to her brother's white friend, Rena Walden has slighted the better man.

Notwithstanding the attention I have given to Frank and Rena's relationship, the novel really pivots on the ill-fated romance of Rena Walden and George Tryon, as Rena tries to follow in her brother's footsteps and live as "Rowena Warwick," a cultured white lady. Found out, after a series of fateful coincidences, she is rejected by Tryon, who cannot reconcile himself to the idea that he had actually planned to marry a black woman. With this Southern aristocrat, affection for a mulatto woman is not the issue, but marriage most assuredly is. Yet as racist as he is, he is still torn in his attitudes toward this beautiful, sensitive woman: "Reason, common-sense, the instinctive ready-made judgments of his training and environment—the deep-seated prejudices of race and caste—commanded him to dismiss Rena from his thoughts. His stubborn heart simply would not let go" (Chesnutt 1900, 173). Finally vowing to make amends to her, he travels to Patesville, only to spy through the window just as she has agreed to dance with Jeff Wain. It is a sight that repulses him, for there she appears, "not pale with grief and hollow-eyed with weeping, but flushed with pleasure, around her waist the arm of a burly, grinning mulatto," whom Tryon knows only too well (198). This single moment is all it takes for him to reconstruct Rena in the stereotypical image of the race he so despises, accusing her in his thoughts of adopting "[w]ith the monkey-like imitativeness of the Negro . . . the manners of white people" for as long as it suited her (200). Even so, once he realizes that she is teaching school close to his own estate, he writes her a letter, wishing to meet with her and set things right between them—an offer she spurns as he had once spurned her and her affections, reminding him that not even friendship is possible between himself as a white man and herself as the black woman she has become in his eyes (231, 232). Yet her letter of rejection only inflames his passions further and he regards it as his right—as one from a superior caste—to see her if he wishes. When he acts on this conviction, he contributes to her delirium and destruction. Although he cannot bring himself to marry this woman he loves, he does honor her brother's secret and informs no one that John Warwick, the lawyer, is really a black man, who, as a young boy had thought matters through and declared in a stunning moment of self-definition, that, indeed, he is no Negro, for, as he puts it to the astonished but sympathetic Judge Straight, a "Negro is black; I am white, and not black" (153).

In Chesnutt's 1901 novel, *The Marrow of Tradition*, Josh Green is a powerful, dark-skinned black man who has vowed to take vengeance on those who have killed his father and driven his mother insane. At the novel's end, he leads his people into battle during the Wellington riot that corrupt white leaders, including the town's newspaper editor, have fomented against their own African American citizens. Although Green's role is crucial to the story, he is not its hero—as the description of the genteel, cultured, and highly educated Dr. Miller makes abundantly clear. For his part, Dr. Miller's "erect form, broad shoulders, clear eyes, fine teeth, and pleasingly moulded features showed nowhere any sign of that degeneration which the pessimist so sadly maintains is the inevitable heritage of mixed races" (Chesnutt 1901, 49). Because of his superior demeanor, Miller has been favorably compared with a white man with whom, at the story's beginning, he has been traveling. In striking contrast to this light-skinned doctor, the angry, uneducated, and rebellious Josh Green, who speaks in heavy dialect, is described as "a great black figure [who] *crawled* off the trucks of the rear car" when the train in which both are riding arrives at the station (62; emphasis added). As the story progresses and the white men work their terrible mischief by inciting a murderous riot in town, during which dozens of black men, women and even children are slaughtered, Josh calls on Miller to lead their resistance. But Miller demurs, advising those who have gathered around Josh to give it up, because their time has not yet come (283). In a passage of indirect discourse that seems attributable to Miller himself, the narrator explains Miller's refusal to act by noting that "[s]o thoroughly diseased was public opinion in matters of race that the negro who died for the common rights of humanity might look for no meed of admiration or glory. At such a time, in the white man's eyes, a negro's courage would be mere desperation; his love of liberty, a mere animal dislike of restraint. Every finer human instinct would be interpreted in terms of savagery" (296). As the white mob, first egged on by the town's first citizens but now dominated by "the baser element of the white population, recruited from the wharves and the saloons" (304), attacks and sets afire the hospital for blacks, which had been founded by Miller's father, the imposing form of Josh Green rises to prominence, still untouched by the flames or the bullets. Driven by rage and a lifelong desire to avenge the wrong done his parents, he drives through the mob to engage his enemy, Captain McBane, in combat that proves fatal to both of them (309). One of the two, the narrative states, "died as the fool dieth"—yet Chesnutt declines to say which and resolve the ambiguity (309). He does assert, however, that "McBane's death was merciful, compared with the nameless horrors he had heaped upon the hundreds of helpless mortals who had fallen into his hands during his career as a contractor of convict labor" (309–10).

Yet, as vivid and climactic as this scene is, the story belongs to those two middle-class, light-skinned African Americans, Dr. Miller and his wife. Not only has Janet Miller been deprived of her patrimony by the duplicitous actions of her white half-sister, but she also loses her young son when he is shot during the riots. Although the riot was instigated by the racist Major Carteret and his cronies, when Carteret's child becomes dangerously ill, out of necessity he must seek Miller's medical attention. When Miller refuses, wracked by his own loss, Carteret's wife comes pleading for help, invoking the aid of Mrs. Miller who is half-sister to Olivia Carteret, the two having had the same white father, but different mothers, one a black one, the other a white one. Establishing beyond all doubt her superior character, Janet Miller sends her husband, against his own wishes, to save the life of Carteret's son. Although Janet sends her husband to aid her estranged sister's child, she bitterly rejects Olivia's desperate and long-overdue acknowledgment of their familial relationship, "extorted from a reluctant conscience by the agony of a mother's fears" (328). Sick with grief at her own loss and contemptuous of this sister for whose loving attention she had once longed, she proudly informs her that she spurns her "father's name, [her] father's wealth, [her] sisterly recognition" (329). The novel's last line refers to the imperiled state of the desperately ill Carteret child, but given the other story lines, it reverberates with additional meaning: "There's time enough, but none to spare" (329). As the symbolically named Judge Straight observes, in a passage of indirect discourse in *The House Behind the Cedars*, "One curse of Negro slavery was, and one part of its baleful heritage is, that it poisoned the fountains of human sympathy. Under a system where men might sell their own children without social reprobation or loss of prestige, it was not surprising that some of them should hate their distant cousins" (Chesnutt 1900, 108).

Nevertheless, human sympathy, human connectedness, and even justice in the flesh are not absent from these post-Reconstruction novels. Although there is not *sufficient* sympathy, connectedness, or justice and many African Americans suffer humiliation, deprivation, and even death (in real life as well as in fiction) because of this shortage, the novels, in their own displaced fashion, do model for us, as the slave narratives before them, that as embodied beings we are all always already predisposed to achieving justice in the flesh. The potential and proclivity for justice, reciprocity, and interconnectedness are already there in our body-selves. Our task is to bring them into the social and political realm by learning (again) to think through and listen to the body. In these remarkable nineteenth-century texts that we have inherited from slaves and the descendants of slaves we have been shown the way.

NOTES

1. For discussion of antebellum African American novels, see Andrews (1990).
2. For another comprehensive account of this era and its racism, see Fredrickson

(1971). For application of these ideas as they pertain to African American women's domestic novels, see also Tate (1992, especially 9–11).

3. For further discussion of the historical meaning and literary treatment of lynching in this country, see Trudier Harris (1984). Of the practice itself, Harris reminds us that originally lynching referred merely to the punishment delivered to an individual without benefit of an officially constituted court hearing; ordinarily such punishment, which was directed at both black and white law-breakers, "consisted of whipping, or tarring and feathering, or being ridden out of town on a rail" (6). As slaves, blacks were largely immune to lynchings because of their value as property. After the Civil War, however, the punishment became more severe—involving mutilation, hanging, burning, and almost certain death—and was reserved predominantly for black people, most particularly black men. "Between 1882 and 1927," according to Harris, "an estimated 4,951 persons were lynched in the United States. Of that number, 3513 were black and 76 of those were black women" (7).

4. On this, see also Giddings (1984).

5. One notable exception to this pattern can be found in Belton Piedmont, the dark-skinned hero of Sutton E. Griggs's 1899 novel, *Imperium in Imperio*. In one extraordinary scene, Piedmont remains alive but unconscious after he has been hanged, shot at the base of his skull, pronounced dead, and removed to a doctor's dissecting table. Feigning death once he regains consciousness, he suffers through the initial stages of the autopsy, only to escape after plunging a knife into the doctor's throat, covering the corpse with a sheet, and leaving a note supposedly written by the doctor himself that instructs his friends not to touch "the nigger" until he returns (155–58). It is significant, however, that Griggs published his own novels and "promoted the sale of his books among the black masses," thus leaving their existence "virtually unknown to white Americans of his time" (Gloster 1969, ii).

6. In her discussion of nineteenth-century sentimental fiction, Sánchez-Eppler describes how even though "the female body, and particularly female sexual desires, are at least covertly inscribed within feminist-abolitionist texts, the paradigmatic body reclaimed in these writings is that of the slave" (Sánchez-Eppler 1988, 30; 1993).

7. Others have described the agendas as exposing the harm done to African American men and women by the socially sanctioned practice of forced concubinage (that is to say, rape) and as furthering in a postbellum venue the original claims of the abolitionists. See, for example, Carby (1987) and Baker (1991). I would not dispute these interpretations; my emphasis simply lies elsewhere.

8. As John Ernest has said admiringly (in a personal communication), this novel has everything—it's all there. For a critique of the novel as "a virtual curiosity cabinet of its era," see Baker (1991), in which he claims further that it appears that "the narrative mind of the text wishes to sound its repleteness, its comprehensive intelligence as a fit complement for the novel's whitened faces" (26, 28). For a thoroughly historicized, more sympathetic, and systematic reading of the novel, see Carby (1987, 128–44).

9. See Yarborough (1988, xli).

10. To those who have argued that Hopkins's intention in this novel was "to glorify the possibilities of the black race if only it would integrate with and eventually lose itself within the white," Carby counters that "the presence of 'mixed' characters in the text did not represent an implicit desire to 'lighten' blacks through blood ties with whites. Hopkins wanted to emphasize those sets of social relations and practices which were the consequence of a social system that exercised white supremacy through the act of rape"

(Carby 1987, 140). Carby reads Hopkins's "Talma Gordon," a short story published in the *Colored American Magazine* in 1900, as making the same case for interconnectedness (Carby 1987, 135). Noting that the desire to establish kinship occurs with regularity in African American narrative forms, she describes how, in *Contending Forces*, Hopkins modifies the pattern by moving outside "racial boundaries" (136).

11. In the opening sentence of her preface she explains that she seeks neither fame nor money in writing her book but is instead attempting "to raise the stigma of degradation from my race" (Hopkins 1900, 13).

12. On the portrayal of these two men as Washington and Du Bois, respectively, see Yarborough (1988). Of Hopkins's sympathetic portrait of Dr. Lewis, Yarborough observes that it shows how far she is able to go in identifying with a wide range of her African American characters and the differing views they represent (xxxix). See also Baker (1991).

13. More critical than I of the novel, Baker faults it and other African American women's novels of the time for conveying "an implicit approval of white patriarchy [that is] inscribed in the very features of the mulatto character's face" (Baker 1991, 25). Comparing what he paternalistically labels the "daughters' strategy" to that of "Washington's manipulations of minstrel discourse" (note that Washington is not a "son" here), Baker claims that a distinction should be made between his "mastery of form insofar as it refuses the split-subject position that comes from inhabiting the black-faced minstrel mask. For the nineteenth-century daughters chose, finally, a moralizing and discursively subservient disguise" (26).

14. For differing views of why characters of mixed races dominated postbellum African American fiction, as occurs especially in *Iola Leroy*, see Christian (1980, 29–30), and Carby (1987, 88–92), or Carby's 1987 introduction to the novel. For a critical view of this fiction, see Baker (1991, 21–28). Claudia Tate has argued that "[e]ven in those instances when the racial designation of the characters was effaced to some degree, the author's racial identity or black cultural markers indirectly racialized the story" (Tate 1992, 11).

15. If I had the space I would argue for the reversibility of touch here, too, with the reader's hands being touched by the body of the text they hold.

16. Perhaps there is good reason that persons in novels are called *characters*.

17. For an historical overview of this phenomenon, see Christian (1980).

18. As I have noted previously, a striking exception to this is Griggs's 1899 *Imperium in Imperio*.

19. For a full discussion of this, see Yarborough (1990).

20. Yarborough reminds us that the degrading role of Pompey "is one that Brown himself filled before his escape and that he describes in his autobiography"; but, given the freedoms of fictionalization, Brown "portrays Pompey in stereotypical terms that he would never have applied to himself" (Yarborough 1989, 113).

Bibliography

Acholonu, Catherine Obianuju. 1989. *The Igbo Roots of Olaudah Equiano: An Anthropological Research*. Owerri, Nigeria: Afa Publications.

Adell, Sandra. 1994. *Double-Consciousness/Double Bind: Theoretical Issues in Twentieth-Century Black Literature*. Urbana, Ill.: University of Illinois Press.

Allison, Robert J., ed. 1995. *The Interesting Narrative of the Life of Olaudah Equiano. Written by Himself*. Boston: St. Martin's Press.

Althusser, Louis. 1970. "Ideology and Ideological State Apparatuses." Reprinted in *Lenin and Philosophy and Other Essays* by Louis Althusser. Trans. Ben Brewster. New York: Monthly Review Press, 1971, 127–86.

Althusser, Louis, and Etienne Balibar. 1968. *Reading Capital*. Trans. Ben Brewster. Reprinted New York: Verso, 1979.

Anderson, James D. 1978. "Political and Scholarly Interests in the 'Negro Personality': A Review of *The Slave Community*." In *Revisiting Blassingame's The Slave Community: The Scholars Respond*. Ed. Al-Tony Gilmore. Westport, Conn.: Greenwood Press, 123–34.

Andrews, William L. 1982. "The First Fifty Years of the Slave Narrative, 1760–1810." In *The Art of Slave Narrative: Original Essays in Criticism and Theory*. Eds. John Sekora and Darwin T. Turner. Macomb, Ill.: Western Illinois University, An Essays in Literature Book, 6–24.

———. 1986. *To Tell a Free Story: The First Century of Afro-American Autobiography, 1760–1865*. Urbana, Ill.: University of Illinois Press.

———. 1988. Introduction. *Six Women's Slave Narratives*. General editor Henry Louis Gates, Jr. New York: Oxford University Press, Schomburg Library of Nineteenth-Century Black Women Writers, xxix–xli.

———. 1989. "The Representation of Slavery and the Rise of Afro-American Literary Realism 1865–1920." In *Slavery and the Literary Imagination*. Selected Papers from the English Institute, 1987. New series, No. 13. Ed. Deborah E. McDowell and Arnold Rampersad. Baltimore: Johns Hopkins University Press, 62–80.

———. 1990. "The Novelization of Voice in Early African American Narrative." *Publica-*

    tions of the Modern Language Association 105.1 (January): 23–34.

——. 1991. Introduction. *Critical Essays on Frederick Douglass*. Ed. William L. An-
    drews. Boston: G. K. Hall, 166–91.

Appiah, [Kwame] Anthony. 1985–86. "The Uncompleted Argument: Du Bois and the
    Illusion of Race." In *"Race," Writing, and Difference*. Ed. Henry Louis Gates,
    Jr. Chicago: University of Chicago Press, 21–37.

——. 1989. "The Conservation of 'Race.'" *Black American Literature Forum* 23.1
    (Spring): 37–60.

——. 1992. *In My Father's House: Africa in the Philosophy of Culture*. New York: Ox-
    ford University Press.

Awkward, Michael. 1990. "Negotiations of Power: White Critics, Black Texts, and the
    Self-Referential Impulse." *American Literary History* 2.4 (Winter): 581–606.

——. 1995. *Negotiating Difference: Race, Gender, and the Politics of Positionality*.
    Chicago: University of Chicago Press.

Baker, Houston A., Jr. 1980. *The Journey Back: Issues in Black Literature and Criticism*.
    Chicago: University of Chicago Press.

——. 1984. *Blues, Ideology, and Afro-American Literature*. Chicago: University of Chi-
    cago Press.

——. 1985. "Autobiographical Acts and the Voice of the Southern Slave." In *The
    Slave's Narrative*. Eds. Charles T. Davis and Henry Louis Gates, Jr. New
    York: Oxford University Press, 242–61.

——. 1985–86. "Caliban's Triple Play." In *"Race," Writing, and Difference*. Ed. Henry
    Louis Gates, Jr. Chicago: University of Chicago Press, 381–95.

——. 1991. *Workings of the Spirit: The Poetics of Afro-American Women's Writing*.
    Chicago: University of Chicago Press.

Bakhtin, Mikhail. 1965. *Rabelais and His World*. Trans. Hélène Iswolsky. Reprinted
    Bloomington, Ind.: Indiana University Press, 1984.

——. 1987. *The Dialogic Imagination: Four Essays*. Ed. Michael Holquist. Trans. Caryl
    Emerson and Michael Holquist. Austin, Texas: University of Texas Press.

Balbus, Isaac D. 1987. "Disciplining Women: Michel Foucault and the Power of Femi-
    nist Discourse." In *Feminism as Critique*. Eds. Seyla Benhabib and Drucilla
    Cornell. Reprinted Minneapolis: University of Minnesota Press, 1988, 110–27.

Banta, Martha. 1987. *Imaging American Women: Idea and Ideals in Cultural History*.
    New York: Columbia University Press.

Barker, Francis. 1995. *The Tremulous Private Body: Essays on Subjection*. Ann Arbor,
    Mich.: University of Michigan Press.

Barrett, Lindon. 1995. "African-American Slave Narratives: Literacy, the Body, Author-
    ity." *American Literary History* 7.3 (Fall): 415–42.

Barthelemy, Anthony G. 1988. Introduction. *Collected Black Women's Narratives*. The
    Schomburg Library of Nineteenth-Century Black Women Writers. New York:
    Oxford University Press, xxix–xlviii.

Barthes, Roland. 1953. *Writing Degree Zero*. Trans. Annette Lavers and Colin Smith.
    Reprinted New York: Noonday Press, 1991.

——. 1957. *Mythologies*. Trans. Annette Lavers. Reprinted New York: Noonday Press,
    1992.

——. 1968. "The Death of the Author." Reprinted in *Image, Music, Text*. Trans. Stephen
    Heath. New York: Hill and Wang, 1986, 142–48.

——. 1971. "From Work to Text." Trans. Josué V. Harari. Reprinted in *Textual Strate-*

gies: Perspectives in Post-Structuralist Criticism. Ed. Josué V. Harari. Ithaca, N. Y.: Cornell University Press, 1979, 73–82.

Baym, Nina. 1984. *Novels, Readers, and Reviewers: Responses to Fiction in Antebellum America.* Ithaca, N. Y.: Cornell University Press.

Beaujour, Michel. 1981. "Some Paradoxes of Description." *Yale French Studies* 61: 27–59.

Beecher, Catherine. 1841. *A Treatise on Domestic Economy.* Reprinted New York: Schocken Books, 1977. (Originally published as *Treatise on Domestic Economy for the Use of Young Ladies at Home and at School.*)

Benjamin, Walter. 1986. *Reflections: Essays, Aphorisms, Autobiographical Writings.* Ed. Peter Demetz. Trans. Edmund Jephcott. New York: Schocken Books.

Berger, Harry, Jr. 1987. "Bodies and Texts." *Representations* 17 (Winter): 144–66.

Bibb, Henry. 1850. *Narrative of the Life and Adventures of Henry Bibb, An American Slave, Written by Himself,* 3rd edn. New York: Published by the author. MacDonald and Lee, Printers.

Birkerts, Sven. 1994. *The Gutenberg Elegies: The Fate of Reading in an Electronic Age.* Reprinted New York: Fawcett Columbine, 1995.

Blassingame, John W. 1977. *Slave Testimony: Two Centuries of Letters, Speeches, Interviews, and Autobiographies.* Baton Rouge, La.: Louisiana State University Press.

——. 1978. "Redefining *The Slave Community*: A Response to the Critics." In *Revisiting Blassingame's The Slave Community: The Scholars Respond.* Ed. Al-Tony Gilmore. Westport, Conn.: Greenwood Press, 135–68.

——. 1979. *The Slave Community: Plantation Life in the Antebellum South.* Revised and enlarged edition. New York: Oxford University Press. (Originally published in 1972.)

——, ed. 1982. *The Frederick Douglass Papers.* Series One: Speeches, Debates, and Interviews. Vol. 2: 1847–54. New Haven, Conn.: Yale University Press.

Bordo, Susan. 1987. *The Flight to Objectivity: Essays on Cartesianism and Culture.* Albany: State University of New York Press.

Boss, Medard. 1979. *Existential Foundations of Medicine and Psychology.* Trans. Stephen Conway and Anne Cleaves. New York: Jason Aronson.

Bourdieu, Pierre. 1972. *Outline of a Theory of Practice.* Trans. Richard Nice. Reprinted New York: Cambridge University Press, 1991.

Braxton, Joanne M. 1986. "Harriet Jacobs' *Incidents in the Life of a Slave Girl*: The Redefinition of the Slave Narrative Genre." *The Massachusetts Review* 27.2 (Summer): 379–87.

Breau, Elizabeth. 1993. "Identifying Satire: *Our Nig.*" *Callaloo* 16.2 (Spring): 455–65.

Brent, Linda (Harriet Jacobs). 1861. *Incidents in the Life of a Slave Girl. Written by Herself.* Ed. L. Maria Child. Reprinted Cambridge, Mass.: Harvard University Press, 1987. (Reprinted edition edited by Jean Fagan Yellin.)

Brown, William Wells. 1847. *Narrative of William W. Brown, A Fugitive Slave. Written by Himself.* Reprinted in *Five Slave Narratives: A Compendium.* Ed. William Loren Katz. New York: Arno Press, 1968.

——. 1853. *Clotel, or The President's Daughter.* Reprinted New York: Macmillan, 1970.

——. 1864. *Clotelle: A Tale of The Southern States.* Facsimile edition reprinted in *William Wells Brown and Clotelle: A Portrait of the Artist in the First Negro*

Novel, by J. Noel Heermance. Hamden, Conn.: Archon, 1969.

——. 1880. *My Southern Home: or, The South and Its People*. Reprinted Upper Saddle River, N. J.: Gregg Press, 1968.

Butler, Judith. 1987. "Variations on Sex and Gender: Beauvoir, Wittig and Foucault." In *Feminism as Critique*. Eds. Seyla Benhabib and Drucilla Cornell. Reprinted Minneapolis: University of Minnesota Press, 1988, 128–42.

——. 1990. *Gender Trouble: Feminism and the Subversion of Identity*. New York: Routledge.

——. 1993. *Bodies That Matter: On the Discursive Limits of 'Sex.'* New York: Routledge.

Butler, Marilyn. 1985. "Against Tradition: The Case for a Particularized Historical Method." In *Historical Studies and Literary Criticism*. Ed. Jerome J. McGann. Madison, Wis.: University of Wisconsin Press, 25–47.

Byerman, Keith. 1982. "We Wear the Mask: Deceit as Theme and Style in Slave Narratives." In *The Art of Slave Narrative: Original Essays in Criticism and Theory*. Eds. John Sekora and Darwin T. Turner. Macomb, Ill.: Western Illinois University, An Essays in Literature Book, 70–82.

Carby, Hazel. 1987. *Reconstructing Womanhood: The Emergence of the Afro-American Woman Novelist*. New York: Oxford University Press.

Carter, Ralph D. 1978. "Slavery and the Climate of Opinion." In *Revisiting Blassingame's The Slave Community: The Scholars Respond*. Ed. Al-Tony Gilmore. Westport, Conn.: Greenwood Press, 70–95.

Chesnutt, Charles W. 1900. *The House Behind the Cedars*. Reprinted Toronto, Ontario: Macmillan, 1969.

——. 1901. *The Marrow of Tradition*. Reprinted Ann Arbor, Mich.: University of Michigan Press, 1969.

Christian, Barbara. 1980. *Black Women Novelists: The Development of a Tradition, 1892–1976*. Westport, Conn.: Greenwood Press.

Clarke, John Henrik. 1978. "*The Slave Community* and the World Community: Some Notes Toward a New Inquiry into the Historiography of the Atlantic Slave Trade." In *Revisiting Blassingame's The Slave Community: The Scholars Respond*. Ed. Al-Tony Gilmore. Westport, Conn.: Greenwood Press, 111–22.

Cobb, Martha K. 1982. "The Slave Narrative and the Black Literary Tradition." In *The Art of Slave Narrative: Original Essays in Criticism and Theory*. Eds. John Sekora and Darwin T. Turner. Macomb, Ill.: Western Illinois University, An Essays in Literature Book, 36–44.

Cornelius, Janet Duitsman. 1991. *"When I Can Read My Title Clear": Literacy, Slavery, and Religion in the Antebellum South*. Columbia, S. C.: University of South Carolina Press.

Cowper, William. 1785. *The Task, A Poem, in Six Books*. Reprinted New York: Printed by William Durell, for Thomas Allen, 1796.

Craft, William. 1860. *Running a Thousand Miles for Freedom; or, The Escape of William and Ellen Craft from Slavery*. Reprinted in *Great Slave Narratives*. Selected and introduced by Arna Bontemps. Boston: Beacon Press, 1969, 269–331.

Csordas, Thomas. 1990. "Embodiment as a Paradigm for Anthropology." *Ethos: Journal of the Society for Psychological Anthropology* 18.1 (March): 5–47.

Culler, Jonathan. 1975. *Structuralist Poetics: Structuralism, Linguistics, and the Study of*

Literature. Ithaca, N. Y.: Cornell University Press.

Davis, Charles T., and Henry Louis Gates, Jr., eds. 1985. *The Slave's Narrative.* New York: Oxford University Press.

Davis, Cynthia J. 1993. "Speaking the Body's Pain: Harriet Wilson's *Our Nig.*" *African American Review* 27.3 (Fall): 391–404.

Delaney, Lucy A. c. 1891. *From the Darkness Cometh the Light or Struggles for Freedom.* Reprinted in *Six Women's Slave Narratives.* General editor Henry Louis Gates, Jr. New York: Oxford University Press, Schomburg Library of Nineteenth-Century Black Women Writers, 1988.

Derrida, Jacques. 1967. *Of Grammatology.* Trans. Gayatri Chakravorty Spivak. Reprinted Baltimore: Johns Hopkins University Press, 1976.

———. 1978. *Writing and Difference.* Trans. Alan Bass. Chicago: University of Chicago Press.

Dillon, M. C. 1988. *Merleau-Ponty's Ontology.* Bloomington, Ind.: Indiana University Press.

———. 1990. "Écart: Reply to Claude Lefort's 'Flesh and Otherness.' " In *Ontology and Alterity in Merleau-Ponty.* Eds. Galen A. Johnson and Michael B. Smith. Evanston, Ill.: Northwestern University Press, 14–26.

Doriani, Beth Maclay. 1991. "Black Womanhood in Nineteenth-Century America: Subversion and Self-Construction in Two Women's Autobiographies." *American Quarterly* 43.2 (June): 199–222.

Douglas, Ann. 1977. *The Feminization of American Culture.* Reprinted New York: Avon, 1978.

Douglass, Frederick. 1845. *Narrative of the Life of Frederick Douglass, an American Slave. Written by Himself.* Reprinted in *Frederick Douglass: Autobiographies.* New York: Library of America, 1994, 1–102.

———. 1853. *The Heroic Slave.* Reprinted in *Violence in the Black Imagination: Essays and Documents.* Ed. Ronald T. Takaki. New York: Oxford University Press, 1993, 37–77.

———. 1855. *My Bondage and My Freedom.* Reprinted in *Frederick Douglass: Autobiographies.* New York: Library of America, 1994, 103–452.

———. 1893. *Life and Times of Frederick Douglass Written by Himself.* Reprinted in *Frederick Douglass: Autobiographies.* New York: Library of America, 1994, 453–1045.

Doyle, Laura. 1994. *Bordering on the Body: The Racial Matrix of Modern Fiction and Culture.* New York: Oxford University Press.

Du Bois, W. E. B. 1897. "The Conservation of Races." Reprinted in *W. E. B. Du Bois: A Reader.* Ed. David Levering Lewis. New York: Henry Holt, 1995, 20–27.

———. 1903. *The Souls of Black Folk.* Reprinted in *W. E. B. Du Bois: A Reader.* Ed. David Levering Lewis. New York: Henry Holt, 1995, 357–547.

———. 1926. "Opinion of W. E. B. Du Bois." *The Crisis* 31.4 (February): 163–65.

duCille, Ann. 1993. *The Coupling Convention: Sex, Text, and Tradition in Black Women's Fiction.* New York: Oxford University Press.

———. 1994. "The Occult of True Black Womanhood: Critical Demeanor and Black Feminist Studies." *Signs* 19.3 (Spring): 591–629.

Dyer, Richard. 1986. *Heavenly Bodies: Film Stars and Society.* New York: St. Martin's.

Eagleton, Terry. 1976. *Marxism and Literary Criticism.* Berkeley: University of California Press.

Elias, Norbert. 1939. *The Development of Manners: Changes in the Code of Conduct and Feeling in Early Modern Times*. Trans. Edmund Jephcott. Reprinted New York: Urizen Books, 1978. Vol. I of *The Civilizing Process*.

Elkins, Stanley M. 1976. *Slavery: A Problem in American Institutional and Intellectual Life*, 3rd. and rev. edn. Chicago: University of Chicago Press.

Equiano, Olaudah. 1814. *The Interesting Narrative of the Life of Olaudah Equiano, or Gustavus Vassa, The African. Written by Himself.* A New Edition, corrected. Reprinted in *The Classic Slave Narratives*. Ed. Henry Louis Gates, Jr. New York: Mentor, 1987, 1–182.

Ernest, John. 1995. *Resistance and Reformation in Nineteenth-Century African-American Literature*. Jackson, Miss.: University Press of Mississippi.

Fahnestock, Jeanne. 1981. "The Heroine of Irregular Features: Physiognomy and Conventions of Heroine Description." *Victorian Studies* 24.3 (Spring): 325–50.

Fanon, Frantz. 1952. *Black Skin White Masks*. Trans. Charles Lam Markmann. Reprinted London: Paladin, 1970.

Fields, Barbara J[eanne]. 1982. "Ideology and Race in American History." In *Region, Race, and Reconstruction: Essays in Honor of C. Vann Woodward*. Eds. J. Morgan Kousser and James M. McPherson. New York: Oxford University Press, 143–77.

——. 1990. "Slavery, Race and Ideology in the United States of America." *New Left Review* 181 (May/June): 95–119.

Fishburn, Katherine. 1977. *Richard Wright's Hero: The Faces of a Rebel-Victim*. Metuchen, N. J.: Scarecrow Press.

——. 1982. *Women in Popular Culture: A Reference Guide*. Westport, Conn.: Greenwood Press.

——. 1995. *Reading Buchi Emecheta: Cross-Cultural Conversations*. Westport, Conn.: Greenwood Press.

Fisher, Dexter, and Robert B. Stepto. 1979. *Afro-American Literature: The Reconstruction of Instruction*. Ed. New York: The Modern Language Association of America.

Foner, Philip S. 1950a. *The Life and Writings of Frederick Douglass: Early Years, 1817–1849*. New York: International Publishers.

——. 1950b. *The Life and Writings of Frederick Douglass. Vol. 2. Pre-Civil War Decade, 1850–1860*. New York: International Publishers.

Foreman, P. Gabrielle. 1990. "The Spoken and the Silenced in *Incidents in the Life of a Slave Girl* and *Our Nig*." *Callaloo* 13.2 (Spring): 313–24.

Foster, Frances Smith. 1985. "Adding Color and Contour to Early American Self-Portraitures: Autobiographical Writings of Afro-American Women." In *Conjuring: Black Women, Fiction, and Literary Tradition*. Eds. Marjorie Pryse and Hortense J. Spillers. Bloomington, Ind.: Indiana University Press, 25–38.

——. 1993. "Harriet Jacobs's *Incidents* and the 'Careless Daughters' (and Sons) Who Read It." In *The (Other) American Traditions: Nineteenth-Century Women Writers*. Ed. Joyce W. Warren. New Brunswick, N. J.: Rutgers University Press, 1993, 92–107.

——. 1994. *Witnessing Slavery: The Development of Ante-bellum Slave Narratives*, 2nd edn. Madison, Wis.: University of Wisconsin Press.

Foucault, Michel. 1970. *The Order of Things: An Archaeology of the Human Sciences*. Reprinted New York: Vintage Books, 1973.

——. 1971. "Revolutionary Action: 'Until Now.'" Reprinted in *Language, Counter-Memory, Practice: Selected Essays and Interviews*. Ed. Donald F. Bouchard. Trans. Donald F. Bouchard and Sherry Simon. Ithaca, N. Y.: Cornell University Press, 1977, 218–33.

——. 1975. *Discipline and Punish: The Birth of the Prison*. Trans. Alan Sheridan. Reprinted New York: Vintage, 1979.

——. 1979. "What Is an Author?" Trans. Josué V. Harari. In *Textual Strategies: Perspectives on Post-Structuralist Criticism*. Ed. Josué V. Harari. Ithaca, N. Y.: Cornell University Press, 141–60.

Fox-Genovese, Elizabeth. 1987. "To Write My Self: The Autobiographies of Afro-American Women." In *Feminist Issues in Literary Scholarship*. Ed. Shari Benstock. Bloomington, Ind.: Indiana University Press, 161–80.

——. 1988. *Within the Plantation Household: Black and White Women of the Old South*. Chapel Hill, N. C.: University of North Carolina Press.

Franchot, Jenny. 1990. "The Punishment of Esther: Frederick Douglass and the Construction of the Feminine." In *Frederick Douglass: New Literary and Historical Essays*. Ed. Eric J. Sundquist. New York: Cambridge University Press, 141–65.

Franklin, John Hope. 1967. *From Slavery to Freedom: A History of Negro Americans*, 3rd edn. Reprinted New York: Vintage Books, 1969.

Fraser, Nancy. 1989. *Unruly Practices: Power, Discourse and Gender in Contemporary Social Theory*. Minneapolis: University of Minnesota Press.

Fredrickson, George M. 1971. *The Black Image in the White Mind: The Debate on Afro-American Character and Destiny, 1817–1914*. New York: Harper and Row.

Fukuyama, Francis. 1992. *The End of History*. New York: Free Press.

Fuss, Diana. 1989. *Essentially Speaking: Feminism, Nature and Difference*. New York: Routledge.

Gadamer, Hans-Georg. 1989. *Truth and Method*. Trans. and revised by Joel Weinsheimer and Donald G. Marshall. 2nd rev. edn. New York: Crossroad.

Garfield, Deborah M., and Rafia Zafar, eds. 1996. *Harriet Jacobs and Incidents in the Life of a Slave Girl*. New Critical Essays. New York: Cambridge University Press.

Gatens, Moira. 1991. "Corporeal Representation in/and the Body Politic." In *Cartographies: Poststructuralism and the Mapping of Bodies and Spaces*. Eds. Rosalyn Diprose and Robyn Ferrell. Sydney, Australia: Allen and Unwin, 79–87, 141.

Gates, Henry Louis, Jr. 1979. "Binary Oppositions in Chapter One of *Narrative of the Life of Frederick Douglass an American Slave Written by Himself*." In *Afro-American Literature: The Reconstruction of Instruction*. Eds. Dexter Fisher and Robert B. Stepto. New York: Modern Language Association of America, 212–32.

——. 1983. Introduction. *Our Nig; or, Sketches from the Life of a Free Black*. By Harriet E. Wilson. New York: Random House, xi–lv.

——. 1985–86. "Writing 'Race' and the Difference it Makes." In *"Race," Writing, and Difference*. Ed. Henry Louis Gates, Jr. Chicago: University of Chicago Press, 1–20.

——. 1987a. "Authority, (White) Power and the (Black) Critic; It's All Greek to Me." *Cultural Critique* 7 (Fall): 19–46.

——. 1987b. Introduction. *The Classic Slave Narratives*. New York: Penguin, ix–xviii.

———. 1989. *Figures in Black: Words, Signs, and the 'Racial' Self.* New York: Oxford University Press.

———. 1990. "From Wheatley to Douglass: The Politics of Displacement." In *Frederick Douglass: New Literary and Historical Essays.* Ed. Eric J. Sundquist. New York: Cambridge University Press, 47–65.

Genovese, Eugene D. 1972. *Roll, Jordan, Roll: The World the Slaves Made.* Reprinted New York: Vintage, 1976.

———. 1978. "Toward a Psychology of Slavery: An Assessment of the Contribution of *The Slave Community.* In *Revisiting Blassingame's The Slave Community: The Scholars Respond.* Ed. Al-Tony Gilmore. Westport, Conn.: Greenwood Press, 27–41.

Geuss, Raymond. 1981. *The Idea of a Critical Theory: Habermas and the Frankfurt School.* New York: Cambridge University Press.

Gibson, Donald B. 1985. "Reconciling Public and Private in Frederick Douglass's *Narrative.*" *American Literature* 57.4 (December): 549–69.

———. 1990. "Faith, Doubt, and Apostasy: Evidence of Things Unseen in Frederick Douglass's *Narrative.*" In *Frederick Douglass: New Literary and Historical Essays.* Ed. Eric J. Sundquist. New York: Cambridge University Press, 84–98.

Giddings, Paula. 1984. *When and Where I Enter: The Impact of Black Women on Race and Sex in America.* New York: William Morrow.

Gilman, Sander. 1985–86. "Black Bodies, White Bodies: Toward an Iconography of Female Sexuality in Late Nineteenth-Century Art, Medicine, and Literature." In *"Race," Writing, and Difference.* Ed. Henry Louis Gates, Jr. Chicago: University of Chicago Press, 223–61.

———. 1990. "'I'm Down on Whores': Race and Gender in Victorian London." In *Anatomy of Racism.* Ed. David Theo Goldberg. Minneapolis: University of Minnesota Press, 146–70.

———. 1991. *The Jew's Body.* New York: Routledge.

Gilmore, Al-Tony, ed. 1978. *Revisiting Blassingame's The Slave Community: The Scholars Respond.* Westport, Conn.: Greenwood Press.

Gilroy, Paul. 1993. *The Black Atlantic: Modernity and Double Consciousness.* Cambridge, Mass.: Harvard University Press.

Gloster, Hugh M. 1969. Introduction. *Imperium in Imperio: A Study of the Negro Race Problem. A Novel.* By Sutton E. Griggs. 1899. Reprinted New York: Arno Press, i–vi.

Goldberg, David Theo, ed. 1990. *Anatomy of Racism.* Minneapolis: University of Minnesota Press.

———. 1993. *Racist Culture: Philosophy and the Politics of Meaning.* Cambridge, Mass.: Blackwell.

Gordon, Lewis R. 1995. *Bad Faith and Antiblack Racism.* Atlantic Highlands, N. J.: Humanities Press.

Gould, Stephen Jay. 1981. *The Mismeasure of Man.* New York: W. W. Norton.

Graff, Harvey J. 1987. *The Legacies of Literacy: Continuities and Contradictions in Western Culture and Society.* Bloomington, Ind.: Indiana University Press.

Gray, James L. 1990. "Culture, Gender, and the Slave Narrative." *Proteus: A Journal of Ideas* 7.1 (Spring): 37–42.

Grayson, Deborah Renée. 1993. "Black Bodies/Black Texts: Critical and Cultural 'Passing' Among Readers of Nella Larsen's *Passing.*" Unpublished Ph.D. dissertation,

Michigan State University.

Griffin, Susan. 1981. *Pornography and Silence: Culture's Revenge Against Nature*. Reprinted New York: Harper Colophon Books, 1982.

Griggs, Sutton E. 1899. *Imperium in Imperio: A Study of the Negro Race Problem. A Novel*. Reprinted New York: Arno Press, 1969.

Grimes, William. 1855. *Life of William Grimes, the Runaway Slave, Brought Down to the Present Time. Written by Himself*. Reprinted in *Five Black Lives: The Autobiographies of Venture Smith, James Mars, William Grimes, The Rev. G. W. Offley, James L. Smith*. Ed. Arna Bontemps. Middletown, Conn.: Wesleyan University Press, 1971, 59–128.

Grosz, Elizabeth. 1994. *Volatile Bodies: Toward a Corporeal Feminism*. Bloomington, Ind.: Indiana University Press.

Gutman, Herbert G. 1976. *The Black Family in Slavery and Freedom, 1750–1925*. New York: Vintage Press.

Guy-Sheftall, Beverly, ed. 1995. *Words of Fire: An Anthology of African-American Feminist Thought*. New York: New Press.

Gwin, Minrose C. 1985a. *Black and White Women of the Old South: The Peculiar Sisterhood in American Literature*. Knoxville, Tenn.: The University of Tennessee Press.

———. 1985b. "Green-eyed Monsters of the Slavocracy: Jealous Mistresses in Two Slave Narratives." In *Conjuring: Black Women, Fiction, and Literary Tradition*. Eds. Marjorie Pryse and Hortense J. Spillers. Bloomington, Ind.: Indiana University Press, 39–52.

Habermas, Jürgen. 1981. "Modernity Versus Postmodernity." Trans. Seyla Ben-Habib. *New German Critique* 22: 3–14.

Hadreas, Peter J. 1986. *In Place of the Flawed Diamond: An Investigation of Merleau-Ponty's Philosophy*. New York: Peter Lang.

Harper, Frances E. W. 1892. *Iola Leroy; or, Shadows Uplifted*. Reprinted Boston: Beacon Press, 1987.

Harris, Susan K. 1993. "'But is it any *good*?': Evaluating Nineteenth-Century American Women's Fiction." In *The (Other) American Traditions: Nineteenth-Century Women Writers*. Ed. Joyce W. Warren. New Brunswick, N. J.: Rutgers University Press, 263–79.

Harris, Trudier. 1984. *Exorcising Blackness: Historical and Literary Lynching and Burning Rituals*. Bloomington, Ind.: Indiana University Press.

Hartman, Geoffrey H. 1981. *Saving the Text: Literature/Derrida/Philosophy*. Baltimore: Johns Hopkins University Press.

Hartsock, Nancy. 1983. *Money, Sex, and Power: Toward a Feminist Historical Materialism*. New York: Longman. Longman Series in Feminist Theory.

———. 1987. "Rethinking Modernism: Minority vs. Majority Theories." *Cultural Critique* 7 (Fall): 187–206.

Hedin, Raymond. 1982a. "The American Slave Narrative: The Justification of the Picaro." *American Literature* 53.4 (January): 630–45.

———. 1982b. "Strategies of Form in the American Slave Narrative." In *The Art of Slave Narrative: Original Essays in Criticism and Theory*. Eds. John Sekora and Darwin T. Turner. Macomb, Ill.: Western Illinois University, An Essays in Literature Book, 25–35.

Hegel, Georg Wilhelm Friedrich. 1956. *The Philosophy of History*. Trans. J. Sibree. New

York: Dover Publications (based on the 1899 edn.).

Heidegger, Martin. 1927a. *Being and Time.* Trans. John Macquarrie and Edward Robinson. New York: Harper Collins, 1962.

——. 1927b. "Introduction: The Exposition of the Question of the Meaning of Being." From *Being and Time.* Trans. Joan Stambaugh. In *Basic Writings,* rev. and exp. edn. Ed. David Farrell Krell. San Francisco: Harper Collins, 1993, 41–87.

——. 1938. "The Age of the World Picture." Reprinted in *The Question Concerning Technology and Other Essays.* Trans. William Lovitt. New York: Harper, 1977, 115–54.

——. 1947. "Letter on Humanism." Trans. Frank A. Capuzzi. In. *Basic Writings,* rev. and exp. edn. Ed. David Farrell Krell. San Francisco: Harper Collins, 1993, 213–65.

——. 1954a. "The Question Concerning Technology." Reprinted in *The Question Concerning Technology and Other Essays.* Trans. William Lovitt. New York: Harper, 1977, 3–35.

——. 1954b. *What Is Called Thinking?* Trans. J. Glenn Gray. Reprinted New York: Perennial Library, 1993.

——. 1961. "On the Essence of Truth." Reprinted in *Basic Writings,* rev. and exp. edn. Trans. John Sallis. Ed. David Farrell Krell. San Francisco: Harper Collins, 1993, 115–38.

——. 1973. *The End of Philosophy.* Trans. Joan Stambaugh. New York: Harper and Row.

——. 1979. *The Will to Power as Art. Nietzsche.* Vol. I. New York: Harper and Row.

Henson, Josiah. 1881. *An Autobiography of the Rev. Josiah Henson ('Uncle Tom') From 1789 to 1881,* with a preface by Mrs. Harriet Beecher Stowe, rev. and exp. edn. Ed. John Lobb. Reprinted in *Four Fugitive Slave Narratives.* General editor Robin W. Winks. Reading, Mass.: Addison-Wesley, 1969, 1–190.

Hernton, Calvin C. 1965. *Sex and Racism in America.* Reprinted New York: Anchor Books, 1992.

——. 1987. *The Sexual Mountain and Black Women Writers: Adventures in Sex, Literature, and Real Life.* Reprinted New York: Anchor Books, 1990.

Herskovits, Melville J. 1990. *The Myth of the Negro Past.* Boston: Beacon Press.

Hohendahl, Peter Uwe. 1982. *The Institution of Criticism.* Ithaca, N. Y.: Cornell University Press.

Holloway, Joseph E., ed. 1990. *Africanisms in American Culture.* Bloomington, Ind.: Indiana University Press.

Holloway, Karla F. C. 1992. *Moorings and Metaphors: Figures of Culture and Gender in Black Women's Literature.* New Brunswick, N. J.: Rutgers University Press.

——. 1993. "Economies of Space: Markets and Marketability in *Our Nig* and *Iola Leroy.*" In *The (Other) American Traditions: Nineteenth-Century Women Writers.* Ed. Joyce W. Warren. New Brunswick, N. J.: Rutgers University Press, 126–40.

Hopkins, Pauline E. 1900. *Contending Forces: A Romance Illustrative of Negro Life North and South.* Boston, Mass.: The Colored Co-operative Publishing Co. Reprinted New York: Oxford University Press, The Schomburg Library of Nineteenth-Century Black Women Writers, 1988.

Hurston, Zora Neale. 1926. "Sweat." Reprinted in *Classic Fiction of the Harlem Renaissance.* Ed. William L. Andrews. New York: Oxford University Press, 1994,

79–89.

——. 1933. "The Gilded Six-Bits." Reprinted in *Classic Fiction of the Harlem Renaissance*. Ed. William L. Andrews. New York: Oxford University Press, 1994, 90–99.

——. 1937. *Their Eyes Were Watching God*. Reprinted New York: Perennial Library, 1990.

Jackson, Mattie J. 1866. *The Story of Mattie J. Jackson; Her Parentage—Experience of Eighteen Years in Slavery—Incidents During the War—Her Escape from Slavery. A True Story*. Reprinted in *Six Women's Slave Narratives*. General editor Henry Louis Gates, Jr. New York: Oxford University Press, Schomburg Library of Nineteenth-Century Black Women Writers, 1988.

Jacobs, Harriet ("Linda Brent"). 1861. *Incidents in the Life of a Slave Girl. Written by Herself*. Ed. L. Maria Child. Reprinted Cambridge, Mass.: Harvard University Press, 1987. (Reprinted edition edited by Jean Fagan Yellin.)

Jaggar, Alison M. 1983. *Feminist Politics and Human Nature*. Reprinted Totowa, N. J.: Rowman and Littlefield, 1988.

Jahn, Janheinz. 1990. *Muntu: African Culture and the Western World*. Trans. Marjorie Grene. Rev. edn. New York: Grove Weidenfeld.

Jameson, Fredric. 1972. *The Prison-House of Language: A Critical Account of Structuralism and Russian Formalism*. Princeton, N. J.: Princeton University Press.

Jehlen, Myra. 1981. "Archimedes and the Paradox of Feminist Criticism." *Signs* 6.4: 575–601.

Johnson, Mrs. A. E. 1890. *Clarence and Corinne; or, God's Way*. Reprinted New York: Oxford University Press, Schomburg Library of Nineteenth-Century Black Women Writers, 1988.

Johnson, Barbara. 1987. *A World of Difference*. Baltimore: Johns Hopkins University Press.

Johnson, Charles. 1982. *Oxherding Tale*. Reprinted New York: Grove Weidenfeld, 1991.

Johnson, Galen A. and Michael B. Smith. 1990. *Ontology and Alterity in Merleau-Ponty*. Evanston, Ill.: Northwestern University Press.

Johnson, James Weldon. 1912. *The Autobiography of an Ex-Coloured Man*. Reprinted New York: Hill and Wang, 1960.

Johnson, Mark. 1987. *The Body in the Mind: The Bodily Basis of Meaning, Imagination, and Reason*. Chicago: University of Chicago Press.

Jordan, Winthrop D. 1968. *White Over Black: American Attitudes Toward the Negro, 1550–1812*. Chapel Hill, N. C.: University of North Carolina Press.

Keckley, Elizabeth. 1868. *Behind the Scenes. Or, Thirty Years a Slave, and Four Years in the White House*. Reprinted New York: Oxford University Press, Schomburg Library of Nineteenth-Century Black Women Writers, 1988.

Kibbey, Ann, and Michele Stepto. 1991. "The Antilanguage of Slavery: Frederick Douglass's 1845 *Narrative*." In *Critical Essays on Frederick Douglass*. Ed. William L. Andrews. Boston: G. K. Hall, 166–91.

Lane, Lunsford. 1842. *The Narrative of Lunsford Lane*. Boston: J. G. Torrey. Reprinted in *Five Slave Narratives: A Compendium*. Ed. William Loren Katz. New York: Arno Press, 1968.

Lang, Candace D. 1988. *Irony/Humor: Critical Paradigms*. Baltimore: Johns Hopkins University Press.

Laqueur, Thomas. 1987. "Orgasm, Generation, and the Politics of Reproductive Biology." In *The Making of the Modern Body: Sexuality and Society in the Nine-teenth Century*. Eds. Catherine Gallagher and Thomas Laqueur. Berkeley: University of California Press, 1–41.

Larison, C[ornelius] W. 1883. *Silvia Dubois, A Biografy of the Slav Who Whipt Her Mistres and Gand Her Freedom*. Trans. and ed. Jared C. Lobdell. Reprinted New York: Oxford University Press, 1988.

Larsen, Nella. 1929. *Passing*. Reprinted in *Quicksand and Passing*. Ed. Deborah E. McDowell. New Brunswick, N. J.: Rutgers University Press, 1986.

Lawrence, William. 1819. *Lectures on Physiology, Zoology, and the Natural History of Man Delivered at the Royal College of Surgeons*. London: Printed for J. Callow.

Leder, Drew. 1990. *The Absent Body*. Chicago: University of Chicago Press.

Lefort, Claude. 1990. "Flesh and Otherness." In *Ontology and Alterity in Merleau–Ponty*. Eds. Galen A. Johnson and Michael B. Smith. Evanston, Ill.: Northwestern University Press, 3–13.

Levin, David Michael. 1985. *The Body's Recollection of Being: Phenomenological Psychology and the Deconstruction of Nihilism*. London: Routledge and Kegan Paul.

———. 1990. "Justice in the Flesh." In *Ontology and Alterity in Merleau-Ponty*. Eds. Galen A. Johnson and Michael B. Smith. Evanston, Ill.: Northwestern University Press, 35–44.

Levine, Lawrence W. 1977. *Black Culture and Black Consciousness: Afro-American Folk Thought From Slavery to Freedom*. New York: Oxford University Press.

Lewandowski, Joseph D. 1994. "Review Essay: Heidegger, Literary Theory and Social Criticism." *Philosophy and Social Criticism* 20.3: 109–22.

Lewes, George Henry. 1875. *On Actors and the Art of Acting*. Reprinted New York: Grove Press, 1957.

Lott, Eric. 1993. *Love and Theft: Blackface Minstrelsy and the American Working Class*. New York: Oxford University Press.

Lyotard, Jean-François. 1984. *The Postmodern Condition: A Report on Knowledge*. Trans. Geoff Bennington and Brian Massumi. Theory and History of Literature, Vol. 10. Minneapolis: University of Minnesota Press.

Macherey, Pierre. 1966. *A Theory of Literary Production*. Trans. Geoffrey Wall. Reprinted London: Routledge and Kegan Paul, 1978.

MacKethan, Lucinda H. 1982. "Metaphors of Mastery in the Slave Narratives." In *The Art of Slave Narrative: Original Essays in Criticism and Theory*. Eds. John Sekora and Darwin T. Turner. Macomb, Ill.: Western Illinois University, An Essays in Literature Book, 55–69.

Madison, Gary Brent. 1981. *The Phenomenology of Merleau-Ponty: A Search for the Limits of Consciousness*. Athens, Ohio: Ohio University Press.

———. 1990. "Flesh as Otherness." In *Ontology and Alterity in Merleau–Ponty*. Eds. Galen A. Johnson and Michael B. Smith. Evanston, Ill.: Northwestern University Press, 27–34.

Masolo, D. A. 1994. *African Philosophy in Search of Identity*. Bloomington, Ind.: Indiana University Press.

McDowell, Deborah E. 1991. "In the First Place: Making Frederick Douglass and the Afro-American Narrative Tradition." In *Critical Essays on Frederick Douglass*. Ed. William L. Andrews. Boston: G. K. Hall, 192–214.

McKay, Claude. 1928. *Home to Harlem*. Reprinted Boston: Northeastern University Press, 1987.

——. 1929. *Banjo: A Story Without a Plot*. Reprinted New York: Harcourt Brace Jovanovich, 1957.

McMillan, Terry. 1989. *Disappearing Acts*. New York: Viking.

Memmi, Albert. 1991. *The Colonizer and the Colonized*, exp. edn. Boston: Beacon Press.

Merleau-Ponty, Maurice. 1964a. "The Child's Relations With Others." Trans. William Cobb. In Maurice Merleau-Ponty, *The Primacy of Perception and Other Essays on Phenomenological Psychology, the Philosophy of Art, History and Politics*. Ed. James M. Edie. Evanston, Ill.: Northwestern University Press, 96–155.

——. 1964b. "The Primacy of Perception." Trans. James M. Edie. In *The Primacy of Perception and Other Essays on Phenomenological Psychology, the Philosophy of Art, History and Politics*. Ed. James M. Edie. Evanston, Ill.: Northwestern University Press, 12–42.

——. 1968a. *The Visible and the Invisible*. Ed. Claude Lefort. Trans. Alphonso Lingis. Evanston, Ill.: Northwestern University Press. (Originally published in 1964 as *Le Visible et l'invisible*).

——. 1968b. "The Intertwining—The Chiasm." In his *The Visible and the Invisible*. Ed. Claude Lefort. Trans. Alphonso Lingis. Evanston, Ill.: Northwestern University Press, 130–55.

——. 1981. *Phenomenology of Perception*. 1962. Trans. Colin Smith. Reprinted London: Routledge and Kegan Paul (New Jersey: Humanities Press).

——. 1982–83. "The Experience of Others" (1951–52). Trans. Fred Evans and Hugh J. Silverman. *Review of Existential Psychology and Psychiatry* 28.1–3: 33–63.

Michie, Helena. 1987. *The Flesh Made Word: Female Figures and Women's Bodies*. New York: Oxford University Press.

Morris, David B. 1991. *The Culture of Pain*. Berkeley: University of California Press.

Morrison, Toni. 1987. *Beloved: A Novel*. Reprinted New York: Plume, 1988.

Moses, Wilson J. 1990. "Writing Freely? Frederick Douglass and the Constraints of Racialized Writing." In *Frederick Douglass: New Literary and Historical Essays*. Ed. Eric J. Sundquist. New York: Cambridge University Press, 66–83.

Neu, Jerome. 1987. "'A Tear Is an Intellectual Thing.'" *Representations* 19 (Summer): 35–61.

Niemtzow, Annette. 1982. "The Problematic of Self in Autobiography: The Example of the Slave Narrative." In *The Art of Slave Narrative: Original Essays in Criticism and Theory*. Eds. John Sekora and Darwin T. Turner. Macomb, Ill.: Western Illinois University, An Essays in Literature Book, 96–109.

Nudelman, Franny. 1992. "Harriet Jacobs and the Sentimental Politics of Female Suffering." *ELH* 59.4 (Winter): 939–64.

Nussbaum, Felicity A. 1989. *The Autobiographical Subject: Gender and Ideology in Eighteenth-Century England*. Baltimore: Johns Hopkins University Press.

Olafson, Frederick A. 1995. *What Is a Human Being? A Heideggerian View*. New York: Cambridge University Press.

Olney, James. 1980. "Autobiography and the Cultural Moment: A Thematic, Historical, and Bibliographical Introduction." In *Autobiography: Essays Theoretical and Critical*. Ed. James Olney. Princeton, N. J.: Princeton University Press, 3–27.

——. 1985. "'I Was Born': Slave Narratives, Their Status as Autobiography and as Literature." In *The Slave's Narrative*. Eds. Charles T. Davis and Henry Louis Gates, Jr. New York: Oxford University Press, 148–75.

———. 1989. "The Founding Fathers—Frederick Douglass and Booker T. Washington." In *Slavery and the Literary Imagination*. Selected Papers from the English Institute, 1987. New series, No. 13. Eds. Deborah E. McDowell and Arnold Rampersad. Baltimore: Johns Hopkins University Press, 1–24.

O'Meally, Robert G. 1979. "Frederick Douglass' 1845 *Narrative*: The Text Was Meant to Be Preached." In *Afro-American Literature: The Reconstruction of Instruction*. Eds. Dexter Fisher and Robert B. Stepto. New York: The Modern Language Association of America, 192–211.

Omi, Michael, and Howard Winant. 1994. *Racial Formation in the United States From the 1960s to the 1990s*, 2nd. edn. New York: Routledge.

Paris, Peter J. 1985. *The Social Teaching of the Black Churches*. Philadelphia: Fortress Press.

———. 1995. *The Spirituality of African Peoples: The Search for a Common Moral Discourse*. Minneapolis: Fortress Press.

Patterson, Orlando. 1982. *Slavery and Social Death: A Comparative Study*. Cambridge, Mass.: Harvard University Press.

Patton, Paul. 1991. "Nietzsche and the Body of the Philosopher." In *Cartographies: Poststructuralism and the Mapping of Bodies and Spaces*. Eds. Rosalyn Diprose and Robyn Ferrell. Sydney, Australia: Allen and Unwin, 43–54, 136–37.

Pêcheux, Michel. 1975. *Language, Semantics, and Ideology*. Trans. Harbans Nagpal. Reprinted New York: St. Martin's Press, 1982.

Pennington, James W. C. 1849. *The Fugitive Blacksmith; or, Events in the History of James W. C. Pennington*, 2nd edn. London: Charles Gilpin. Reprinted in *Five Slave Narratives: A Compendium*. Ed. William Loren Katz. New York: Arno Press, 1968.

Peterson, Carla L. 1993. "'Doers of the Word': Theorizing African-American Women Writers in the Antebellum North." In *The (Other) American Traditions: Nineteenth-Century Women Writers*. Ed. Joyce W. Warren. New Brunswick, N. J.: Rutgers University Press, 183–202.

Piccinato, Stefania. 1994. "The Slave Narrative and the Picaresque Novel." In *The Black Columbiad: Defining Moments in African American Literature and Culture*. Eds. Werner Sollors and Maria Diedrich. Cambridge, Mass.: Harvard University Press, 88–98.

Picquet, Louisa. 1861. *Louisa Picquet, The Octoroon: or Inside Views of Southern Domestic Life*. By H. Mattison, Pastor of Union Chapel, New York. New York: Published by the author. Reprinted in *Collected Black Women's Narratives*. General editor Henry Louis Gates, Jr. New York: Oxford University Press, Schomburg Library of Nineteenth-Century Black Women Writers, 1988.

Polanyi, Michael. 1961. "Knowing and Being." In Michael Polanyi, *Knowing and Being: Essays by Michael Polanyi*. Ed. Marjorie Grene. Chicago: University of Chicago Press, 1969, 123–37.

———. 1964. "The Logic of Tacit Inference." In *Knowing and Being: Essays by Michael Polanyi*. Ed. Marjorie Grene. Chicago: University of Chicago Press, 1969, 138–58.

———. 1969. *Knowing and Being: Essays by Michael Polanyi*. Ed. Marjorie Grene. Chicago: University of Chicago Press.

Polhemus, Ted, ed. 1978. *The Body Reader: Social Aspects of the Human Body*. New York: Pantheon Books.

Preston, Dickson J. 1980. *Young Frederick Douglass: The Maryland Years*. Baltimore: Johns Hopkins University Press.

Prichard, James Cowles. 1813. *Researches into the Physical History of Man*. London: J. and A. Arch.

——. 1843. *The Natural History of Man: Comprising Inquiries into the Modifying Influence of Physical and Moral Agencies on the Different Tribes of the Human Family*. London: H. Bailliere.

Prince, Mary. 1831. *The History of Mary Prince, A West Indian Slave. Related by Herself*. London: F. Westley and A. H. Davis. Reprinted in *Six Women's Slave Narratives*. General editor Henry Louis Gates, Jr. New York: Oxford University Press, Schomburg Library of Nineteenth-Century Black Women Writers, 1988.

Prince, Nancy. 1853. *A Narrative of the Life and Travels of Mrs. Nancy Prince*. Written by Herself, 2nd edn. Boston: Published by the author. Reprinted in *Collected Black Women's Narratives*. General editor Henry Louis Gates, Jr. New York: Oxford University Press, Schomburg Library of Nineteenth-Century Black Women Writers, 1988.

Rampersad, Arnold. 1989. "Slavery and the Literary Imagination: Du Bois's *The Souls of Black Folk*." In *Slavery and the Literary Imagination*. Selected Papers from the English Institute, 1987. New series, No. 13. Eds. Deborah E. McDowell and Arnold Rampersad. Baltimore: Johns Hopkins University Press, 104–24.

Reising, Russell J. 1986. *The Unusable Past: Theory and the Study of American Literature*. New York: Methuen.

Rich, Adrienne. 1977. *Of Woman Born: Motherhood as Experience and Institution*. 1976. Reprinted New York: Bantam.

Roach, Joseph R. 1985. *The Player's Passion: Studies in the Science of Acting*. Newark, Del.: University of Delaware Press.

Rockmore, Tom, and Joseph Margolis, eds. 1992. *The Heidegger Case: On Philosophy and Politics*. Philadelphia: Temple University Press.

Rorty, Richard. 1982. *Consequences of Pragmatism (Essays: 1972–1980)*. Minneapolis: University of Minnesota Press.

——. 1985. "Habermas and Lyotard on Postmodernity." In *Habermas and Modernity*. Ed. Richard J. Bernstein. Reprinted Cambridge, Mass.: The MIT Press, 1988.

——. 1989. *Contingency, Irony, and Solidarity*. New York: Cambridge University Press.

Ross, Catherine Sheldrick. 1987. "Metaphors of Reading." *Journal of Library History: Philosophy and Comparative Librarianship* 22.2 (Spring): 147–63.

Russo, Mary. 1986. "Female Grotesques: Carnival and Theory." In *Feminist Studies/Critical Studies*. Ed. Teresa de Lauretis. Bloomington, Ind.: Indiana University Press, 213–29.

Sánchez-Eppler, Karen. 1988. "Bodily Bonds: The Intersecting Rhetoric of Feminism and Abolition." *Representations* 24 (Fall): 28–59.

——. 1993. *Touching Liberty: Abolition, Feminism, and the Politics of the Body*. Berkeley: University of California Press.

Scarry, Elaine. 1985. *The Body in Pain: The Making and Unmaking of the World*. New York: Oxford University Press.

Schiebinger, Londa. 1987. "Skeletons in the Closet: The First Illustrations of the Female
       Skeleton in Eighteenth-Century Anatomy." In *The Making of the Modern
       Body: Sexuality and Society in the Nineteenth Century*. Eds. Catherine Gal-
       lagher and Thomas Laqueur. Berkeley: University of California Press, 42–82.
——. 1989. *The Mind Has No Sex? Women in the Origins of Modern Science*. Cam-
       bridge, Mass.: Harvard University Press.
Serequeberhan, Tsenay, ed. 1991. *African Philosophy: The Essential Readings*. New
       York: Paragon.
Smith, Herbert F. c. 1980. *The Popular American Novel 1865–1920*. Boston: Twayne.
Smith, James L. 1881. *Autobiography of James L. Smith, Including, also, Reminiscences
       of Slave Life, Recollections of the War, Education of Freedmen, Causes of the
       Exodus, etc.* Reprinted in *Five Black Lives: The Autobiographies of Venture
       Smith, James Mars, William Grimes, The Rev. G. W. Offley, James L. Smith*.
       Ed. Arna Bontemps. Middletown, Conn.: Wesleyan University Press, 1971,
       139–240.
Smith, Sidonie. 1974. *Where I'm Bound: Patterns of Slavery and Freedom in Black
       American Autobiography*. Westport, Conn.: Greenwood Press.
——. 1993. *Subjectivity, Identity, and the Body: Women's Autobiographical Practices in
       the Twentieth Century*. Bloomington, Ind.: Indiana University Press.
Smith, Stephanie A. 1994. *Conceived by Liberty: Maternal Figures and Nineteenth-
       Century American Literature*. Ithaca, N. Y.: Cornell University Press.
Smith, Valerie. 1987. *Self-Discovery and Authority in Afro-American Narrative*. Cam-
       bridge, Mass.: Harvard University Press.
——. 1990. "'Loopholes of Retreat': Architecture and Ideology in Harriet Jacobs's *Inci-
       dents in the Life of a Slave Girl*." In *Reading Black, Reading Feminist: A Criti-
       cal Anthology*. Ed. Henry Louis Gates, Jr. New York: Meridian, 212–26.
Smith, Venture. 1897. *A Narrative of the Life and Adventures of Venture, a Native of Af-
       rica, But Resident Above Sixty Years in the United States of America. Related
       by Himself*. Originally published in 1798. Reprinted in *Five Black Lives: The
       Autobiographies of Venture Smith, James Mars, William Grimes, The Rev.
       G. W. Offley, James L. Smith*. Ed. Arna Bontemps. Middletown, Conn.: Wesle-
       yan University Press, 1971, 1–34.
Soyinka, Wole. 1990. *Myth, Literature and the African World*. Reprinted New York:
       Cambridge University Press.
Spanos, William V. 1993. *Heidegger and Criticism: Retrieving the Cultural Politics of
       Destruction*. Minneapolis: University of Minnesota Press.
Spelman, Elizabeth V. 1988. *Inessential Woman: Problems of Exclusion in Feminist
       Thought*. Boston: Beacon Press.
Spillers, Hortense J. 1987. "Mama's Baby, Papa's Maybe: An American Grammar
       Book." *Diacritics* 17 (Summer): 65–81.
Stallybrass, Peter, and Allon White. 1986. *The Politics and Poetics of Transgression*.
       Ithaca, N. Y.: Cornell University Press.
Stepan, Nancy Leys. 1982. *The Idea of Race in Science: Great Britain 1800–1960*. Lon-
       don: Macmillan Press.
——. 1990. "Race and Gender: The Role of Analogy in Science." In *Anatomy of Racism*.
       Ed. David Theo Goldberg. Minneapolis: University of Minnesota Press, 38–57.
Stepto, Robert B. 1979. "Narration, Authentication, and Authorial Control in Frederick
       Douglass' *Narrative* of 1845." In *Afro-American Literature: The Reconstruc-*

tion of Instruction. Eds. Dexter Fisher and Robert B. Stepto. New York: Modern Language Association of America, 178–91.

——. 1991. *From Behind the Veil: A Study of Afro-American Narrative*, 2nd. edn. Urbana, Ill.: University of Illinois Press.

Stuckey, Sterling. 1990. "'Ironic Tenacity': Frederick Douglass's Seizure of the Dialectic." In *Frederick Douglass: New Literary and Historical Essays*. Ed. Eric J. Sundquist. New York: Cambridge University Press, 23–46.

Sundquist, Eric J., ed. 1990. *Frederick Douglass: New Literary and Historical Essays*. New York: Cambridge University Press.

Tate, Claudia. 1992. *Domestic Allegories of Political Desire: The Black Heroine's Text at the Turn of the Century*. New York: Oxford University Press.

Taylor, Susie King. 1902. *Reminiscences of My Life in Camp With the 33d United States Colored Troops Late 1st S. C. Volunteers*. Boston: Published by the author. Reprinted in *Collected Black Women's Narratives*. General editor Henry Louis Gates, Jr. New York: Oxford University Press, Schomburg Library of Nineteenth-Century Black Women Writers, 1988.

Thompson, John B. 1984. *Studies in the Theory of Ideology*. Berkeley: University of California Press.

Thoreau, Henry David. 1982. *The Portable Thoreau*. Ed. Carl Bode. New York: Penguin.

Thorpe, Earl E. 1978. "*The Slave Community*: Studies of Slavery Need Freud and Marx." In *Revisiting Blassingame's The Slave Community: The Scholars Respond*. Ed. Al-Tony Gilmore. Westport, Conn.: Greenwood Press, 42–60.

Tompkins, Jane. 1985. *Sensational Designs: The Cultural Work of American Fiction 1770–1860*. New York: Oxford University Press.

Truth, Sojourner. 1993. *Narrative of Sojourner Truth*. Ed. Margaret Washington. New York: Vintage. (Originally published in 1850.)

Turner, Bryan S. 1984. *The Body and Society: Explorations in Social Theory*. Oxford: Basil Blackwell.

Van Leer, David. 1990. "Reading Slavery: The Anxiety of Ethnicity in Douglass's *Narrative*." In *Frederick Douglass: New Literary and Historical Essays*. Ed. Eric J. Sundquist. New York: Cambridge University Press, 118–40.

Veney, Bethany. 1889. *The Narrative of Bethany Veney A Slave Woman*. Worcester, Mass. Reprinted in *Collected Black Women's Narratives*. General editor Henry Louis Gates, Jr. New York: Oxford University Press, Schomburg Library of Nineteenth-Century Black Women Writers, 1988.

Wald, Priscilla. 1995. *Constituting Americans: Cultural Anxiety and Narrative Form*. Durham, N. C.: Duke University Press.

Walker, Alice. 1974. "In Search of Our Mothers' Gardens." Reprinted in Alice Walker, *In Search of Our Mothers' Gardens: Womanist Prose*. New York: Harcourt Brace Jovanovich, 1983, 231–43.

Warhol, Robyn R. 1992. "As You Stand, So You Feel and Are: The Crying Body and the Nineteenth-Century Text." In *Tattoo, Torture, Mutilation, and Adornment: The Denaturalization of the Body in Culture and Text*. Eds. Frances E. Mascia-Lees and Patricia Sharpe. Albany: State University of New York Press, 100–125.

Washington, Booker T. 1901. *Up From Slavery*. Reprinted New York: Penguin, 1986.

Washington, Margaret, ed. 1993. *Narrative of Sojourner Truth*. New York: Vintage.

(Originally published in 1850.)

Welter, Barbara. 1976. "The Cult of True Womanhood, 1820–1860." In her *Dimity Convictions: The American Woman in the Nineteenth Century*. Athens, Ohio: Ohio University Press, 21–41.

White, Barbara A. 1993. "'Our Nig' and the She-Devil: New Information about Harriet Wilson and the 'Bellmont' Family." *American Literature* 65.1 (March): 19–52.

White, Hayden. 1979. "Michel Foucault." In *Structuralism and Since: From Lévi-Strauss to Derrida*. Ed. John Sturrock. New York: Oxford University Press, 81–115.

———. 1987. *The Content of the Form: Narrative Discourse and Historical Representation*. Baltimore: Johns Hopkins University Press.

Wilentz, Gay. 1992. *Black Women Writers in Africa and the Diaspora*. Bloomington, Ind.: Indiana University Press.

Williams, Raymond. 1977. *Marxism and Literature*. New York: Oxford University Press.

Williams, Sherley Anne. 1986. *Dessa Rose: A Novel*. Reprinted New York: Berkley Books, 1987.

Wilson, Harriet E. 1859. *Our Nig; or, Sketches from the Life of a Free Black, In a Two-Story White House, North. Showing that Slavery's Shadows Fall Even There*. Reprinted New York: Random House, 1983.

Winks, Robin W. 1969. General Introduction. *Four Fugitive Slave Narratives*. Reading, Mass.: Addison-Wesley, v–vii.

Wright, Richard. 1940. *Native Son*. Reprinted in *Richard Wright: Early Works*. New York: Library of America, 1991, 443–850.

Yarborough, Richard. 1988. Introduction. *Contending Forces: A Romance Illustrative of Negro Life North and South*. By Pauline E. Hopkins. Boston: The Colored Co-operative Publishing Co., 1900. Reprinted New York: Oxford University Press, Schomburg Library of Nineteenth-Century Black Women Writers, xxvii–xlviii.

———. 1989. "The First-Person in Afro-American Fiction." In *Afro-American Literary Study in the 1990s*. Eds. Houston A. Baker, Jr. and Patricia Redmond. Chicago: University of Chicago Press, 105–21.

———. 1990. "Race, Violence, and Manhood: The Masculine Ideal in Frederick Douglass's 'The Heroic Slave.'" In *Frederick Douglass: New Literary and Historical Essays*. Ed. Eric J. Sundquist. New York: Cambridge University Press, 166–88.

Yellin, Jean Fagan. 1985. "Text and Contexts of Harriet Jacobs' *Incidents in the Life of a Slave Girl: Written by Herself*." In *The Slave's Narrative*. Eds. Charles T. Davis and Henry Louis Gates, Jr. New York: Oxford University Press, 262–82.

———. 1987. Introduction. *Incidents in the Life of a Slave Girl. Written by Herself*. By Harriet Jacobs ("Linda Brent"). Ed. L. Maria Child. Reprinted Cambridge, Mass.: Harvard University Press, xiii–xxxiv.

———. 1989. *Women and Sisters: The Antislavery Feminists in American Culture*. New Haven, Conn.: Yale University Press.

Ziolkowski, Thad. 1991. "Antitheses: The Dialectic of Violence and Literacy in Frederick Douglass's *Narrative* of 1845." In *Critical Essays on Frederick Douglass*. Ed. William L. Andrews. Boston: G. K. Hall, 148–65.

Index

abolitionist audience, 20 n.3, 77
abolitionist discourse, 117, 119
abolitionist lecture circuit, 65, 120, 145
abolitionist movement, 65, 85 n.50, 117
Abolitionist sponsors, 27 n.50, 35, 121
abolitionists, 35, 63, 65, 77, 85 n.49, 87 n.64, 88 nn.68, 70, 90–91 n.85, 97, 155 n.7
abolitionist texts, 97, 101
absence, 25–26 n.42, 26 n.48, 130 n.31, 133 n.69; of author, 120; of body, 95, 115; of details, 116, 124. *See also* bodies, absence of, in African American narrative; bodies, absence of, in bourgeois fiction; bodies, as absent to us; body, absence of
absent signifier, 139; body as, 121
Acholonu, Catherine Obianuju, 80 n.10, 81 n.13, 82 n.19. *See also* bodies, marked; body, culture inscribed in the
Adell, Sandra, 21 n.8, 22 n.22, 51 n.46
African American narrative, origins of, 2
African customs, 43, 80; as memorialized in the body, 55–56, 80–81 n.12

African dances, 42, 53, 55
Africanisms, 24, 35–37, 52 nn.53, 54
Africans: purported lasciviousness of, after Reconstruction, 138; purported natural inferiority of, 138. *See also* Hegel, G. W. F.
African traditions, 87 n.65
Afro-American Literature (Fisher and Stepto), 21 n.14
Age of Enlightenment. *See* Enlightenment, Age of
"The Age of the World Picture" (Heidegger), xi, 11–12
aletheia, 41
Allison, Robert J., 80 n.10, 82 n.19. *See also* bodies, marked; body, culture inscribed in the
alterity, 42–43; in a text, 42; in ontology, 3, 43, 64, 145. *See also* chiasm; Dillon, M. C.; flesh, the; intertwining; Levin, David Michael; Madison, Gary Brent; Merleau-Ponty, Maurice; reciprocity; slave-master relationship (Hegel)
Althusser, Louis, 9, 24–25 n.34, 109, 115, 133 n.71. *See also* interpellation; ISAs
Amnesty International, 92 n.94
Anderson, James D., 87 n.66

19, 22 n.18, 44. *See also* anti-
humanism; humanism, critique of;
metaphysics, critique of
différance, 121, 135–36 n.88
Dillon, M. C., 34. *See also* alterity;
chiasm; flesh, the; intertwining;
Levin, David Michael; Madison,
Gary Brent; Merleau-Ponty,
Maurice
distrust: of white readers, 17, 96, 128
n.20
domestic fiction, 17; 155 n.2. *See also*
bodies; Genteel School; middle-
class novel; post-Reconstruction
writers; proto-Genteel School; sentimental novelists
domesticity, 127 n.14, 145; habitus of,
93; myth of, 95, 113, 117
Doriani, Beth Maclay, 128 n.21
double-consciousness, 33
Douglas, Ann, 128 n.22
Douglass, Frederick, 24 nn.31, 33, 25
nn.35, 40, 57–79, 82 nn.21, 24–27,
29, 83 nn.30, 35, 83–84 n.36, 85
nn.46–50, 85–86 n.51, 87 nn.62–
65, 88 nn.68 ,71, 93, 98–99, 119–
20, 125; ability of his body-self to
see otherwise, 10; appearance of,
65–66; as ministered to by Lucretia
Auld, 65, 71–73; as Representative
Man, 92 n.97; attack on ethnology
by, 20 n.4, 80 n.8, 85–86 n.51; biography of, 87 n.59; body of, as
text, 90–91 n.85; body of, taught
by bodies of others, 76; body of,
unmarked, 73; body-self of, 58,
64–65, 85 n.49, 95; calling on others to work with their hands, 64–
65; challenge to metaphysics in,
70, 92 n.97; community of, 83–84
n.36, 88 n.68; compassion experienced by, 67–69, 71–75, 77, 90
n.85; connectedness of, to other
slaves, 59, 68; critique of dominant
ideology by, 28 n.56; critique of
liberal humanism by, 23 n.24, 91
n.89, 106; destructive hermeneutics
of, 19; embodiment of, 65; experi-

ences with Covey of, 63–66, 71,
75–76, 85 nn.47–48, 90 n.81, 91
n.88; exposure of body of, 86 n.55;
function in literary history of, 82
n.21; grandmother of, 69–70, 72–
73, 87 n.65, 102; identification
between audience and, 86 n.52;
importance of family to, 67; importance of material experience to, 22
n.20; importance of physical
strength to, 64; individualism in,
86 n.53; meditation on slave music
by, 84 n.37 (*see also* slave songs);
mother of, 69; narratives of (*see
individual titles*); onset of thinking
in, 72, 89 n.75; openness-for-*being*
in, 69, 71–73, 74; physique and
physiognomy of, 120; pride of, in
his body, 17; questioning of metaphysics by, 65, 91 n.89; questioning of subjectivity by, 86 n.53;
rebuttal to Hegel by, 21 n.8; rejection of chattel principle by, 84 n.43
(*see also* chattel principle); relationship of, to Sandy Jenkins, 70–
71; relationship of, to Sophia Auld,
74–77; reshaping of body of, 74;
rhetorical use of his body by, 93;
self-conscious writing in, 51 n.49,
62, 75–76, 79, 84 n.39; sense of
justice known in body of, 34;
shaping of body of, into that of a
slave, 59; speeches of, 22 n.19, 23
nn.24, 30; 26 n.43, 47 n.16, 49
n.29, 63–66, 80 n.8, 86 n.55, 87
n.63, 88 n.68, 135 n.85 (*see also
individual titles of*); tensions in narratives of, 22 n.19, 84 n.38; thinking through the body in, 73; view
of hands in, 46 n.9; wandering in,
72–73, 78 (*see also* Hedin, Raymond); women in, 89 n.78; writing
of, 75–79. *See also individual titles
of his narratives and stories*
Doyle, Laura, 2
dread, 12; as experienced by slaves,
12–14, 26 n.47; differences from
fear, 13–14

See also alterity; chiasm; Dillon,
M. C.; intertwining; justice in the
flesh; Levin, David Michael; Madison, Gary Brent; Merleau-Ponty,
Maurice; reciprocity

The Flight to Objectivity (Bordo), 46
n.4

fold, 48 n.20; of the visible, 33, 145–
46

Foner, Philip S., 47 n.16, 49 n.29, 85
n.50

Foreman, P. Gabrielle, 121, 128 n.21,
133–34 n.76, 134 n.80

forgetting the body, 15; impossibility
of, 36, 39

Foster, Frances Smith, 21 n.9, 80 n.6,
84 n.39, 87 n.58, 88 n.68, 89
nn.76, 89, 125 n.1, 127 n.9, 128
n.20, 131 n.46, 134 nn.78, 80

Foucault, Michel, 6–12, 23 n.29, 24
n.32, 89 n.73, 108, 115, 132 n.52;
critique of, 25 n.41. *See also* anti-
humanism

Fox-Genovese, Elizabeth, 86 n.53, 127
n.13, 128 n.20

Franchot, Jenny, 82 n.27, 84 n.39, 86
n.55, 87 nn.59, 63

Franklin, John Hope, 137–38

Fraser, Nancy, 22 n.19, 24 n.32

Fredrickson, George M., 24 n.33, 49
n.36, 138, 154–55 n.2

freedom, 1, 3–4, 6, 8–10, 22 n.18, 24
n.33, 25 nn.36–37, 35–38, 46 n.4,
49 n.32, 63, 72, 76, 79 n.4, 83
n.33, 85 n.48, 88 n.72, 89 n.78, 90
n.83, 91 n.89, 105, 116–18, 123;
essence of, 10, 105, 131 n.42, 134
n.80; goal of, problematic in
women's texts, 134 n.80; slaves'
inability to find, 131 n.42. *See also*
liberty

from-to phenomenon, 29, 60, 104

The Fugitive Blacksmith (Pennington),
66–67

Fukuyama, Francis, 22 n.17

Fuss, Diana, 27 n.52

Gadamer, Hans-Georg, 42, 110, 114,

132 nn.63–63; notion of prejudices
in, 80 n.7, 110–11; understanding
in, as involving bodies, 51 n.48,
78. *See also* understanding

Gage, Frances, 127 n.11

gaps and silences, 103, 117, 124,
133n.77

Garfield, Deborah M., 134 n .80

Garrison, William Lloyd, 85 n.50

Gatens, Moira, 85 n.49

Gates, Henry Louis, Jr., 1–2, 37–39,
44, 54, 80 n.9, 91 n.91, 92 nn.93,
98, 103, 127 n.12, 127–28 n.15,
128 n.21, 130 nn.30, 34, 132 n.65;
on Phillis Wheatley, 82 n.21

Genovese, Eugene D., 20–21 n.8, 35,
52 n.52, 81 n.12, 87–88 n.67

genteel discourse, 101, 103. *See also*
domestic fiction; genteel fiction;
Genteel School; middle-class
novel; proto-Genteel School

genteel fiction, 148; admirable dark-
skinned characters in, 148–49. *See
also* domestic fiction; genteel discourse; Genteel School; middle-
class novel; proto-Genteel School

Genteel School, 18, 28 n.63, 96; con-
trasted to Bohemian School, 18–
19; view of bodies in, 96. *See also*
bodies; domestic fiction; middle-
class novel; proto-Genteel School

gesture, 30–31, 35; as emotion, 97; of
compassion, 107, 109–10; reading
as a, 42, 46 n.9; speech as a, 61;
thoughtful, 69; writing as, 43, 46
n.9, 74. *See also* care; compassion;
hands; handshake; justice in the
flesh; language; motility

Geuss, Raymond, 27 n.56

Gibson, Donald B., 85 nn.47–48

Giddings, Paula, 21 n.11, 125 n.1, 155
n.4

gift of our hands. *See* hands

gifts of the past, 46 n.11

"The Gilded Six-Bits" (Hurston), 128
n.19

Gilman, Sander, 81 n.18, 86 n.54, 125
n.3, 126–27 n.8

body; body-self; body-selves
sentimental discourse: as manipulated
by Douglass, 82 n.24; in Jacobs,
117–18, 123. *See also* sentimental
novel; sentimental novelists
sentimental novel, 96–97; body of
slave in the, 155 n.6; recuperation
of, 128 n.22. *See also* bodies; domestic fiction; middle-class novels;
Genteel School; postbellum writers; post-Reconstruction writers;
proto-Genteel School; sentimental
discourse; sentimental novelists
sentimental novelists, 17; rehabilitation
of writing of, 50 n.45. *See also*
bodies; domestic fiction; Genteel
School; middle-class novels; postbellum writers; post-
Reconstruction writers; proto-
Genteel School
sentimental romance, 139, 142, 145.
See also sentimental discourse;
sentimental novel; sentimental
novelists
Serequeberhan, Tsenay, 52 n.54
sexuality: black female, 126–27 n.8;
black male, 127 n.8; of all blacks,
138–39; of working women, 125
n.3; white female, 93–94. *See also*
cult of true womanhood; embodiment; motherhood; myth of domesticity; womanhood; women;
work; working bodies; working-
class blacks; working-class women
shame: as cause for silence about body,
16
signature: as mark of embodiment, 43,
51–52 n.50, 120. *See also* handwriting
Sims, J. Marion, 94
singing. *See* slave songs
slave: redefinition of term, 11
The Slave Community (Blassingame)
24 n.33, 86 n.51
slave families, 87 n.66
slave-master relationship, 24 n.33, 33,
72; Hegelian concept of, 20–21
n.8; in Douglass, 59, 61, 67. *See*

also alterity; intertwining
slave narratives, 51 n.49, 77, 78–79,
120, 122, 154; as counter-
hegemonic discourse, 10; as
stereotyping slave women, 127 n.9;
conventions of, 132 n.53, 134 n.80;
differences in depiction of beatings
in male and female, 82 n.27; gaps
in, 82 n.23; genre of, 96, 126 n.21;
male-authored, 49 n.28, 85 n.48;
plot of, 85 n.48, 107; metaphysical
claims of, 122; themes in, 132–33,
n.65, 148; voice in, 84 n.40. *See
also under specific titles and individual authors*
slave narrators: differences between
male and female, 19, 65, 124–25,
125 n.1. *See also under specific titles and individual authors*
slavery, 105; being of, 49 n.31; *being
unconcealed by*, 43–44; essence of,
30, 64, 99–100; establishment of,
21 n.11; marking itself on bodies
of slaves, 60; thematizing flaws of
humanism, 9, 30
slave songs, 35, 61–63, 83 n.35, 83–84
n.36, 84 n.37–38, 89 n.79
slave trade, 56–57
slave woman: as sexual victim, 127
n.9; as stereotyped in slave narratives, 127 n.9
Smith, Herbert F., 97
Smith, James L., 83 n.31, 88–89 n.72,
92 n.92, 94
Smith, Michael B., 34
Smith, Sidonie, 22 n.18, 23 n.29, 24
n.31, 27 n.50, 85 n.49, 116, 126
n.5, 127 n.8, 128 n.18, 131 n.42
Smith, Stephanie A., 21 n.16, 22 n.18,
24 n.30, 28 n.56, 48 n.22, 82
nn.22, 24–25, 27, 84 n.39, 85 n.48,
88 n.68, 91 n.89
Smith, Valerie, 80 n.11, 81 n.19, 85
n.48, 92 n.98, 116, 128 n.21, 133
n.75, 134 n.80
Smith, Venture, 17, 36–37, 49 n.32,
130 n.29
sociability: the body's inherent, 31, 34,

About the Author

KATHERINE FISHBURN is Professor of English at Michigan State University, where she teaches courses in African American literature, twentieth-century literature, women's literature, and cultural studies. She is author of a book on Richard Wright, a monograph on Doris Lessing, and three Greenwood Press titles: *Reading Buchi Emecheta: Cross-Cultural Conversations* (1995), *The Unexpected Universe of Doris Lessing: A Study in Narrative Technique* (1985), and *Women in Popular Culture: A Reference Guide* (1982).

ISBN 0-313-30359-2

90000>

EAN

9 780313 303593

HARDCOVER BAR CODE